FREDRIC WERTHAM
AND THE CRITIQUE OF MASS CULTURE

FREDRIC WERTHAM
AND THE CRITIQUE OF MASS CULTURE

BART BEATY

UNIVERSITY PRESS OF MISSISSIPPI / JACKSON

www.upress.state.ms.us

The University Press of Mississippi is a member of the
Association of American University Presses.

First edition

Library of Congress Cataloging-in-Publication Data
Beaty, Bart.
  Fredric Wertham and the critique of mass culture / Bart Beaty.— 1st ed.
    p. cm.
  Based on the author's dissertation, MaGill University.
  Includes bibliographical references and index.
  ISBN 1-57806-810-X (cloth : alk. paper) — ISBN 1-57806-819-3 (paper : alk. paper) 1. Mass media
and culture. 2. Mass media—Influence. 3. Wertham, Fredric, 1895–1981. I. Title.
  P94.6.B43   2005
  306'.0973'09045—dc22   2005005448

British Library Cataloging-in-Publication Data available

In any contemporary study of the effect of mass-media violence and brutality, comic books must be included. It is a kind of snobbishness, an indication of estrangement from the masses, that in studies of mass-communication effects, comic books are so often left out.

—FREDRIC WERTHAM, *A Sign for Cain*

CONTENTS

ACKNOWLEDGMENTS

In undertaking a lengthy project such as this one, the research inevitably will at times be driven by unforeseen circumstances and odd coincidences. Case in point: Fredric Wertham's final book was his 1973 study of comic book and science fiction fandom, *The World of Fanzines.* In that work, he quoted a young fan named Will Straw. It is perhaps only coincidence that a quarter of century later Will Straw would be teaching in the Graduate Program in Communications at McGill University, where he would supervise a dissertation that investigated Wertham's work. Nonetheless, chance played little role in my choice of supervisors. Over the course of my years as his student and colleague, Will has been a constant source of inspiration, encouragement, and support and a model of intensive and committed scholarship. Without his unwavering enthusiasm for this project, its completion would have been inconceivable. I am extremely grateful for his interest in this work and in my career, even if he never did come to grips with the question of violence in Conan's world.

Other faculty at McGill's Graduate Program in communications also played an important role in shaping this research. Much of the thinking that has gone into this book was refined in Gertrude Robinson's seminar on mass culture, and I am grateful for her insights and for the rigorous model of historiography that she presented. My interest in postwar theories of mass culture was influenced by the courses I took with George Szanto, and I thank him for his comments on earlier versions of this work. Outside the program, this work was particularly influenced by discussions with Janine Marchessault and John Jackson that guided me toward my ultimate destination. To them, my thanks.

A number of friends and colleagues have been instrumental in developing these arguments, and I particularly thank Keir Keightley for providing research materials and for his ongoing interest in this project. I also appreciate the efforts of Danielle Comeau, Joe Jackson, and Anne Whitelaw to help me keep things in their proper perspective.

For their ongoing interest in my work and useful comments on earlier drafts of this material presented at various conferences, I thank the small coterie of scholars actively engaged in researching comics-related subjects. I have found the observations of Paul Gravett, Charles Hatfield, Gene Kannenberg, and Nick Nguyen particularly helpful. I am deeply indebted to John Lent, whose careful reading of the manuscript benefited me tremendously and who was an early supporter of my research into Fredric Wertham's career as editor of *The International Journal of Comic Art*. I am grateful to Keith Logan, Michael Rhode, and Tom Spurgeon for research assistance. I extend a special thanks to Mark Nevins for his insights and his enthusiasm.

An archival project such as this one is built through the strength of libraries and with the assistance of highly skilled librarians. During the course of writing this work, I read more than two hundred articles written by Wertham in his lengthy career. This could not have been accomplished without the outstanding work of the staff of the Interlibrary Loan office at McGill's McLennan-Redpath Library, who worked tirelessly to track down many of the articles that are the basis for my research into the postwar debate about the status of comic books. In addition, my initial research was augmented by a month spent in the Manuscript Reading Room at the Library of Congress, the repository of Wertham's papers. I am deeply indebted to Fred Bauman and the staff of the Manuscript Division for their able assistance, and I particularly thank Charles Noonan for allowing me to access the papers in a timely manner.

The dissertation on which this manuscript is based was completed with the assistance of a fellowship from the Social Sciences and Humanities Research Council of Canada, and I gratefully acknowledge the council's financial support of this research. The University Research Grant program at the University of Calgary funded my trip to the Library of Congress. Without the generous support of these programs, this book would never have been completed.

This book has been considerably strengthened by the close attention that it has received at the University Press of Mississippi. I am grateful to Seetha

Srinivasan for her insights into the material and for her constructive comments that have allowed me to focus and refine the argument presented here. I also wish to acknowledge the work of Walter Biggins, whose diligence constantly reminded me that my choice of presses for this project was always the right one. The copyediting performed by Ellen D. Goldlust-Gingrich significantly improved this text, and I thank her for her hard work. I am exceedingly grateful to Rusty Witek, whose insights into two drafts of this manuscript have benefited the work immeasurably. His dedication to this project went well above and beyond the expectations that I had of a reader.

My parents, Harry and Dianne Beaty, have never faltered in their encouragement of my studies, and I am extremely grateful for their support and assistance during my years at McGill. I also acknowledge the contribution of my grandfather, Don Beaty, who never hesitated to lend a hand when it was necessary.

Finally, this book would not exist today were it not for the efforts of Rebecca Sullivan. The impact of her constant presence in my life can be felt on every page of this work. She has taught me more than she will ever know about how to succeed in scholarship and in life. I am grateful to her beyond measure, and I dedicate this work to her with all my love.

FREDRIC WERTHAM
AND THE CRITIQUE OF MASS CULTURE

INTRODUCTION

A ghostlike figure haunts the history of postwar debates on American popular culture. That ghost is Fredric Wertham, a German-born psychiatrist and once well-known and widely-respected expert in the areas of psychiatry, criminality, juvenile delinquency, and civil rights. For more than half a century, from the 1920s until the 1970s, Wertham published extensively in both scholarly journals and mainstream newspapers and magazines, emerging in the mid-1950s as one of America's best-known commentators on the purported effects of the mass media. Today, however, readers must be forgiven if the name rings few bells. A search of library catalogs will turn up a few of his books with vaguely lurid and somewhat threatening titles: *Dark Legend* (1941), *The Show of Violence* (1949), *Seduction of the Innocent* (1954), *The Circle of Guilt* (1956), and *A Sign for Cain* (1966). At present, little secondary material exists that assesses his contribution to the debates about popular culture. Examining the histories of communications studies, the discipline with the clearest engagement in the study of media effects, imparts little further information. While the first two editions of the seminal text-book *Milestones in Mass Communication Research: Media Effects* (Lowery and DeFleur 1983, 1988) discuss Wertham at length, the most recent edition of the book (1995) entirely omits his contribution to the development of the field. Wertham's name fails to even emerge in recent histories of communication research (Rogers 1994), suggesting that he has become a nonentity as far as the history of communications is concerned.

This is not, however, an entirely recent phenomenon. Even as the field of popular culture was crystallizing in the immediate postwar decades, Wertham's contributions were marginalized as the discipline sought professionalism

3

and legitimacy. In Bernard Rosenberg and David Manning White's *Mass Culture: The Popular Arts in America* (1957), the first significant collection of writings on popular culture in the United States, Wertham's contribution had already lost much of its corporeality, and he had begun to assume the form of a specter whose ideas required little serious contemplation. Throughout that text, Wertham's name was repeatedly evoked by the contributors, only to be dismissed (White 1957:13; Fiedler 1957:537; Van Den Haag 1957:530). Wertham was the subject of Robert Warshow's contribution, "Paul, the Horror Comics, and Dr. Wertham" (199–211), which dismissed the psychiatrist's work. Nothing written by Wertham appeared in the book's section on comic books despite the fact that he was undeniably the best-known commentator on that form of popular culture at the time the book was published.

Wertham's absence from current histories of popular culture studies and his negative presence in the early canonical texts are the structuring poles of this book. In the pages that follow, I offer an explanation for the way in which Fredric Wertham's work has been systematically excluded from the mainstream of research into popular culture, both as it was consecrated as a legitimate area of academic inquiry in the 1950s and 1960s and as it has been critically reassessed by subsequent generations. Situating Wertham's work in this history elucidates many of the submerged connections in the development of the field, most notably the historical association of mass communication research and the media-effects paradigm with increasingly conservative Cold War discourses about mass society and the negative aesthetic influences of popular culture.

In determining who has exorcised the ghost of Fredric Wertham from the house of popular culture research, it is important to note that both historical and contemporary commentators on his work agree on its relative valuelessness. Negative assessments of Wertham's arguments can be found in the writings of social scientists beginning only a few years after the publication of his best-known book, *Seduction of the Innocent*. Writing in 1957, for instance, Reuel Denney suggested that Wertham may have been sensitive to a real problem when he identified mass culture generally, and comic books specifically, as an influence on juvenile criminality. Nonetheless, Denney maintained that Wertham's work lacked scientific evidence "of any weight" and that his appeal lay primarily with cultural lowbrows already predisposed to be suspicious of print (164–65). A few years later, Joseph Klapper declared in *The Effects of Mass Communication* (1960), the definitive elaboration of the limited-effects thesis that would come to dominate communications research for decades, that

> Explicit mention must be made of Dr. Frederick [*sic*] Wertham, who is probably the world's most voluble castigator of media-depicted violence, and in particular of comic books. Wertham claims to have diagnosed or treated numerous delinquent children in whose downfall comic books were the chief impetus. He does not seem to consider that emotional disturbance or abnormal aggressive tendencies are necessary prerequisites to comic book influence but rather seems to believe, as the title of his best known work asserts, that such fare in and of itself achieves "Seduction of the Innocent." Wertham is not generally regarded, however, as having substantiated his very extreme views. Thrasher (1949), for example, is typical of the critics in pointing out that Wertham provides no description of his samples of comic books or of human cases, apparently deals only with a small and highly deviant minority of both, provides no description of his case study techniques, uses no control groups, and, in short, provides no acceptable scientific evidence for his ascription of comic book influence. (290)

While the substantive disagreement between Frederic M. Thrasher and Wertham on the nature and quality of Wertham's proofs cited by Klapper will be addressed specifically in chapter 4, of greater importance at this point is the use of the term *apparently* in reference to *Seduction of the Innocent*. It suggests that Klapper had not read Wertham's text and used Thrasher's denunciation of it as the basis of his opinion. Klapper erroneously argued that Wertham's conclusions were unfounded because he had studied material that did not qualify as mass media, a claim that could not be supported by a reading of the book itself. Klapper's opinion was symptomatic of a dual refusal that would come to characterize discussions of Wertham's work. Klapper not only denounced Wertham's book without apparently reading it but, based on his incorrect assumptions, implied that it did not even merit reading before it was to be condemned to the junk heap of subscholarly achievement.

Klapper's partially-informed dismissals eventually became the primary template through which the vast majority of commentators on media and popular culture would address Wertham's work. Contemporary fans of comic books, for instance, largely remember Wertham as a McCarthyite, a censorious moralizing crusader on a witch hunt against comic books in the 1950s (Daniels 1971), despite the fact that Wertham was an outspoken postwar liberal and opponent of censorship. Catherine Yronwode spells out the commonly held view of Wertham among comic book fans: "We hate him, despise him. He and he alone virtually brought about the collapse of the comic book industry during the 1950s. . . . [E]ven the younger of us know the legend well, for it is repeated among us like some tribal myth" (Reibman 1990:18). Other recent scholarship, while failing to address Wertham's work in any systematic way, tends to view him as emblematic of larger cultural themes in the postwar era: as evidence of a national anxiety over mass culture during the 1950s (Gorman 1996) or as a "forerunner of the kind of media-oriented pop-psychiatrist later to be in vogue on television talk shows and syndicated self-help programs" (Savage 1990:96). That these descriptions and labels obscure more than they clarify goes almost without saying. A small number of recent scholars have sought to come to terms with Wertham's writing within a larger framework of inquiry. Amy Nyberg, for instance, rejects traditional fannish accounts of Wertham and his influence on comic books in her history of the American Comics Code. While Nyberg correctly identifies Wertham as a part of an ongoing debate in communications research about the effects of media, she ultimately cannot overcome the temptation to denounce his scholarship as "clearly censorship" and the man as a "skillful manipulator" who targeted comic books for investigation because they constituted an easy target rather than a cause for genuine scholarly interest (1996:156–57).

Nyberg's account of Wertham's studies relies heavily on the evaluations put forward by James Gilbert in his study of American concerns about postwar juvenile delinquency, *A Cycle of Outrage* (1986). Gilbert has the distinction of being one of a very small group of commentators to have taken Wertham seriously, rooting his analysis not only in his readings of Wertham's published work but also in a survey of his archives and in interviews with Wertham and his colleagues. Unlike other commentators on Wertham's work, Gilbert offers arguments that help explain why a well-known media critic should have fallen so decidedly out of favor with both the general public, which had previously embraced him, and the intellectual community, which at one time had at least been forced to acknowledge him, if only in negative terms.

In Gilbert's analysis, Wertham's fall from grace with the public simply resulted from shifting public opinion in the late 1950s and early 1960s as new attitudes toward popular culture developed (9). From this point of view, *Seduction of the Innocent* capitalized on a cyclic or recurrent moral panic about youth behavior and mass culture that focused for a brief period on comic books before dissipating and taking Wertham with it. While there is some merit to seeing Wertham's postwar fame as a matter of timing, this explanation does not, however, adequately address the ongoing friction between Wertham's conception of media effects and those of his contemporaries in the American social sciences who continued to research media influence even as public interest in the topic abated. On this question, Gilbert suggests that Wertham's analyses were "too direct and sweeping, his conclusions too positive for many of the psychologists and sociologists engaged in considering the impact of mass media on American culture" (91). Once again, Gilbert stops short of addressing the systematic way in which Wertham has been excluded from the history and practice of mass communication and popular culture research.

Discussing the origins of American psychoanalysis, Peter Berger argues, "the root platitude of the sociology of knowledge is ideas do not succeed in history by virtue of their truth but by virtue of their relationship to specific social processes" (1965:32). In this volume, I will demonstrate the conscious and systematic exclusion of Fredric Wertham's conception of media effects as part of deliberate strategies to codify research into a coherent field of mass culture studies. It is not enough to suggest that Wertham's fall occurred because his conclusions were too positive. Rather, structural biases can be located in the specific social processes through which mass media research was brought into professional and academic realms by scholars working in concert with funding agencies, the broadcasting industry, and governmental committees investigating the effects of the mass media.

Gilbert's contention that anxiety about mass culture was an episodic notion unnecessarily minimizes the notion that the differential evaluation of culture forms a continuous thread through history. Far from episodic, the mass culture debate can be seen as an ongoing background to the intellectual discussions that have characterized American cultural discourse throughout history. In the twentieth century, this debate was amplified by the emergence of a growing number of intellectuals working outside the academy. Termed "public intellectuals" by Russell Jacoby (1987), these men (in the vast majority of cases) were "writers and thinkers who address a general and educated audience" (5). Although the specific political objections to the mass media shifted during the course of the twentieth century, the attitude that the mass media should be viewed with alarm remained largely constant.

Concomitant with these criticisms was the understanding that something could and should be done to ameliorate the condition of the mass media. Yet professional sociological methodologies did little to appease nonacademic critics and public intellectuals, who continued to condemn the mass media even as researchers entered into agreements with media industries and governments seeking to solve the perceived problems. Quite the contrary—as the social sciences became increasingly practical and wedded to the New Deal's social-engineering policies, public intellectuals stepped up their rhetoric and calls for change, ultimately producing a critique of the bureaucratic policies that their initial objections had helped to bring about. As the media-effects paradigm developed as a specialty within the academy, researchers increasingly neglected their roles as critics. These roles were subsequently taken up by public intellectuals while social scientists limited themselves to practical questions. In addressing the history of the media-effects debate, therefore, it is necessary to keep in mind the fact that two distinct groups joined the discussion. The first was the scholarly researchers from a social scientific background, whose work revolved around traditional methodologies developed in the natural sciences. They were at odds with the second group, public intellectuals with a literary or aesthetic interest in protecting elite culture from the ostensibly degrading influence of mass culture.

To get to the heart of that dialogue, it is necessary to focus on a figure who bridged the divide between the public intellectuals and the researchers. The unique career of Fredric Wertham permits just such an analysis. He lies at the intersection of a number of movements and debates about mass culture as it played out in the midcentury era. Wertham himself could, by Jacoby's definition, be cited as a public intellectual. Although Wertham wrote dozens of articles for scholarly and medical journals during his career, he should also be remembered for his more popular, accessible writings in magazines ranging from *The Nation* to *Ladies' Home Journal*. Furthermore, although he is never counted among the most famous postwar public intellectuals, the fact remains that Wertham had connections with many of them, including H. L. Mencken, Walter Lippman, and Clarence Darrow.

On the other side of the mass culture divide, it needs to be noted that Wertham, a psychiatrist by training, dedicated much of his life in the 1940s and 1950s to clinically studying the effects of media on the psychological development of children and spent much of the 1950s and 1960s trying to have his clinical research methodologies recognized as valid by proponents of experimental and survey methodologies. Ultimately, of course, Wertham failed in these attempts and, despite the important contributions that psychiatry and psychoanalysis have made to the study of popular culture in the United States, the clinical method has never been regarded as scientifically rigorous enough to qualify as valid by the researchers of media effects. Consequently, over the years, Wertham's findings have been systematically excluded until little more than faint traces haunt the contemporary landscape. As a figure who was both a researcher and a public commentator on the media but who was ultimately excluded from the developing paradigm, Wertham can instructively highlight certain submerged tendencies in the development of research into mass media and popular culture. In reinserting Wertham, I seek to make a historiography of these fields that pays particular attention to the institutionalization of the media-effects paradigm in American research into popular culture.

This book is divided into five chapters, each of which will critically engage with some aspect of Wertham's published writings to illuminate key tensions in the establishment of the paradigm. The first chapter addresses the foundational element of Wertham's thinking, his training as a psychiatrist. Gilbert's argument that Wertham's writings represented a European tradition of criticism that was alien to the United States can be considered correct only if he were discussing Wertham's training in psychiatry. Laura Fermi argues that the intellectual migration from Europe to the United States in the 1920s and 1930s represents the most significant event of the second quarter of the twentieth century. She identifies the two biggest forces brought from Europe to America as atomic science and psychoanalysis (1971:141). While it is true that American psychoanalysis predated the waves of German and Austrian psychiatrists who arrived in the United States between 1932 and 1941, this rapid influx undeniably shifted the center of global psychoanalysis from Europe to America.

Chapter 1 outlines the history of American uses of psychoanalysis and psychiatry following the sudden growth of the field in the 1920s and the 1930s. Furthermore, the chapter examines the close connection between psychiatry and social-reform movements, paying attention to psychiatrists' early efforts to link their field to the study of juvenile delinquency. Psychoanalysis became an important factor in American jurisprudence as psychiatrists increasingly testified as expert witnesses in criminal trials. This history is tied to Fredric Wertham's experiences as an immigrant psychiatrist in the United States in a number of important ways, and Wertham's arguments about the relationship between the legal system and the psychiatrist are examined in the context of his books on psychiatry and criminality, *Dark Legend, The Show of Violence,* and *The Circle of Guilt.* This link is further investigated through an analysis of Wertham's ongoing debate with conservative psychiatrist Gregory Zilboorg about the future direction of American psychiatry as it pertained to the criminal act generally and criminal insanity specifically.

Chapter 2 broadly addresses American cultural commentators' and intellectuals' longstanding antipathy to various forms of popular culture on primarily aesthetic grounds. Following Patrick Brantlinger (1983), this chapter argues that the division between elite and popular cultures is a centuries-long tradition that culminated in postwar debates about the status and effects of television. The specific postwar anxieties about the role of mass culture in society, rooted in a rhetoric of democracy and inclusiveness, are examined in relation to the work of a coterie of writers collectively known as the "New York Intellectuals." Wertham's writings enter into this chapter through an analysis of his relatively limited yet nonetheless informative works on the role of high culture in shaping society and his fraught relationship to this group. These efforts include extensive commentaries on the interpretation of Shakespeare's *Hamlet,* psychological analyses of the fiction of Richard Wright and the drama of Arthur Miller, and Wertham's explanatory notes in *The World Within: Fiction Illuminating the Neuroses of Our Time* (1947), a short story collection edited by Mary Louise Aswell. Wertham's thoughts on the artist's social responsibility are addressed in an examination of his conception of artistic and literary production as either pro- or antiviolence. While Wertham shared many of the same traits and aesthetic predispositions as the New York Intellectuals, he was never actively integrated into that circle and was in fact often criticized by them. Chapter 2, therefore, outlines the critical discursive backdrop out of which the media-effects paradigm emerged and identifies the specific ways in which Wertham can be seen to be both working inside and outside of that tradition at various points in his career so that his legacy as a mass culture critic is perpetually placed into question.

Chapter 3 explores how Wertham's association with the mass culture critics who dominated the American intellectual scene in the postwar period was further jeopardized as attention turned away from purely aesthetic concerns toward a more overtly political critique of mass society. The immediate postwar years were characterized by a culture of affluence and consumption that witnessed the culmination of the progressivist goals for the nation. As the Truman administration began to put into place the final elements of Roosevelt's New Deal, critical intellectuals who had called for mass involvement in the state during the 1920s and 1930s increasingly began to see government itself as a potentially totalitarian threat to individual liberties. As American social problems were declared solved by postwar accommodations among government, industry, and organized labor, the intellectuals of the 1950s transferred their attention from labor to leisure and emphasized the need for individuals to free themselves from the threat posed by society. Shifting their emphasis from the social structure to the individual allowed intellectuals to displace economic problems with questions that were increasingly moral and psychological.

The difficulty of achieving autonomy within a mass society was conceptualized in a variety of ways. New conceptions of bureaucracy led to the elaboration of several important critiques of American society, including David Riesman's other-directed man (1950) and William Whyte's organization man (1956). These transformations took place within an increasingly conservative Cold War political climate and helped to lend immediacy to concerns about mass culture that otherwise might have been absent had the critiques remained at the level of the abstract or aesthetic. In an era in which intellectuals were increasingly loathe to criticize American social and economic institutions, the perception that mass society posed an inherent threat of totalitarianism energized concerns regarding the shape of American culture and fostered an interest in ongoing research into the effects of the mass media. If Wertham was sometimes at odds with other intellectuals where aesthetic questions were concerned, he was truly the odd man out in terms of political orientation. At a time when the majority of intellectuals reconciled with the American Cold War consensus of the 1950s, Wertham increased his calls for reform and actively supported causes that were seen as unpopular or even unpatriotic. The individualistic and anticommunist political underpinnings of accepted mass culture critiques are contrasted here with Wertham's call for broad-based collective social reforms, particularly in his 1966 book *A Sign for Cain,* and his support for Ethel Rosenberg. Wertham's important contributions to the desegregation trials in Delaware, which culminated in the Supreme Court's *Brown v. Board of Education* decision, are discussed in relation to efforts by the New York Intellectuals and others to displace civil rights following the Second World War. Wertham's political differences with this group ultimately enabled the marginalization of his arguments about mass culture as prevailing ideas about the effects of the media were consolidated in harmony with the Cold War consensus of the postwar period.

Chapter 4 brings the elements discussed in the first three chapters together around a single case study of his most famous and controversial book. The chapter examines Wertham's claims about the effects of comic book reading on children in various articles and *Seduction of the Innocent.* These claims are contrasted with competing analyses of comic books from a vast array of commentators, including literary critics, educators, librarians, psychologists, sociologists, and communication scholars. In total, more than two hundred separate articles written between 1938 and 1960 are surveyed. Furthermore, government and industry reactions to the work of Wertham and others concerned with the comic book question are documented to critically assess Wertham's role in shaping changes in the field of comic book publishing. By addressing Wertham's specific objections to American crime comic books in the postwar period, it is possible to come to terms with the particular reasons why his work would later be dismissed.

Wertham's theoretical foundations in reformist psychiatry and progressivist liberal political traditions allowed his work to be doubly discounted by social scientists. First, Wertham's work was assailed as nonscientific and impressionistic because of its failure to rely on the dominant experimental and survey methodologies. Second, Wertham's reformist politics allowed critics to characterize him as a moral crusader rather than a researcher. His detractors suggested that he had done no scientific or legitimate research but had merely helped to foster a moral panic, an irrational fear caused by social change. Thus, researchers in the social sciences began to disengage themselves from the critical intellectuals whose denunciations of mass culture had helped to spawn the field of popular culture studies. By characterizing Wertham and the intellectuals as moralizing crusaders and aesthetes, this field ultimately marked itself as a distinct area of study with a unique set of research methodologies that could be used to understand the media.

This shift is best seen through a comparison between Wertham's writings on the media and the institutionalized standards established by government hearings. In 1954 the Senate Subcommittee to Investigate Juvenile Delinquency looked into the role of comic books, television, and other social factors in fostering youth criminality. Wertham was one of the experts called to testify at the hearings on comic books, which were attended by a number of industry professionals and a very small number of social scientists, few of them communication scholars. The 1972 Senate Subcommittee on Communication hearings to investigate the surgeon general's report on the relationship between violence and television, conversely, was largely dominated by communication scholars. This shift in emphasis indicates how the quantitative social scientific method had triumphed as a way of thinking about popular culture in the intervening decades.

Chapter 5 specifically addresses the rise to dominance of this paradigm through reference to investigations of the effects of television on the lives of children from the end of the Second World War until the 1972 follow-up hearings on the surgeon general's report. Key to the development of popular culture research as a field of study has been the historical split between critical and empirical schools of thought. The critical school that viewed the mass media as manipulating society focused its attention over time on macrolevel studies of media ownership and control. The empirical school, however, viewed the media as potentially ameliorating social problems and was consequently more amenable to working with the broadcasting industry in an effort to direct social change through microlevel investigations concerned with effects. While the critical school has remained a constant force in American mass communication research, the empirical school has come to dominate the field. This chapter explains the ways in which the intersection of industry interests, the scientific method, and the desire to legitimate the study of popular culture in the eyes of governments and funding agencies led to a focus on the phenomenalistic approach to the media. The chapter traces the debate over the status of television by examining Wertham's responses to the foundational texts in the subcategory of television studies, Schramm, Lyle, and Parker (1961) and Himmelweit, Oppenheim, and Vince (1958). Wertham's commentaries on television from the late 1950s and 1960s are discussed to demonstrate the specific ways that they diverged from emergent quantifiable research methodologies. In addition, his unpublished manuscript on the effects of television on youth, *The War against Children,* is assessed in relationship to the success of *Seduction of the Innocent.* Finally, Wertham's work on fanzines is introduced to suggest the full degree to which his work diverged from the dominant modes of conceptualizing media audiences. This work enables the clearest possible picture of the extent to which Wertham's research represented the potential for an alternative paradigm that failed to materialize in his lifetime.

J. D. Peters argues that the media-effects paradigm developed in a scientific culture that emphasized the cleavage of facts and values (213). The rules of the social sciences insist that when political content is explicit in research, objectivity has been relinquished. Further, that authority rests on the researcher's ability to bracket values out of his or her findings. For someone like Fredric Wertham, concerned as he was with the ongoing and urgent need for progressive social change, such a bracketing was all but impossible. As a consequence, popular culture researchers whose interests remained tied to traditional notions of scientific validity and authority generally degraded Wertham's work. However, Wertham was also denied the possibility of emerging as a critical voice among the humanistic cultural commentators of his era insofar as those critics had occupied political positions that were at odds with Wertham's reformist intentions. The creeping neoconservatism of the New York Intellectuals and the insistence on valueless and quantitative methodologies from midcentury academic scholars left Wertham without any ground to occupy in the postwar debates about popular culture. Insofar as he was to have any influence, therefore, it was to be found at the level of the lay reader, in particular with inflamed parents' organizations and other crusaders caught up in a furor over comic books that quickly subsided in the wake of the industry's self-regulation. Unacceptable to his would-be colleagues and quickly passed over by a fickle public moving on to newer concerns, Wertham remains little more than a ghost in the history of American commentaries on the mass media. Yet where Wertham failed, the media-effects paradigm thrived. Shaped by industry needs and political ambivalence, communications researchers promised that the methodologies of the behavioral and social sciences that would solve the problems of public anxiety about mass culture through science. As Willard Rowland points out, this was a false hope that ultimately forced research into popular culture down a narrow and limiting path without resolving any of the questions that were intended to be solved: "The accommodations during the process of legitimizing mass communication research meant that short-term practical research such as audience attendance levels, communication and political persuasiveness, and reliable, readily administered methodologies came to displace long-term, more complex issues of societal and cultural impact and significance. The service of those interests militated against any comprehensive, intellectually grounded discussion of the role and meaning of mass communications in society and culture" (1983:294). The ability to have this "comprehensive, intellectually grounded discussion" depended on the inclusion of nonscientific and humanistic critical voices in the rigorous social scientific research that defined communications as a scholarly field in the 1950s. In short, such a nuanced version of popular culture research would have necessitated the inclusion and recognition of alternative scholars such as Fredric Wertham, whose qualitative methodologies and reformist tendencies were regarded as beyond the pale by the majority of effects researchers. Until such time as that research can be recognized as a historically important and potentially productive alternative to the dominant paradigm, it seems unlikely that the ghosts that haunt the study of the popular culture will be fully exorcised.

This book situates the work of Fredric Wertham within a series of twentieth-century cultural and critical histories. It is in no way intended to be a comprehensive biography of Wertham as a scholar or as a man. While the structure of the book is roughly chronological—beginning with Wertham's work on psychiatry and ending with his work on television some fifty years later—a number of instances of historical discontinuity have been brought about by the fact that Wertham never really abandoned any of his research interests at any point in his life. Thus, a certain level of familiarity with Wertham and his career will assist readers by allowing developments in his writings to be understood more easily.

Born on 20 March 1895 in Nuremberg as one of five children of Sigmund and Matilde Wertheimer, nonreligious, assimilated middle-class German Jews, Fredric Wertheimer was raised in Germany and England. He was studying medicine at King's College London, when he was briefly interred as a German national at the outbreak of the First World War. After the war, he continued his studies at the Universities of Munich and Erlangen in Germany and ultimately received his M.D. from the University of Würzburg in 1921. He did postgraduate work in psychiatry in Vienna, London, and Paris before landing in Munich as an assistant to Emil Kraepelin, Wertham's first significant mentor. Kraepelin (1856–1926) was one of the leading authorities on brain physiology as it related to the study of psychopathology. He rejected the dominant psychiatric orthodoxy of the day, in which psychiatrists made diagnoses based on symptomatic readings and theoretical assumptions. Instead, Kraepelin believed that context—family history, culture, environment, and economic and social factors—had to be considered in the treatment of a patient.

In 1922 Wertham moved to the United States on the invitation of Adolf Meyer, Kraepelin's best-known student and the director of the Phipps Psychiatric Clinic at Johns Hopkins University. Wertham became an American citizen in 1927 and remained at Johns Hopkins for seven more years. His positions during that time included chief resident in charge of psychiatry and assistant in charge of the Mental Hygiene Clinic. He also taught psychotherapy and brain anatomy. During that period he married Margaret Hesketh, a sculptor and illustrator, who collaborated with him on some of his earliest medical publications. Wertham was the first psychiatrist in the United States to receive a National Research Council fellowship, and he used the funding to return to Europe and complete the research he would publish in 1934 in the medical textbook *The Brain as an Organ*. While at Johns Hopkins, Wertham became friendly with Clarence Darrow because Wertham was one of the only psychiatrists willing to testify in court on behalf of indigent blacks accused of crimes.

In 1934, Wertham moved to New York, where he became a professor of clinical psychiatry at New York University as well as the head of the Court of General Sessions (later known as the State Supreme Court) psychiatric clinic, which gave examinations to every convicted felon in the city. From 1934 to 1936 he worked at Bellevue Hospital as the senior psychiatrist in the alcoholic, children's, and then prison wards. In 1936 Wertham became the director of Bellevue's Mental Hygiene Clinic, but he left that position in 1940 to become the director of psychiatric services at Queens Hospital Center, a job he held until his retirement in October 1952. During this period his interests gradually shifted from brain physiology to forensic psychiatry, and he became well known as an expert witness in criminal trials. In the ensuing decades, Wertham published three books—*Dark Legend* (1941), *The Show of Violence* (1949), *The Circle of Guilt* (1956)—and numerous articles on the role of the psychiatrist in judicial proceedings.

From 1946 to 1958 Wertham ran a psychiatric clinic in Harlem three nights per week. Fourteen volunteer psychiatrists and twelve social workers operated the Lafargue Clinic, situated in the basement of St. Philips Parish House on West 133d Street. The clinic charged twenty-five cents for a consultation—if the patient had the money. In 1947 he opened the Quaker Emergency Service Readjustment Center, which specialized in the treatment of sex offenders. In 1951, Wertham studied the effects of segregation on schoolchildren in Delaware, and his testimony was cited in the famous *Brown v. Board of Education* Supreme Court decision that desegregated American schools. Wertham also used his influence to interject himself into a number of public debates, acting as the psychiatrist to Ethel Rosenberg and as an adviser to the Hendrickson-Kefauver committee hearings on juvenile delinquency in the 1950s. Wertham continued to work in New York until the 1970s, when he retired to a farm in Pennsylvania. There, he passed away on 18 November 1981 at the age of eighty-six. He was cremated in Allentown, Pennsylvania, on the following day.

CHAPTER ONE

FROM FREUD TO SOCIAL PSYCHIATRY

Fredric Wertham opened a January 1953 article in the *Saturday Review* by observing, "At present this nation has more psychoanalysts—and incidentally more murders and more comic books—than any other two or three nations combined" (1953a:16). More succinctly than any other single sentence, this statement summarizes Wertham's preoccupations in the postwar period. The conjunction of psychoanalysis, human violence, and mass culture lay at the heart of his thinking. Moreover, it was virtually impossible for him to separate these interests from each other. To come to terms with Wertham's thinking on the effects of mass culture as they related to human violence in the form of comic books, it is necessary to first come to terms with the particular ways in which his approach to the study of the mass media was informed by his career as a psychiatrist.

In *White Collar,* C. Wright Mills argued that the postwar psychoanalytic literature promising peace of inner mind fit the "alienating process that has shifted from a focus on production to consumption" (1951:283). Wertham shared this concern. He rejected those aspects of Freudianism that drew heavily on conservative or aristocratic critics of mass society such as Gabriel Tarde and Gustave Le Bon and advanced in their stead a conception of "social psychiatry" that placed equal emphasis on the biological, familial, and societal influences on mental illness (Wertham 1963a:410). Indeed, it is impossible to come to terms with *Seduction of the Innocent*'s clinically based intervention into the media-effects debates without acknowledging

Wertham's unorthodox position in postwar psychiatry. Examining Wertham's writings on psychoanalysis and psychiatry during the first half of the twentieth century demonstrates the ways in which psychiatric issues—especially those derived from the mental hygiene movement—reinforced his unique critique of mass culture. The ways in which Wertham negotiated the intellectual and professional paradigms of psychiatry suggest the ways in which he similarly negotiated those of media effects and the critique of mass culture. Examining Wertham's relationship to pre- and postwar psychoanalysis and psychiatry lays a foundation for understanding his specific intervention into the postwar debates about comic books and other aspects of mass culture.

The intersection of scientific knowledge and psychoanalysis connected in the mental hygiene movement was largely influenced by a number of doctors at Johns Hopkins University, where Wertham began teaching in 1922. Hopkins director Adolf Meyer had long urged psychiatry to move away from its roots in philosophy and toward clinical research that would help to legitimate its scientific orientation. Specifically, he advocated a holistic approach to mental illness based on an understanding of the dynamic interplay between a patient's mental and physical faculties. Meyer termed this approach "psychobiology" and helped make it the central premise of the American mental hygiene movement (Richardson 1989:23). This movement was an extension of existing public health movements in the field of psychiatry and emphasized the application of scientific knowledge to the nation's social life in much the same way as the media-effects paradigm did later in the century. Meyer coined the term "mental hygiene" for the movement that he suggested should concentrate on preventative psychiatry (Richardson 1989:49).

The linking of human biology and psychiatry allowed Meyer and his followers to approach the patient as an integrated whole. As with psychoanalysis, Meyer stressed the importance of childhood on mental development, but he went beyond Freud in insisting on the equal importance of the home, the school, and the community in shaping the development of young minds. Meyer insisted on the need to study all features of a patient's life to arrive at a proper diagnosis and plan of treatment. To this end, Meyer appreciated Freud for the way in which he had helped to broaden and humanize psychiatry but at the same time criticized him for failing to take account of the "social formulation" of mental processes (Dreyer 1972:109).

In 1923 Wertham copublished his first medical/scientific article, "Concerning Psychoanalysis" (Wertham and Meyer 1923). This article argued for a greater interdependence between physicians and psychiatrists in the treatment of patients, a theme that would resonate in Wertham's subsequent medical work. In the following years, Wertham published extensively on medical and scientific topics in several journals, including *Annales Medico-Psychologiques, Mental Hygiene,* the *American Journal of Psychiatry,* and *State Hospital Quarterly.* Wertham's indebtedness to Meyer can be seen in the fact that the journal to which he contributed the majority of his early writing was *Archives of Neurology and Psychiatry,* on whose editorial board his mentor served. These publications formed the basis for his first important monograph, *The Significance of the Physical Constitution in Mental Disease* (Wertham and Hesketh 1926). This booklet outlined the fundamental assumptions of Wertham's early research as a psychiatrist and expounded many of the formal beliefs on which his subsequent work in cultural psychiatry rested.

Briefly, *The Significance of the Physical Constitution in Mental Disease* suggested, following the work of Meyer and Emile Kraepelin, that while individual persons are unique, people themselves are classifiable with regard to habitus (body form), inner organs, and psychobiology. In his study of sixty-five randomly chosen men from the Phipps Clinic, Wertham, following Kretschmer's typologies, identified four morphological body types. Moreover, Wertham proposed that while a correlation existed between morphological constitution, mental disease, and personality (65), a fundamental connection suggesting biological determinacy was inconceivable unless one were to ultimately believe in the power of fate over science. In short, Wertham stressed the biological factor of mental disease without adopting an absolute or eugenic position that would minimize the importance of the interpersonal or social elements of psychiatry.

Wertham's career path took a major turn at the beginning of the 1930s when he became the first psychiatrist in the United States to be awarded the prestigious National Research Council Fellowship. Wertham used these funds to undertake the research that would go into the writing of his medical textbook, *The Brain as an Organ* (Wertham and Wertham 1934), which contained an introduction by Meyer. Wertham's research at this time was almost exclusively forensic and scientific, focusing on brain lesions. Wertham's textbook opened by suggesting that the prevailing method of studying the brain had reached an impasse and that progress could only be made if a simpler conception were devised. Fundamental to Wertham's argument was the then-radical suggestion that the brain was an organ of the body similar to other organs and not, as had previously been assumed, something unique unto itself in anatomical terms. *The Brain as an Organ,* like the vast majority of Wertham's earliest publications, is best seen as the writing of a physician and scientist concerned with questions that are primarily medical rather than social. Although these works were informed by his political and social convictions, they do not directly address questions of significance for the study of popular culture. In his later works, however, Wertham forged an alliance among medical research, psychoanalytic therapy, and social theory that would lead to his interest in mass culture.

While he was writing *The Brain as an Organ,* Wertham relocated from Baltimore to New York, where the New York Department of Hospitals named him the senior psychiatrist at Bellevue Hospital. He also organized and directed the Court of General Sessions, a clinic responsible for screening every felon convicted in the city. In 1936 he became director of Bellevue's Mental Hygiene Clinic, and four years later he moved to the Queens Hospital Center, where he became director of psychiatric services. In coming into contact with career criminals, Wertham's attention slowly moved away from strictly medical questions and toward the work for which he would be best known. Wertham's dramatically reduced medical writings over the course of the next decade provide evidence of this shift. Nonetheless, Wertham made a number of noteworthy minor interventions into the psychiatric study of human behavior.

First, Wertham developed the mosaic test, a projective test intended as an aid in psychiatric diagnosis. He first described this test in an article published in the *American Journal of Psychiatry* (Wertham and Golden 1941). This test utilized a series of multicolored geometric pieces with which patients were asked to design an image that would be analyzed by the psychiatrist, often in conjunction with the analysis of a patient's other artworks. Wertham used this test on many of his patients, including Zelda Fitzgerald.

Second, Wertham diagnosed a psychiatric syndrome that he suggested went a considerable way toward fostering an understanding of the means through which fantasies of violence are transmuted into acts of violence. Wertham's studies in what he ultimately termed the catathymic crisis (from the Greek *kata* meaning "according to" and *thymos* meaning "wish") found their origins in his belief that psychiatry needed to bring psychopathology to bear on the criminal mind (Wertham 1937). The catathymic crisis was seen as a specific behavioral manifestation in patients who acquired the idea that they must carry out a violent act against themselves or another person. He described this not as obsessional but as a specific urge that met a resistance in the conscious mind that caused a delay. According to Wertham, "Practically, the conception of the catathymic crisis as a clinical entity seems indispensable for the understanding of certain forms of violent crime and suicide. Theoretically, it leads to interesting sidelights on general psychopathology. The period following the crime, for example, has a superficial appearance of normality. But it can be demonstrated that during this time a profound inner adjustment is taking place which finally leads to a complete shift in the person's attitude and results in the gain of insight and the reestablishment of an equilibrium which is lasting" (977). The biologic and intrapsychic basis of the catathymic crisis stands as an important juncture between Wertham's strictly medical writings and his later socially oriented work on the nature and character of human violence.

Finally, Wertham wrote a much-cited study of the relationship between psychiatry and physical pain. In 1944, he developed a nearly fatal case of thrombophlebitis in his right leg that required emergency surgery. The specifics of the case were such that he was unable to receive anesthetic and was awake for the entire procedure as well as for a second operation on his left leg conducted shortly thereafter. During these operations Wertham had his spoken utterances recorded by a stenographer for later analysis. His subsequent study of the pain he had endured was one of the first to record such a psychologically abnormal experience from the inside point of view of the patient. In two articles (Wertham 1945a, c) he argued that Freud's contention that a "sick man withdraws his libido" was oversimplified and that the dissociation between mood and behavior can be complex to a degree that the available literature had not demonstrated. For example, Wertham wrote that during the operation he laughed with the surgeons and made puns ("Don't get demoralized; get demerol-ized" [1945c:171]). These observations on his own mental state were well received and subsequently reprinted, and his experience was written up by *Time* in the magazine's medical section ("Speaking" 1945).

Wertham's self-study was related to the mosaic test and the catathymic crisis insofar as it demonstrated the ways in which he sought to unite intrapsychic complexes to interpersonal relations in the furtherance of a scientific
psychiatry. From that basis in scientific psychiatry, Wertham would seek to
make real interventions into his social and cultural environment, and scientific
thinking remained a constant background for the developments of his later
career even as he moved away from strictly medical and scientific writings.

Wertham's transition from medical researcher to socially oriented psychiatrist occurred after his move to New York and the start of his work with
that city's court system. He wrote on a number of occasions that his desire
to pursue psychiatry as a profession had been profoundly influenced by his
correspondence with Freud while in college. It is somewhat surprising,
therefore, that so little of Wertham's earliest writings touch on Freud's work
in any serious fashion. Not until 1949 did he publish his definitive article on
Freudian analysis. This timing, however, coincides with the significant rise
to prominence of Freudianism in the United States following the Second
World War. Indeed, if psychoanalysis was born in Vienna in the 1890s, it
grew strongest in the United States of the mid–twentieth century.

Following the German *Anschluss* of 11 March 1938, Freud and many of his
followers who had remained in Vienna emigrated to England, and when
Freud died the next year, a number of the remaining analysts moved on to
the United States. An estimated two-thirds of all European psychoanalysts
emigrated to the United States during the 1930s, thereby ending the continental stranglehold on psychoanalysis and shifting the base of power to
America (Fermi 1971:142). In America, Freud's argument for progressive
sexual reform found a receptive audience in a nation emerging from its
puritanical roots. At the same time, America's decentralized medical establishment, emphasis on the individual, and progressivist traditions lent psychoanalysis an air of legitimacy that it might have otherwise lacked. In
short, the United States and psychoanalysis provided each other with the
tools necessary to develop in new directions.

The First World War had provided a seedbed for psychoanalysis in the
United States insofar as the conflict seemed to confirm a number of Freudian
hypotheses relating to the nature of conflict, catharsis, and instinctual
drives. Following the war, the role of psychoanalysis rapidly advanced in the
United States as treatments were sought for shell shock and other postwar

trauma syndromes. The development of the mental hygiene movement in the 1920s combined behaviorism and psychoanalysis in an attempt to stem mental illness and delinquency, which was increasingly regarded as a medical problem. While psychoanalysis was ascendant in America in the first decades of the twentieth century, the Second World War truly conferred legitimacy. Psychiatrists were drafted into service in an effort to weed the psychologically unfit from the armed forces and to treat returning veterans suffering from war neuroses. Following the wartime successes of psychiatry, the National Institute of Mental Health was formed in 1946. Increasingly, psychotherapy was becoming the treatment of choice for dealing with mental illness, and psychoanalysis was becoming the dominant model of psychotherapy.

At the same time, psychiatric practice was seriously shifting away from the mental hospital toward private practice. In 1947, half of all American psychiatrists were affiliated with hospitals, but a decade later that number had dropped to 16 percent (Hale 1995:246), likely as a result of the fact that psychoanalysis was undergoing tremendous popularization, with hundreds of books and articles published each year. Interest in psychoanalysis peaked in 1956 with the celebration of Freud's one hundredth birthday. The new popularizers were generally uncritical of Freudian thought; as a consequence, some observers have argued, the United States became more conservative, orthodox, and Freudian than even Freud ever was (Hale 1995). As Freud increasingly replaced Marx as the intellectual forefather of choice among American intellectuals, a number of psychoanalysts, including Erich Fromm and Fredric Wertham, voiced criticisms of the conservative tenor of psychoanalysis in the United States.

Wertham's statement on Freud and Freudianism, "Freud Now," was published in *Scientific American* and was presented as the views of a "noted psychoanalyst" on the "present condition of Freud's legacy" (1949c). According to Wertham, Freud's significant accomplishments in psychoanalysis included the development of the appreciation of the role of sexuality in personality development; the development of the distinctions among the unconscious, preconscious, and conscious minds; and the development of ideas including repression, condensation, displacement, and sublimation. Moreover, Freud effected a massive change simply by speaking of psychological processes. That he did so with a logic of science evidenced by the idea of the unconscious and a practical method of investigation helped to advance the understanding of the mind by bringing humanity to science, an attitude previously expressed by Meyer.

Yet in Wertham's eyes, Freud and more importantly Freudianism were hardly beyond reproach. Wertham suggested that Freud's thinking moved from a materialist basis rooted in the natural sciences toward a mechanistic idealism that paved the way for the reactionary mysticism of Carl Jung. Wertham alleged that the Freudian notion of the death instinct was "off the deep end," arguing that in that instance Freud strayed close to the thought of Heidegger, "the most influential Nazi philosopher" (53). In contemporary usage, Wertham suggested that politically conservative psychiatrists in private practice had emphasized the conservative tendencies of late Freudian thought to such a degree that Freudianism was no longer a help to anyone: "The great discovery of psychoanalysis was the discovery of the individual. The great error of late orthodox psychoanalysis is to see the problems, the processes and the solutions only within the individual" (54). He argued that one way of reversing this trend was through an expansion of Freudian logic. While Freud correctly focused on the formative power of the family, Wertham wanted psychiatrists to expand the social circle to encompass the personality-shaping influence of society as a whole. This new conception of personality development, he suggested, necessitated regarding Freudian thought as historically situated and open to dialogical development:

> We psychoanalysts who wish to guard the true heritage of Freud and develop in a truly progressive manner do not visualize the future scientific development of psychoanalysis in terms of a formalistic allegiance to dogmatic doctrine as it stands. One must reconstruct Freud's work on the basis of a realistic philosophy, of newer and broader clinical observations, and on the full utilization of the experiences of mankind during the last two decades. Neglect of the social element in psychoanalysis is based largely on the too-mechanical separation of biological and social. Such a psychological phenomenon as the Oedipus complex gains its real force from the very fact that it indicates both the social and biological points of greatest tension. (54)

Of note in this instance are not only Wertham's use of the term *we* to describe Freud's "true heritage" but more importantly the emphasis on the interrelationship of biology and society that marked the intersection of his medical training and writing with the liberal politics and social conscience that would structure the majority of his best-known scholarship. That type of scholarship would come to the fore as he increasingly turned his attention away from purely theoretical debates with the orthodox Freudians and toward the application of psychoanalysis in forensic psychiatry.

Wertham's 1932 move from Baltimore to New York marked a significant shift in his writings. He became less concerned with medical subjects and increasingly cognizant of the important role society played in the structuring of individual personalities. His work with the Court of General Sessions helped to spark interest in the ways in which psychiatry could potentially benefit the courts. By 1934 Wertham emerged as a well-known forensic psychiatrist who had testified in a number of notorious New York murder trials and emerged as a leading critic of the poor administrative relationship between the courts and medical experts. Wertham's experiences as an expert witness in various murder trials were the subject of two books published during the 1940s, *Dark Legend* (1941) and *The Show of Violence* (1949). In each of these books, he argued that the psychiatrist's role in the court of law was to bring out the psychiatric background of murder in relationship to the law and the society it represented.

The relationship of murder, law, and society particularly fascinated Wertham and became the subject of much of his writing. His interest in murder as a social phenomenon was articulated concisely in a 1949 essay, "It's Murder," published in the *Saturday Review* (1949d) as a preview to *The Show of Violence*. In this essay, Wertham suggested that America as a nation was fascinated with murder and murderers and that this fascination had led to a view that crime was an exceptional circumstance divorced from social origins and unique unto itself. He reminded readers that, divorced from its mythologies, murder was not exceptional but commonplace. He argued that the idea that murderers were hounded by guilt was seriously held only by "romantic poets and conservative psychoanalysts" (8), suggesting instead that every murderer had a justification or rationalization for his acts. Wertham further argued that rationalizations for murder did not merely constitute the fictions of individuals but rather symbolized "the ideology of a previous stage of society" (8).

The relationship of murder to the criminal's social background was similarly highlighted by the historical status of murder. Wertham suggested that history could be written in terms of the ways with which societies dealt with murders and murderers. Following this logic, Wertham condemned the American postwar period as an era in which murder was not taken seriously as a crime—as evidenced by unsolved cases relating to racially motivated killings, particularly in the South—and in which there existed a general devaluation of human life that prevented the possibility of changing society in any significantly progressive fashion: "There is no healing murder. The real problem is prevention. That requires not only the changing of man but the changing of conditions, the modification not only of individual impulses but of social institutions. The question is not only why one does it, but how one justifies it. Those dangers of violence that threaten us come not from the heads of individual men but from social circumstances. Murder is an embolus. The disease lies elsewhere. It is not so much a matter of episodic violence as a continuous violation of human life, which even now is no more than a vaguely professed ideal" (34). Wertham's thoughts on the relationship between the act of murder and the social context from which it emerged formed one of the central concerns of his first books written for nonspecialist audiences.

Dark Legend, his first book-length general interest publication, was a case history of a matricide. Gino, a young Italian immigrant living with his family in New York, surrendered for arrest after stabbing his mother thirty-two times with a bread knife. Wertham testified on Gino's competence to stand trial, arguing that the youth did not know the difference between right and wrong and therefore was by definition legally insane. Gino was ultimately committed to a hospital for psychiatric observation, and Wertham was his psychiatrist. Wertham's conclusions regarding Gino's motives for the murder depended on an interpretation of the crime that equally emphasized Gino's life history and his social status as an impoverished Italian immigrant living in New York. Although Wertham considered the possibility of a biological basis for Gino's mental disorder, Wertham ultimately placed little stock in the possibility, arguing that the disorder was psychological rather than physical (127–29). The psychological drives that factored into the murder in this instance were largely the result of Gino's life history, which Wertham recorded in the first-person testimony of the killer for more than 60 pages in this 233-page book.

Gino was the oldest of three children of a New York man who died when Gino was only six years old. At that time, his mother relocated the family to

Borda, Italy, where she began to neglect the children while spending time with the father's married brother, Aiello. This neglect enraged Gino, who prayed to his father for the strength to avenge his family name by killing his uncle, an act that he never carried out. At the age of thirteen, Gino and his family returned to New York, where his mother began a series of relationships with different men, all of whom Gino despised and feared. At the same time, he became his family's sole financial supporter. Although he felt unable to disobey his mother by leaving the family or quitting his job, Gino also felt an overwhelming urge to restore his family honor. Gino ultimately murdered his mother as she slept, an act for which he told Wertham he had no remorse: "I never slept so well like I slept now. I was glad I did it. I did what I thought was right. I will never be sorry. Nothing bothers me now. I am sorry I didn't do it a long time ago. I don't believe in forgiving. When I am good to somebody I am really good. I can forgive anybody who would give me a slap, but not one who dishonors my family. I can't take it. About my honor I don't forgive" (120–21). Wertham interpreted Gino's prayers to his father for strength and his fixation on the question of family honor as a fantasy identification with his father. Wertham further suggested that the image of the father—of the adult—had been interrupted by the father's untimely death. The question of family honor, following this line of reasoning, was simply a rationalization rooted in the particular ideology of a previous historical era (153).

According to Wertham, the rationalization of family honor was likely instilled in Gino during his time in Borda, a period in which his sense of family became badly confused and deeply associated with violence. From this point of view, the social world was implicated in the causes of the murder but did not itself take on a proximate role. The impulse that actually led to the murder, Wertham argued, stemmed from Gino's inability to successfully negotiate the sense of degradation he felt by the usurpation of his father's role by his uncle. In this way, Gino's story remarkably resembled the stories of Hamlet and Orestes, the two most famous matricides in fiction. To support this connection, Wertham placed significance on a number of facts related to the actual murder as well as to Gino's life history. First, Gino killed his mother while she slept, an act that Wertham interpreted as the slaying of the mother image rather than of the mother. This was related to a general misogyny present in Gino and rooted in his deep-seated hatred of his sexuality that manifested as a connection between sex and death.

The threads that bound Gino's fantasies of sex and revenge were incest and the dread of incest. Wertham suggested that the development of incest taboos was historically situated late in the development of civilization and was bound to the right to own women under patriarchy. Gino's jealousy of his mother's lovers, therefore, took the form of a subconscious awareness that he was losing the ownership of his mother that was his due under patriarchal authority as he entered adulthood. This led to destructive fantasies about her that were aggravated by the impoverished living conditions in which the family found itself. Unable to negotiate the entry into adulthood because of the traumatic impact of the behavior of his mother, his emotional conflict necessitated some resolution. Wertham suggested that Gino found an "illusory path" related to vindicating the family honor by clearing his father's name (189). Thus, killing his mother became for Gino an act symbolic of adulthood that was rooted in his continuing deeply held love/hate relationship as both son and symbolic patriarch: "He could no longer see his mother apart from all other women nor other women apart from his mother. He could not run away because he loved his mother and could not leave her. The mother-image, loved and hated at the same time, overshadowed all his life. It had to be destroyed" (190). Wertham's conclusions based on this interpretation were twofold: first, Gino was the victim of a catathymic crisis in which an act of violence against his mother was the only way he could relieve his profound unconscious emotional conflict; second, Gino's actions were related to the historical ritual injuries inflicted on tribal mothers under patriarchy. Wertham termed this hostility to mothers based on excessive attachment and patriarchal feelings the Orestes complex and suggested that it be seriously considered by psychoanalysts in addition to the Oedipal complex described by Freud.

Wertham's second book on the subject of murder, *The Show of Violence* (1949i) differed from the first insofar as it gave the case histories of six different murder cases or trials along with opening and closing chapters that generally discussed the question of murder and specifically looked at the psychiatrist's role in the murder trial. Briefly, Wertham argued that psychiatrists could play a central role in murder trials because murder was a crime that grew from negative emotions such as fear, anxiety, anger, and frustration. As the science best equipped to deal with emotions, psychiatry could provide tremendous fact-finding insight that could transform the nature of society: "Psychiatry and jurisprudence must be parts of a planned social response to an individual anti-social action" (19).

The murder cases detailed in the volume varied, but each contained a touch of the lurid or the sensational. The first was the case of a woman whom Wertham diagnosed as having had a catathymic crisis after she murdered her two children and attempted to end her own life. Another case of bureaucratic incompetence related by Wertham was the case of a man named Forlino who had murdered his nephew but who received inadequate treatment from the authorities. The case of Martin Lavin cemented Wertham's stature as a forensic psychiatrist. Lavin had been charged with the murder of a man during a bar holdup, and Wertham contended that Lavin was not insane in any way and that he was faking his symptoms. This case brought Wertham a degree of fame in New York at the time when he staked his professional reputation—under oath at the trial—on his absolute belief that Lavin would kill again if he were released into society. Three months later, Lavin killed a police officer, and Wertham was praised in the press as the one man who had understood the real problem, although no one had listened to him.

Two other cases were more notorious. In 1935, Albert Fish became one of the most notorious serial killers in the United States, a sexual predator who cannibalized his victims. Wertham testified at Fish's trial that he suffered from paranoid psychosis, but the jury ultimately ruled that Fish was sane and sentenced him to death. Wertham cited the case as an example of exceptional mishandling of jurisprudence and crime prevention because Fish had been institutionalized at least eight times for minor offenses and was never properly diagnosed but rather was released each time to resume his murders.

According to Wertham, authorities similarly mishandled the Robert Irwin case. Irwin, dubbed the "Mad Sculptor" by the tabloid press, had been in and out of mental institutions for a decade before he murdered three people in a New York boardinghouse. Irwin was a self-castrator whom Wertham diagnosed as suffering from catathymic crisis, while other psychiatrists had diagnosed schizophrenia. Irwin's case became widely known after he sold his confession to the Hearst newspaper chain, which ran large stories on the case over several days in the summer of 1937 before turning Irwin over to the authorities.

Perhaps the most interesting case in *The Show of Violence* was the story of a woman who attacked her two children, killing one of them. Wertham wrote that the case reminded him of the tragedy of Medea, the legendary wife of Jason who killed her children rather than face the shame of abandonment. Wertham suggested that the various myths of Medea should be understood as a parable in which a woman asserts her womanhood in a misogynist world but nonetheless loses that womanhood by this assertion. He saw much the same pattern in this case. The accused was an impoverished woman with two children whom she had not wanted in the first place. She was unable to care for them, but social workers denied her adequate assistance and discouraged her from giving the children up for adoption. Wertham argued that the community that denied this woman assistance in caring for her children was culpable in their deaths because it had neglected to come to the assistance of the children and the mother before she took such extreme actions: "When a physical explosion occurs and a person gets killed you want a complete inquiry into the causes. You are not satisfied with just knowing about the last spark. You want to know about the location, the circumstances, the inspection, the reason why inflammable material was kept where it was, and so on. In a murder case we don not usually do that, though in addition to the responsibility of the individual there is a responsibility of the community as well" (234).

By denying this woman her dignity as an individual—just as Jason had denied the dignity of Medea by sentencing her to exile—the community had precipitated the murder of those children. The difference between Medea and this woman, Wertham argued, was that "the ancient temples are in ruins, and times and human nature have changed. There was nothing heroic about her—not even anything tragic. The tragedy lies elsewhere, in the contrast between our civilized morality and our uncivilized social responsibility" (235). Wertham concluded by stating that the maternal instinct did not operate in a social vacuum and announced that he would testify on the woman's behalf to the effect that the crime could have been prevented with the aid of the community. This case led Wertham to conclude that most psychiatrists undervalued the way that inner conflicts in individuals were linked to social conflicts and that individual and social factors in psychology were not opposing forces but were bound together. In support of this observation, he suggested that the problem of infanticide had historically related to patriarchy and its manifestations in successive societies. In the contemporary situation, Wertham extended that argument to suggest that the higher rate of infant mortality among blacks in the United States reflected the way that America as a nation devalued certain lives and facilitated an ongoing climate of murder and violence.

Wertham's condemnation of a generalized devaluation of human life led to a series of prescriptive measures intended to curb violence in the United States. For example, Wertham wrote a number of articles suggesting ways in which sex crimes might be curtailed. A 1938 article, "Psychiatry and Prevention of Sex Crimes," one of Wertham's first publications on the relationship of psychiatry and criminality that would structure later writings such as *Seduction of the Innocent,* claimed that neither of the two existing orthodoxies relating to prevention had merit (Wertham 1938). The legal perspective on prevention advocated greater degrees of punishment but failed to safeguard the community. The psychological perspective, which suggested that sex crimes stemmed from personality quirks in individual perpetrators, similarly failed because it did not address the role of society in the development of social ills.

Wertham contended that most sex criminals were caught between "crime and disease" (849) and that "psychiatrically speaking there is no such thing as a single individual all by himself. One can neither understand nor treat a man alone; one can only study man-in-society" (850). The key to prevention, therefore, was cooperation between psychiatric and legal agencies directed at the understanding and correction of the social circumstances in which individuals found themselves. Interestingly, his conclusion foreshadowed the arguments that he would mobilize more than a decade later in relation to the influence of comic books: "a child is like a flower; the vast majority of human beings will grow up to a healthy enough sexual development if all the social circumstances and surroundings are favorable. Let us not begin by dissecting and delving into the minds of children. Let us first correct and improve the circumstances under which they grow up" (853).

Twenty-three years later, Wertham's position had evolved in the details, yet the underlying assumptions remained the same. In a *Ladies' Home Journal* article, "Sex Crimes Can Be Prevented" (Wertham 1961), he outlined five "practical measures" that parents, the media, and public authorities could take to safeguard children from sexual predators. Wertham's recommendations included the warning of children by parents, the reduction of mass media sadism, adequate psychiatric treatment for all persons convicted of both major and minor sexually related offenses, more community-based psychiatric clinics, and a greater exchange between experts in all fields of violence prevention.

Throughout his writing on violent crimes generally and murder specifically, Wertham carefully reminded his readers that violence was a social condition. One example that he provided on a number of occasions was the fact that anthropologists have pointed out that in some societies it was not a crime to kill a stranger to the tribe, while in others accidental killings were subject to the same treatment as deliberate homicides. In a 1954 article in the *New York Times Magazine*, Wertham (1954l) addressed the question of how death wishes were translated into action. He argued that a catalyst was required to transform thought into act; more importantly, however, the whole life experience and personality of a killer were also required. Wertham suggested that the difference between a thought and an action was never as simple as a single impulse because murder required an impulse strong enough to allow it to overcome social and moral inhibitions. More to the point, Wertham maintained that while the question of why men kill might remain eternal, society already knew enough about the answer to better prevent the crime in the first place. In a well-ordered society, insane murderers and sex murderers would present the smallest problem because "most of these people come to the attention of the authorities long before they murder. Instead of quibbling about legal insanity after the event, we should provide treatment or guidance before it" (50).

Moreover, Wertham announced his belief that the end of murder as a social phenomenon was foreseeable. He suggested that historically the incidence of incest had been reduced by society's adoption of it as a major taboo and that murder could similarly be minimized. Wertham's response to the question of why humans kill was tied to his reformist belief that killing itself could be stopped: "Buried in the works of Freud is this sentence: 'Conflicts of interests among human beings are principally decided by the application of violence.' Undoubtedly that was true. But I don't believe it always will be. Even though we live in a violent period, I am certain that the ways of violence will eventually be replaced by reason" (50). Wertham's liberal faith in the possibility of far-reaching social reform clearly consisted of a near-utopian view of humanity's potential to effect the broadest conceivable social changes. This belief was closely related to the mental hygiene perception of juvenile delinquency as a curable social problem. Crucial to this attitude was the notion of the *parens patriae* principle as an expression of the common good.

Adopted at the end of the nineteenth century, this principle redefined the child not as a criminal offender but as a juvenile delinquent and thereby granted the child the protection of the court. Under this new understanding, instead of punishment, prevention of juvenile delinquency through "child guidance" became the paramount concern. The idea of child guidance sought to apply psychiatry to the identification of abnormal emotional development at a young age so that potential deviants might be corrected or redirected. By 1930 there were more than five hundred permanent child guidance clinics in the United States (Richardson 1989:107). Tying the scientific study of emotions and human relations to specific interventions into the social realm, Wertham suggested, would necessitate a view of psychiatry that was at odds with America's dominant individualist paradigm of the time. That particular paradigm was supported by orthodox Freudians, and Wertham spent considerable energy engaged in an effort to redirect American psychoanalysis after Freud.

The question of whether psychiatry and psychoanalysis were to make specific interventions into the social realm or were to be limited to the treatment of individual patients was the subject of much of Wertham's writing. Specifically, this question was the source of Wertham's ongoing disagreement with Gregory Zilboorg, an orthodox Freudian psychiatrist who served as chairman of the influential New York Psychoanalytic Society. Over the years, the two men's disagreements ranged across a number of topics in many venues.

Their most public encounter occurred in the pages of *The Nation* in 1950, when both men responded to an article in which Dorothy Ferman argued that psychoanalysis had destroyed her marriage. This public debate spilled out of the magazine and was reported on by *Time* ("Couch Cult" 1950). Ferman wrote that her marriage had ended on the recommendation of her husband's analyst, whom she blamed for needlessly rehashing grievances and life experiences from her husband's childhood rather than attempting to cure him. Ferman argued that psychoanalysis had become caught up in its own "hoopla" and that although it might help some individuals, it could also be destructive to others (1950:185). In his response, Wertham contended that what Ferman wrote rang true, suggesting that "ordinary problems" of the type that Ferman described her husband as having suffered did not require orthodox analysis. He also suggested that psychiatrists were the only doctors who when they could not cure their patients, blamed them or their families; furthermore, he wrote, eight out of ten orthodox analyses were entirely unwarranted. He concluded that psychiatrists seemed to seek to adjust people to mass society (1950c:205–7). Zilboorg, responding to both Ferman and Wertham, took an entirely different position. Deeming Ferman an "unfortunate, unhappy, bitter person" and Wertham an "excellent clinician" who nonetheless suffered from an antipsychoanalytic bias, Zilboorg argued that little could be achieved by attacking psychoanalysis in the pages of a national magazine (1950:207–8). He concluded that true psychoanalysis was orthodox psychoanalysis and that the establishment of a national board for psychotherapists that would enforce orthodox training could correct the problems of the type outlined by Ferman.

While this dispute between two psychiatrists of differing methodological outlooks might appear to be minor on the surface, it was in fact symptomatic of a far deeper dispute between Wertham's conception of a social psychiatry and orthodox Freudianism. This dispute played out around criminal questions generally and specifically around the utility of the McNaughton rule, which at that time governed determinations of legal insanity. The rule had its origins in English law. In 1843 a man named M'Naghten had shot and killed a man named Drummond, the private secretary of Sir Robert Peel, the intended victim. The defense at the trial was insanity, and the court established that the purpose of criminal law was to punish willfully committed wrongdoing. As a result, McNaughton was committed to an asylum until his death but was acquitted of the charge. By the mid–twentieth century in the United States, however, this basis for legal insanity was increasingly under siege by psychiatrists, who proposed new understandings that would give psychiatric testimony and expertise greater weight in the courtroom.

This group included Zilboorg, who, in a 1951 book on Sigmund Freud, argued that criminology had come thoroughly under the psychoanalytic influence and the McNaughton rule was being undermined by more recent, Freudian understandings of mental processes (1951:8). In his 1955 book, *The*

Psychology of the Criminal Act and Punishment, dedicated entirely to the relationship between psychoanalysis and criminality, Zilboorg contended that "the future historian will some day assess the true harm that the McNaughton rule has done to justice as well as to scientific criminology and forensic psychiatry" (1955:8–9). Zilboorg argued that a more modern approach to forensic psychiatry would necessarily come to terms not only with criminal deeds but also with perpetrators who acted out of an innate aggressive desire to do injury. He recommended the establishment of a board of unbiased expert witnesses who would diagnose all accused criminals and testify at all trials. This board would be run by the American Psychiatric Association and would be charged with classifying criminals based on the danger they posed to society. Some criminals charged only with minor offenses would ultimately be condemned to life in asylums, while others would be cured and released (130–37). Zilboorg's proposals would clearly have placed near-total authority over life and death matters in the hands of a small group of psychiatric experts.

Wertham was similarly interested in the legal definition of insanity, although he did not advocate the overthrow of the McNaughton rule but instead sought some changes in its interpretation. His position was most clearly enunciated in the first chapter of *The Show of Violence.* There he traced the history of the insanity defense in criminal cases, settling on four key eras: the scholastic/theological view of right and wrong that dominated the Middle Ages and was ended by Erskine; the metaphysical view of right and wrong that was ended by McNaughton in 1843; the psychological perspective of Freudian theories that violence was an irresistible impulse; and the scientific social view that he argued was defined by Judge Cardozo in his challenge to the McNaughton ruling. Cardozo challenged the McNaughton rule by placing the question of responsibility in a secondary position. Instead, Cardozo suggested that the law test the "true capacity" of the individual. The proof of mental disorder—regardless of degree—would increasingly supplement and replace the test of personal responsibility.

In championing Cardozo's legal interpretation of insanity, Wertham suggested that the McNaughton rule still retained a degree of medieval retribution and refused to draw the type of clear distinctions between the ill and the well that would be necessary in a humane and just society. Society's response to the sick must differ from its response to the well insofar as society must ensure that individuals with morbid impulses were protected from themselves as much as society was protected from them. To do this, psychiatrists would need to develop a social orientation corresponding to the growing awareness of social responsibility in a changing world. They could no longer shirk their duty to determine "where individual guilt resolves itself into social responsibility" (Wertham 1949i:18). In this way, psychiatrists would make themselves truly useful to the courts in their capacity as fact finders rather than advocates, thereby helping to end the "cancer of present-day hyper-individualistic psychiatry" (Wertham 1953c:51), which, Wertham believed, had done nothing to solve the problem of violence.

Wertham's embrace of Cardozo's interpretation of the McNaughton rule did not extend to the elimination of the rule itself. While admitting various faults with the rule, Wertham opposed efforts to repeal it altogether and replace it with the Durham rule of 1954 or the American Law Institute ruling of 1962, both of which many states adopted. In Wertham's eyes, the McNaughton rule was a highly elastic safeguard against abuse that would be curtailed by newer rulings. Although Wertham allowed that many judges had interpreted the McNaughton rule too narrowly, he continued to suggest that the problem lay not with the rule itself but with its interpretation by the courts and the inability of psychiatrists and the legal system to reconcile their differing needs and assumptions.

Ultimately, Wertham's critique of the relationship of psychiatry and the law pointed to three deficiencies that he perceived as paramount: first, the area of procedures, which were too often left unclear or contradictory and which allowed the system to ignore potentially violent offenders; second, the area of jurisprudence, where legal cases were handled administratively rather than scientifically; and finally in the area of psychiatry, which had failed the courts by not undertaking adequate follow-up studies and consequently had overemphasized projective tests and imprecise terminologies—such as "antisocial"—in the place of the significant clinical studies, which Wertham argued should be the mainstay of psychiatric research.

Wertham's tempered embrace of the McNaughton rule went hand in hand with his absolute refusal of the proposals put forward by Zilboorg. His disdain for Zilboorg was evidenced in his frequent negative references to his rival in his articles and book reviews, even when discussing entirely different subjects. On one occasion he accused Zilboorg of misleading the public

(1963b:514). Another time Wertham chastised Zilboorg for his prewar Freudian assertion that the Nazis simply needed to release their aggressive tendencies (1965:837). More substantial treatments of Zilboorg's thought appear in book reviews written by Wertham.

In a 1943 *New Republic* review of Zilboorg's *Mind, Medicine, and Man,* for example, Wertham argued that the book was the culmination of a modern trend in orthodox Freudian circles that denied that social forces exerted influence on the psychological makeup of individuals (Wertham 1943). Wertham contrasted his politics—"I must confess, not without shame, that I still am an unregenerate 'idealist' and 'would-be reformer'" (707)—with those of Zilboorg, whom Wertham suggested "adds fuel to the subtlest kind of political and economic reaction" (708). Wertham's alignment of orthodox Freudianism with political conservatism would become crucial in defining his social psychiatry as a divergent form of Freudian-derived psychiatry.

Yet more than simple conservative tendencies in orthodox Freudianism troubled Wertham. In an extremely lengthy review of *The Psychology of the Criminal Act and Punishment,* he argued that Zilboorg's work was more romantic than scientific and that he had confused social problems with emotional problems (Wertham 1955d:569). Specifically rebutting Zilboorg's arguments for changes to the McNaughton rule, Wertham termed the Freudian approach to criminality "psycho-authoritarianism" and raised a number of objections. First, he pointed out that the idea of unbiased psychiatric experts was ludicrous given the number of psychiatrists who would not treat black patients (570). He also disagreed with Zilboorg's assumption that an individual's life was the history of struggle with the aggressive instinct, suggesting that Zilboorg had failed to consider the effects of economic and social deprivations on criminality. Wertham dismissed Zilboorg's arguments as speculative, noting that Zilboorg had never worked on criminal wards as Wertham had. He also condemned him for misrepresenting the facts relating to Albert Fish, whose case Wertham had discussed in *The Show of Violence* and whom Zilboorg had never met (573).

Ultimately, Wertham drew the distinction between his approach and Zilboorg's theoretically unbiased Freudian expertise by asking, "If I am asked to determine whether a patient is sick, and I find that he is sick, why shouldn't I be on the side of the patient? If a patient suffers from a genuine illness, I fight for him. If he is ill, I say so. The difficulties of the situation lie elsewhere. They are obscured by such statements as '[p]sychiatry is predestined to reject . . . legal tests' or 'psychiatry cannot really take sides'" (579). Taking sides, whether in murder trials or civil rights hearings, was the essence of Wertham's conception of a social psychiatry and formed the crucial distinction between his philosophy and that of the more orthodox Freudians, who sought to intervene in the criminal process in a more neutral fashion.

Wertham's tendency to take sides on the major issues relating to the intersection of psychiatry and the law of his day was never more in evidence than when he combined his progressive politics and his views on psychiatry to publicly condemn the judgment that the poet Ezra Pound was unfit to stand trial for treason. Pound was arraigned in November 1945 as a result of a series of wartime broadcasts on Italian radio aimed at American servicemen in Europe. He was ordered for psychiatric observation at St. Elizabeth's Hospital in Washington, D.C., where he was diagnosed by four psychiatrists, three working for the federal government and one hired by the defense. The lead government psychiatrist on the case was Winfred Overholser, who had been approached previously by defense counsel to testify on Pound's behalf but had convinced the others that it would be advantageous if they submitted a single unified report. Over the objections of the staff of St. Elizabeth's, the report stated that Pound was unfit to stand trial. As a result he was committed to the hospital for treatment and was eventually released in 1958 without ever coming to trial for treason.

Wertham's critique of the report authored by Overholser did not rest entirely on the idea that the case had been erroneously decided, although that certainly accounted for many of his substantial objections. Wertham also discussed the controversies that had erupted around Pound following his commitment to the hospital. The first of these began in March 1946, when Pound's work was omitted from the Modern Library edition of Conrad Aiken's influential anthology of modern poetry despite the fact that an earlier edition had included twelve of Pound's poems (Cornell 1966:112). A larger scandal supplanted that one in 1949, however, when the Library of Congress awarded Pound the Bollingen Foundation Prize for poetry for *The Pisan Cantos*. This action meant that one branch of the U.S. government had awarded a prize to a man who was facing treason charges brought by another branch of the government. The scandal was broadened when it was learned that the name Bollingen referred to the vacation home of Carl Jung, who was similarly accused of collaboration with the Nazis.

In two articles (Wertham 1949g, h) Wertham argued that the Pound case was a warning signal that wartime violence was being brushed under the carpet. He said sarcastically that Pound deserved the prize because he had so clearly earned it (1949h:589). Wertham meant that the prize was named for a home owned by a fascist and that it was given to a fascist author for a fascist book. He went on to suggest that the Pound case raised the most vital problems of the epoch:

> the security of people; the prevention of mass hatred and mass violence; the social responsibility of the writer and the artist; the relationship of a poet to his poem; the life of an artist in relation to the work of art; the administration of justice to satisfy the sense of justice of the people; the safeguards of democracy; the unsolved question of why so many intellectuals in different countries—writers, musicians, painters, psychiatrists—have succumbed to the blandishments of Fascism, from Knut Hamsun and Paul Morand to Dr. Alexis Carrel and Carl G. Jung. Rational scrutiny of all these questions was cut off with one work: INSANITY. *Psychiatria locuta, causa finita.* Psychiatry has spoken, the case is closed. (593)

Wertham contended that to reconcile violence—especially violence on a grand scale—it had to be judged and condemned. That had not occurred in this instance because the psychiatrists had found Pound unfit to stand trial despite the fact that they offered no supporting evidence for that view. Wertham's condemnation of the forces at work in the Pound controversy—antisocial and individualistic psychiatry, a minimization of fascist tendencies, and a point of view from the Bollingen jurors drawn from the Fellows of American Letters that utterly divorced aesthetic concerns from political realities—illustrated his primary complaints about the work of others in this period. What remained to be seen was the type of positive contribution Wertham would strive to make with his personal conception of a social psychiatry.

The history of psychoanalysis is intricately and inextricably linked to the biography of a single man, Sigmund Freud. Trained as a medical doctor but forced to find work elsewhere because he was Jewish, Freud began to see neurotic patients and to search for ways to cure them. Psychoanalysis is largely a result of these efforts, an attempt to explain human behavior by examining the individual generally and the unconscious mind specifically. Psychoanalytic theory is based primarily on a small number of detailed case studies assembled by Freud, who relied on a "talking cure" methodology developed by a colleague, Joseph Breuer, that stressed the purging of emotions through catharsis. Together Breuer and Freud penned *Studies in Hysteria* (1895), the first book on psychoanalysis. Perhaps the single most important text for the development of psychoanalytic thought, however, was Freud's 1899 book, *The Interpretation of Dreams*, which suggested that dreams were a window onto the unconscious mind.

In the decade following the publication of this volume, Freud made a number of crucial contributions to the development of psychoanalysis, including the identification of the conflicting pleasure and reality principles, the enunciation of the theory of the three stages of childhood development and the Oedipus complex, and the idea that the human personality is derived from the interaction of three systems, the id, the ego, and the superego. As Freud continued to work and attract followers, psychoanalysis began its rise in Europe, originating in Vienna before extending to Germany and Switzerland. Freudian techniques were seen as the essential elements of psychoanalytic practice insofar as it was held that the solutions to neuroses lay with an inward-looking and individualistic explanation of behavior that rejected social causation. Orthodox Freudian psychoanalysis, therefore, did not seek to change society, as Wertham would seek to do, but sought to help neurotic individuals understand the causes of their dysfunctions and get on with their lives. In this regard, therefore, it can be suggested that Freudian psychoanalysis sought to help spread rather than combat the rise of conformism in the twentieth century.

H. Stuart Hughes suggests that Freud demonstrated an "Olympian detachment" from politics (1975:189). Most commentators on Freud's notion of the interaction between social and internal psychic forces agree that while he paid lip service to the idea that social factors played an important role in shaping the individual personality, it is clear that he never developed these ideas in his own writings. Arthur Berliner argues, for instance, that Freud seemingly ignored Marx's writings and that Freudian liberation concentrated exclusively on the individual (1983:165). Freud's extreme individualism can be seen in his argument that social life was detrimental to the individual because it necessitated the subordination of individual pleasure seeking and exacted a heavy toll through conformity. To this end, therefore, Freud saw all social structures as essentially coercive.

To develop these ideas, Freud drew heavily on the crowd psychology of Gustave Le Bon and Gabriel Tarde, with particular emphasis on Le Bon's 1895 book, *The Crowd*. He developed Le Bon's notion of the group as a primal horde in *Group Psychology and the Analysis of the Ego* (1921), in which Freud argued that the mob is highly sensitive to suggestions from a leader. To counteract irrational group tendencies, societies required an elite that would take control of the masses to ensure the continued survival of the social order: "It is just as impossible to do without control of the mass by a majority as it is to dispense with coercion in the work of civilization. For masses are lazy and unintelligent; they have no love for instinctual renunciation. . . . It is only through the influence of individuals who can set an example and whom masses recognize as their leaders that they can be induced to perform the work and undergo the renunciations on which the existence of civilization depends" (Freud 1927:7). Because his social thought depended on a clear demarcation between an elite and a mob, Freud contributed to the development of a conservative, aristocratic understanding of social relations. Subsequent efforts by writers such as Erich Fromm, Herbert Marcuse, and Theodor Adorno to link Freudian psychoanalysis with Marxism, therefore, constituted a truly radical effort to reinterpret the basis of Freudian thought for a new era. To this end, however, the Marxist Freudians were only one of many groups struggling to define psychoanalysis in the United States in the first half of the twentieth century.

In a series of articles written for the *New Republic* in 1945, Wertham began to lay a foundation for much of his later writing that would take issue with postwar tendencies in psychiatry and psychoanalysis (Wertham 1945b, d). Here, Wertham wondered whether psychoanalysis was becoming an opiate, drawing particular attention to psychiatrists who seemed content to label entire societies as "anal" or "oral," a position that Wertham called "absurd" (1949c:540). His critique of psychoanalysis, while specific to more conservative tendencies, often seemed to blend into a general dismissal of popularization. In the *New York Times Book Review*, Wertham asked what was to be gained from the popularization of psychiatry. His answer was an image of man, specifically of *homo psychoanalyticus*, the man without a social world and the man with orifices in the place of flesh and blood (1948h). Similarly, writing in the *New Republic* a few months later, Wertham derided psychoanalysis' new status as "cocktail chatter" and attacked both prominent anti-Freudian psychiatrist Harry Stack Sullivan for his "platitudes and pseudo-erudite announcements" and Sullivan's publisher for the "unparalleled lack of criticism and responsibility" that would allow a book such as *Conceptions of Modern Psychiatry* to be published at all (1948d:29).

Wertham ultimately opposed what he saw as a politically conservative tendency among popularized psychoanalytic works to sell what he termed "peace of mind literature" (1949e:6). Reviewing Norman Vincent Peale's *The Art of Real Happiness,* Wertham noted that "we may live in a complex civilization but this is a simple book. The reader is promised as much as he would be by a pocketbook introduction to modern physics: 'The Expanding Universe, Condensed'" (1950b:38). He recognized that the vogue for these books indicated the presence of a large number of significantly unhappy people who were being denied proper psychiatric attention because of the high cost of analysis. This is not, however, to suggest that Wertham opposed in toto the popularization of psychiatric thought. Indeed, he engaged in just this sort of activity when he wrote articles such as "10 Ways a Child May Tell You He Is Headed for a Troubled Teen Age" in *Ladies Home Journal* (1959a), and in 1953 he worked on a proposed monthly series for *Ladies Home Journal* on "What's Worrying You?" with articles on topics ranging from guilt to depression. Rather, Wertham reserved his criticism of psychiatric writing for the lay reader for those writers whom he suggested were in the business of promoting a "conservative dogma" regarding the relationship between infants and their excreta in the place of analysis rooted in the individual's intersection with the social world (Wertham 1953a:16).

Wertham's most extensive critique of the conservative tendency of postwar psychoanalysis was published in his *American Journal of Psychotherapy* article, "Society and Problem Personalities: Praetorian Psychiatry" (1963a). The "problem personalities," according to Wertham, were troubled youths whose behavior placed them somewhere on a continuum between mental disease and normalcy. The imprecision of such a definition had opened the door to unlimited subjectivism in psychiatry, leading to an inadequate state of psychopathology with regard to the problem personality and an equation of the term with the more vaguely defined "antisocial" type. Diagnoses of problem personalities, therefore, were apt to be neither strictly scientific nor psychiatric but administrative and rooted in the moral judgments of psychiatric practitioners. More importantly, however, Wertham extended his criticism to demonstrate who benefited from the kinds of labeling he was decrying in this instance. Wertham suggested that differences in the social status of individual psychiatrists within the field structured their views. He went on to note that the highest-paid psychiatrists had the "greatest ideological influence" (409).

As a privileged social group, Wertham argued, psychiatrists had a vested interest in obscuring class divisions within society. While Wertham acknowledged that "the existence of social classes is a historical fact" (409), he also observed that most psychiatrists attempted to minimize class tensions by speaking of social strata and by enumerating quantitative rather than qualitative differences amongst various groups. Moreover, Wertham suggested that in personal analysis, the psychoanalyzed absorbed the ideological slant of the analyst, leading to a situation in which "more and more psychiatrists are developing an organization man mentality" (410).

The ability to think around the development of psychoanalytical conformism was rooted in a rethinking of the relationship between the individual and the masses. Wertham noted that the "masses" was a very ambiguous term with historically variant meanings and that current usage in psychiatry was heavily influenced by Ortega y Gasset, Vilfredo Pareto, Otto Spengler, and especially Gustave Le Bon. According to Wertham, Le Bon's influence on Freud had led to the development of a twofold dogma widely accepted by analysts: first, that the masses were always inferior in comparison with the individual; second, that the masses had certain unalterable qualities. Wertham suggested that to regard only the negative characteristics of the mass—as Freud, following Le Bon, did—was prejudicial and intellectually unsound. Wertham reminded his readers that masses are simply agglomerations of individuals and that their reactions depend on many different factors.

The inability to think through the distinction between the individual and the mass—or the individual and society—had led to the exclusion of the social process from psychoanalytic writing because writers took for granted that social forces did not exist independently of the individual. Yet Wertham maintained that "the pressures of our present society are very great" (1963a:411) and that in both the normal and problem personality, these pressures evoked almost automatic responses. The reality of social pressures on the individual obligated the scientific psychiatrist, in Wertham's eyes, to become a social critic.

The need for social criticism in psychiatry led Wertham to his most significant break with postwar psychiatric orthodoxies and the development of his own notion of "social psychiatry," or a medical practice that sought to transform both the individual and society. Wertham argued that while the majority of psychiatrists espoused self-expression and self-actualization, they really desired, by virtue of their privileged class position, conformism. For Wertham this was best noted, obviously, in the contemporary relationship between psychiatry and the legal system. He suggested that psychiatric attacks on the definition of insanity and legal concepts such as responsibility, punishment, and deterrence that were presented as progressive and humanitarian were actually reactionary, or what he termed "psychoauthoritarianism," the rule of an expert elite.

Key to psychoauthoritarianism was complacency toward negative social forces such as violence. Wertham argued that in promoting a psychological view of social forces that suggested, for example, that Nazism was the result of Hitler's individual neuroses, psychiatry has allowed "wrong or reactionary" social values to develop within society (413). Psychiatry, therefore, performed a social function in society regardless of whether individual practitioners were aware of it. Wertham termed the American postwar context of psychiatry a "praetorian" function insofar as psychiatrists acted not unlike the Praetorian Guard of ancient Rome, who prevented social changes toward the new. Psychiatry was not simply a rationale, as C. Wright Mills referred to it, but actually acted as a powerful adjunct to the constituted instruments of social control. What was progressive in Freud's Vienna, Wertham suggested, was reactionary in the atomic age: "By leaving problem personalities to the highly subjective, discriminatory labels of an expert elite, by separating the psyche from its social roots, by attacking rational ideas of responsibility, by diverting interest in social affairs into preoccupations and activities with mental health and psychopathology, by placing all faults in the individual, by suggesting, as sociologist Maurice Stein put it, that all social settings are the same and social resistance hopeless—by all such means psychiatry and psychoanalysis play a praetorian role, upholding power and privilege" (414).

Wertham suggested that the reactionary character of postwar psycho-analysis could be seen in both theory and practice. To Wertham, the explanation of historical events by reference to the Oedipus complex was just as reactionary as the ongoing segregation of psychiatric hospitals. In the place of these praetorian tendencies, Wertham suggested that analysts needed to remember that it was possible to speak of the mental health only of the individual and not of the group because, despite Erich Fromm's protestations, no such thing as a sane society existed. Wertham further suggested that social ills could not be solved through psychiatry. Yet by the same token, it was reckless to ignore the wider social dimension in the analysis of individual patients. Wertham concluded, "If we do our best clinical work for the individual, and face social problems scientifically with equal concreteness on their own level, we shall make progress in better understanding the relationship between the two" (415). The key here was Wertham's connection between science and criticism and the equal emphasis on the individual and the social that he set against a conservative Freudian psycho-analysis characterized as overly individualistic, uncritical, and asocial. Thus, Wertham called for a socially grounded psychiatry that nevertheless maintained its connection to the scientific domain. In this way, Wertham's earliest writings on science and medicine played a crucial formative role in the development of his position as a socially concerned postwar psychiatrist and cultural critic.

In many ways, Wertham became almost totally isolated as a psychiatric thinker. His constant denunciations of orthodox Freudianism as asocial, reactionary, and needlessly individualistic certainly separated him from the mainstream of psychoanalytic societies and organizations. At the same time, he was equally critical of most other notable critics of Freudian ortho-doxy. In *The Circle of Guilt,* for instance, he complained that the best known Freudian apostates—Erich Fromm, Harry Stack Sullivan, Karen Horney, Clara Thompson, and Abram Kardiner—did not "go far enough and [did] not take account of the full extent of the underlying dynamic interaction between personal and impersonal factors" (1956:69). Reviewing Fromm's *Man for Himself,* Wertham argued, "what prevents Fromm from attaining a really progressive psychiatry is his attachment to the idea of a psychosocial parallelism. By that term I mean the current frame of reference according to which psychological experiences and social events form two series of cause and effect that run parallel to each other. It is not enough to concede that the two may meet somewhere. . . . What is important is that they are inseparable, that they run not in two parallel streams but in one single stream. They are not two processes, but one" (1948f:27).

Wertham's essential position was that people's thoughts and actions were determined not only by subjective wishes but in equal measure by their objective social positions. This left Wertham virtually alone despite the fact that his work obviously intersected with so many of the most important debates in psychiatry and psychoanalysis of his day. He was involved at various moments in the mental hygiene movement, debates about the future of forensic psychiatry, and efforts to combine psychoanalysis and science through neurology and projective psychology. Nonetheless, his relentless insistence on combining psychiatry with progressive politics and concern for culture often left him as the odd man out.

In many ways, Wertham's widely reported involvement with the Ezra Pound case ("Wertham Assails" 1949) could have been the culmination of Wertham's writings on social psychiatry because the case so clearly combined his primary interests: a concern with fascism and the politics of human violence; the role of the intellectual in relation to politics and culture; and the intersection of psychiatry and the legal system. Yet the Pound case remains little more than a footnote to Wertham's career. Instead, the culmination of these interests would reappear in the mid-1950s and eclipse everything else that Wertham had written or accomplished. With the publication of *Seduction of the Innocent* and the campaign to reform the comic book industry, Wertham brought together all the strands that had run through his work until that time. Specifically, the book married his interest in mental hygiene and the prevention of human violence with an overriding concern for the relative merits and effects of high and mass culture on society. The combination of these interests and Wertham's particular background and training made *Seduction of the Innocent* both an important and an idiosyncratic intervention into postwar debates about mass culture and the effects of the mass media on the lives of children.

CHAPTER TWO

MASS CULTURE IN THE TWENTIETH CENTURY

To understand the specific ways in which *Seduction of the Innocent* intersected with the dominant media-effects paradigm in the midcentury United States, it is necessary first to come to terms with the intellectual climate of the time. Twentieth-century analyses of U.S. culture were dominated by a single framework that tended to cast the tastes of various audiences in opposition to each other. This conception of culture elevated so-called high culture, the preferred taste of a minority of Americans who comprised a cultural elite, to a level of prestige and legitimacy while denigrating the cultural choices of the majority public. The critique of mass culture was shaped by a variety of forces that created connections between art and politics.

Commentators who had a hand in shaping the direction of the mass culture debate ranged across the political spectrum from ardent conservatives to liberal reformers and radical Marxists. Similarly, critics of popular culture approached the subject from a number of disciplinary perspectives, including the social scientific (specifically, anthropology and sociology) and the humanistic (primarily literary studies and philosophy). Each of these groups addressed itself to a variety of questions pertaining to the development and structure of the mass media as well as to the relationship of audiences to society at a time when the mass media were becoming increasingly enmeshed in people's everyday lives. Because the questions remained fairly limited and the binary opposition between high and low cultures was such a constant in the discourse across political lines, it should not be entirely surprising that a considerable degree of overlap existed, causing Marxist and conservative critiques to resemble one another and sociological and literary interpretations of culture to use the same sets of assumptions.

Despite these considerable overlaps, Fredric Wertham's work fits only unevenly into the mass culture critique. Thus, while he shared a large number of interests with the intellectuals who framed the cultural debate of his time, he was never particularly well received by those critics. Charting the establishment of the dominant intellectual framework for understanding culture in the postwar period and relating that framework to the writings of Wertham enables us to come to terms with the ways in which his work both illuminates and problematizes the triumph of a conservative and elitist approach to the study of popular culture that views audiences as examples of masses.

During a 1957 discussion panel at New York's Museum of Modern Art examining "The Role of the Intellectual in Modern Society," W. H. Auden surveyed the panelists and remarked on the fact that all of the assembled commentators were literary critics. In centuries past, Auden noted, similar panels might have brought together clergymen or, later, natural scientists. However, in the postwar period the widely held synonym for intellectual seemed to be cultural critic. Jackson Lears argues that during the 1950s, the "touchstones of cultural criticism became questions of style and taste—questions, it was assumed, that literary intellectuals were well equipped to answer" (1989:46).

The fact that literary scholars dominated the intellectual field is evidenced by the extraordinary importance of mass culture criticism in the public debates of this era. Herbert Gans argues that in the United States, the longest-running cultural struggle has been between advocates and consumers of high and low cultures (1974:3), and in the postwar period this long-standing and one-sided debate emerged among public intellectuals as among the most important questions facing the nation. Shaped by a variety of influences both ideological and disciplinary over the first half of the twentieth century, the anti-mass-culture discourse emerged in the midcentury period as the only viable lens through which it seemed possible to examine questions relating to the intersection of culture and society. As such, the anti-mass-culture point of view exerted a phenomenal influence over every area of scholarly investigation in the humanities and social sciences in the United States at that time. To come to terms with the development of the media-effects paradigm as a way of conceptualizing cultural relations, therefore, it is necessary to give attention to the important structuring elements of the mass culture debates that elevated Auden's literary scholars to the position of supreme cultural commentators for the entire nation.

In a 1961 essay on the relationship between the intellectual and the mass media, Leo Rosten conceded that "the deficiencies of mass media are a function, in part at least, of the deficiencies of the masses." However, he also suggested that a problem remained insofar as intellectuals could not reconcile themselves to the fact that the vast majority of the population did not and never would share the intellectuals' tastes and predilections (1961:72). While Rosten's derogatory remarks about the qualities of the so-called masses were in tune with the general intellectual sentiments of the postwar period, his condemnation of the narrow-mindedness of the intellectuals, however timid, was at odds with the general tenor of the times. In suggesting that part of the problem be laid at the feet of the critics rather than the criticized, Rosten challenged one of the more common assumptions of the mass culture critique. As he pointed out, mass culture criticism had always been shaped more by critics' social concerns, biases, and presuppositions than by empirical research into the varying uses and effects of the mass media.

Insofar as criticism of mass culture in the postwar period constituted, as Gans argues, an attack by the culturally powerful on the culturally weak (1974:4), its purpose can perhaps best be understood as an attempt, however clumsy, to negotiate the proper relationship of intellectuals to the public in a democracy. Rooted as this critique was in the intellectual's disdain for the aesthetic content of the mass media, the critique can be understood as an argument on behalf of an ideal way of life that traces its roots to the Enlightenment (52). Gans identifies four major themes of the mass culture critique in the postwar period: mass culture is profit-minded and mass-produced; mass culture has a negative effect on higher forms of culture through its tendency toward debasement; mass culture has a negative effect on its audience; and mass culture has a negative effect on society that leads to antidemocratic or totalitarian tendencies (19). The issues pertaining to the intellectuals' evaluations of the status of mass culture and its relationship with other taste cultures are critical to understanding the cultural and political discourses that influenced the development of the media-effects paradigm.

Interestingly, despite its lengthy history in the United States, the anti-mass-culture point of view has long been associated with a particularly European way of conceptualizing social and class distinctions through culture. Gans, for instance, argues that because the critique had European roots, most mass culture critics have been Europeans or Americans who modeled themselves on the European elite (1974:54). The argument that seeks to displace the origins of the mass culture debate far away from the traditions of American pluralism and democracy continues to find safe havens. The historiography of comic books, for instance, tends to dismiss Wertham's critique of that industry as foreign to American ways of conceptualizing the mass media. Wertham's view is dismissed as an alien—specifically European or Germanic—critique at odds with American postwar sensibilities. Amy Kiste-Nyberg claims that "Wertham's arguments were a popularization of 'some of the most radical European criticisms of mass society.'" Nyberg extends that argument to suggest that Wertham deliberately deemphasized the radical, European roots of his argument "to ally himself with the conservative groups who seemed to be most willing to take action against comic books" (1998:97).

Both of these arguments have their origins in James Gilbert's 1986 book, *A Cycle of Outrage*. Gilbert's argument is fuller than Nyberg's paraphrase of it insofar as he suggests some actual, albeit glancing, connections between Wertham and Frankfurt School scholars. Yet neither Gilbert nor Nyberg demonstrates this supposition through evidence. Gilbert asserts the claim and Nyberg repeats it without any supporting documentation despite the many vast and obvious differences between the theories of culture advanced by Wertham on the one hand and scholars such as Max Horkheimer, Theodor Adorno, and Herbert Marcuse on the other. Close attention to Wertham's writings as a whole, however, supports a position that is at odds with the analysis put forward by Gilbert and Nyberg. Indeed, Wertham's writings generally and *Seduction of the Innocent* specifically were rooted in particularly American anxieties about the status of mass culture in the postwar period. The permanence of the mass culture critique in the United States, from its emergence following the revolution until its culmination after the Second World War, suggests that episodic models of analysis overlook key continuities over time that are related to the formation of a unique national culture. Furthermore, the distinctions between various specific formulations of the mass culture critique can best be understood in a context of the history of American progressivism rather than in a generally European articulation of the relationships among cultural levels. Finally, the important role of a small group of intellectuals in directing the shape of postwar evaluations of culture and in determining the subsequent development of social science research into the field of culture can be seen in a new light when refracted through the lens of Fredric Wertham.

Despite the fact that Wertham shared many concerns about American culture with the so-called New York Intellectuals—a loose-knit collection of journalists and public intellectuals affiliated with small political and cultural magazines such as the *Partisan Review*, the *New Republic*, and *Commentary*—and despite the fact that *Seduction of the Innocent* is often regarded as a key text in the history of the postwar mass culture critique dominated by that coterie of writers (Gorman 1996:2), Wertham clearly never quite belonged. Although Wertham published no fewer than twenty articles and book reviews in the *New Republic* on the subject of psychoanalysis between 1943 and 1950, the critics who dominated the pages of these journals generally subjected him to disapproval. Leslie Fiedler, for instance, wrote dismissively about Wertham in "The Middle against Both Ends," suggesting "that the undefined aggressiveness of disturbed children can be given a shape by comic books, I do not doubt; and one could make a good case for the contention that such literature standardizes crime woefully or inhibits imagination in violence, but I find it hard to consider so obvious a symptom a prime cause of anything" (1957:537). This contention falls something short of a full refutation of Wertham's argument but is also typical of the New York Intellectuals' casual dismissal of Wertham.

Robert Warshow was one of the few who attempted to engage with Wertham's writings in *Seduction of the Innocent* in any systematic way, and Warshow's commentaries demonstrate the limits of tolerance shown to the psychiatrist by his critics. In "Paul, the Horror Comics, and Dr. Wertham," originally published in *Commentary* in 1954, the same year as the release of *Seduction of the Innocent*, Warshow argued that his son, Paul, a comic book fan, was not seriously affected by reading comic books, although Warshow as the boy's father would have preferred that he not read them anyway. Having established his limited opposition to the mass media (comics are bad but not necessarily harmful), Warshow addressed a number of claims from Wertham's book, chastising him for his "humorless dedication" to reformism, for his tendency to accept statements made by children in therapy sessions as valid, and for his tendency to argue as if the comic book industry were monolithic.

In the end, Warshow rejected a caricature of Wertham's argument about causality but nonetheless advocated some degree of censorship for the "worst of the comic books" (1957:210) that were conceptualized in traditional high/low terms. Indeed, throughout the essay, Warshow imposed a series of high and low distinctions on comic books to shift the terrain of Wertham's critique somewhat away from the question of social and psychological damage and toward aesthetic concerns. Warshow argued that a valid value distinction existed between comic books and canonical literature: "It remains true that there is something questionable in the tendency of psychiatrists to place such stress on the supposed psychological needs of children as to encourage the spread of material which is at best subversive of the same children's literacy, sensitivity, and general cultivation. *Superman* and *The Three Musketeers* may serve the same psychological need, but it still matters whether a child reads one or the other" (1957:209). Warshow's suggestion that "it still matters" only appears sensible through the lens of the mass culture critique. In failing to take seriously Wertham's various claims about media effects, the only possible line of dissent accorded a critic such as Warshow was a recourse to traditional, near-Manichaean conceptions of good and bad culture. While Wertham often relied on these same sorts of divisions in his writing, the fact remains that his work also moved beyond a narrowly aesthetic conception of culture. Therefore, while Wertham's work clearly needs to be understood within the general context of the New York Intellectuals' common postwar American mass culture critiques, it is by no means entirely contained by those understandings.

Another New York Intellectual and member of the Frankfurt School, Leo Lowenthal, argued that although popular culture was not a strictly modern phenomenon (it could be dated back at least to the era of feudalism), specific controversies about popular culture were in fact particular to early-twentieth-century modernism. Controversy about the popular arts, Lowenthal suggested, arose only after cultural contact between the elite and masses became a reality (1961:28). Lowenthal's observation reinforced the suggestion that the basis for the intellectual's critique of mass culture was primarily political rather than aesthetic and was rooted in apprehensions about the intellectuals' cultural status.

Patrick Brantlinger, whose 1983 book *Bread and Circuses* traces the evolution of the critique of popular culture, argues that cultural critics' specific concern with mass culture was linked to the emergence of the perception that the masses posed a revolutionary threat in the nineteenth century and a totalitarian threat in the twentieth (1983:30). The term *mass culture* emerged just prior to the Second World War, and similar terms—*mass art, mass entertainment,* and *mass communication*—also stem from the 1930s, when they were framed in reference to totalitarian political movements, giving the terms negative connotations from their origins. Brantlinger suggests that all critical theories of mass culture have implied the existence of a superior culture that can be judged positively and, further, that culture is usually located historically in the Enlightenment, the Renaissance, the Middle Ages, or in Periclean Athens (1983:17). These backward glances at mythically utopian cultures constitute what Brantlinger terms "positive classicism." The corollary to that phrase is "negative classicism," an umbrella term that signifies a concern with the "decline and fall" trajectory associated with ancient Rome and other extinct civilizations (9). According to Brantlinger, negative classicism has been the major myth since at least the French Revolution. A form of utopian recollection and sentimentality, negative classicism is expressed as the debate between an ancient high culture and a contemporary mass culture that ultimately uses the former to disparage the latter (42–44). In seeking to protect the image of intellectual transcendence associated with Athens while avoiding the sense of Roman decay, negative classicists promote simultaneous critiques of democracy, the common individual, and mass culture. Because the common or average contradicts the good, the true, and the beautiful, negative classicism has posited that the best is the few, the bad is the many, and the worst is the mass. The point of view that presumes that an individual can be good while many individuals together must be bad has led to a rejection of pluralist and democratic values in artistic criticism. Furthermore, negative classicism has remained unable to conceptualize the mass of the population in positive terms, relying instead on politically conservative images of barbarians (53–55).

In the nineteenth century, warnings about the threat of the masses appeared in the thought of men such Jakob Burckhardt, Friedrich Nietzsche, and Henry Adams, but the most influential commentary on the American mass culture question perhaps originated with Alexis de Tocqueville and his 1835 book, *Democracy in America.* Tocqueville outlined a number of ideas about the relationship between artistic production and democracy that would come to dominate nineteenth- and twentieth-century thinking about culture in the United States. He argued, for instance, that the creation of a mass audience for culture had shifted cultural producers' emphasis away from quality and toward cheapness. He argued, therefore, that democracy would never create great literature (1957:27–34). Not only have these arguments historically contributed to underlying justifications for political theories that privilege monarchies, oligarchies, and aristocracies, but such elitist conceptions of the relations between social groups permeated—consciously or unconsciously—the mass culture debates in the midcentury United States. The result was a rather unique period of deeply entrenched, highly public, and volatile cultural politics that viewed the mass media and popular culture as particularly denigrating forces within American society.

The roots of the American critique of mass culture reside in conservative and aristocratic European social thought at the turn of the twentieth century. The sheer quantity of the mass media in the century's first decade—more than twenty-five hundred daily newspapers and six thousand magazines in the United States—alarmed a number of conservative cultural critics, who accused the media of pandering to base passions and interfering with social discipline. In denouncing the mass media for their reliance on the twinned evils of criminality and sensuality, genteel critics such as T. S. Eliot and Matthew Arnold sought to defend social institutions rooted in ideas of moral fitness and dependent on the uplifting and enlightening aspects of high culture.

Eliot's specific concerns in *Notes Towards a Definition of Culture* (1948) were that only high culture could be considered genuine and that mass culture threatened to impose a uniform or leveled culture in an increasingly classless society. Eliot was convinced that society was on the precipice of total decline into a state of no culture. To this end, he offered a triple defense of cultural elitism based on divisions among classes, elites, and "*the* elite," which bore considerable resemblance to the work of Italian fascist intellectuals such as Gaetano Mosca and Vilfredo Pareto (Brantlinger 1983:206).

These politics found their clearest expression in the work of Spanish philosopher and politician José Ortega y Gasset. In his 1932 book, *The Revolt of the Masses,* Ortega y Gasset argued that culture cannot flourish under the masses. From Ortega y Gasset's point of view, mass culture was the product of the mass man, which itself was the product of nineteenth-century society. Ortega y Gasset's division of society into two camps—the specially qualified and the unqualified, those who makes demands on themselves and those who are "mere buoys that float on the waves" (1993:15)—would be repeated ad nauseam by an almost endless parade of subsequent commentators on mass culture.

Gans argues that in its trajectory from the eighteenth century to the 1950s, it is possible to see in the mass culture critique a rise and fall of the power of intellectuals (1974:7). If, as Gans maintains, the criticism of mass culture subsides in periods when intellectuals have social power, the ferocity of the critique in the 1950s would indicate that the postwar period represented a low point in the history of American intellectuals' influence. Yet several recent scholars have argued against a simple reading of intellectual decline and in favor of a view that sees the postwar era as one of transition for what Russell Jacoby has termed "public intellectuals" (1987:5) and Steven Biel has called "independent intellectuals" (1992:2). These terms are roughly congruent, and both authors point to a group of intellectuals who were, in the immediate postwar period, not affiliated with universities but who congregated around a small number of influential New York–based magazines and journals. These intellectuals, whose audience was generally presumed to be the educated but nonspecialist public interested in culture and current affairs, were the stalwarts of the mass culture debate and largely shaped the direction that the discussion would take. By the mid-1950s, the era of the independent intellectual had been largely—though not entirely—concluded, as professional academics began to replace the former group and public intellectuals moved into universities. Nonetheless, these writers have had a pervasive impact on common understandings of culture's role in society.

The possibility that mass culture could be regarded as anything other than a problem to be managed by elites appears only sporadically in the debate on the subject that characterized the first half of the twentieth century. Perhaps the strongest possibility for the overthrow of this point of view came from the cultural radicals, whose embrace of aesthetic modernism was found in the so-called little magazines of the 1910s and 1920s and who challenged the assumptions of the genteel critics. The most influential of the American modernist journals of the 1920s was *The Dial,* which celebrated a number of popular entertainers such as Charlie Chaplin, Fanny Brice, and W. C. Fields. The *Dial*'s managing editor and theater critic was Gilbert Seldes, one of the few champions of mass entertainment to have emerged from the mass culture debates in this period.

Seldes's influential 1924 book, *The Seven Lively Arts*, sought to rescue the best elements of popular culture from the scorn of the conservative genteel critics. The elements of popular culture that Seldes praised included the films of Charlie Chaplin and George Herriman's comic strip *Krazy Kat*. While Seldes limited his embrace of mass entertainments to those aspects that he considered exceptional, his insistence on integrating new forms of culture into appreciations of the classics constituted a radical challenge to earlier critics. Nonetheless, Seldes and the other American modernists provided only an extremely limited contribution to the mass culture debate. Because they validated popular culture in a very restricted fashion by challenging the cultural critics' range but not their, the modernists could only praise elements of mass culture in those instances where they perceived such elements to be the unique expressions of particular artists. Furthermore, the cultural radicals of the American little magazines had little to say about the relationship between artists and audiences and, consequently, refrained from entering one of the central aspects of the debate as it played out in subsequent decades. Nonetheless, the modernist writers associated with magazines such as *Seven Arts* and *The Dial* pointed to the ways in which the debate about mass culture had increasingly been framed as a problem intrinsic to American rather than European culture and suggested the narrowness of the possibilities for the embrace of mass culture on any level. Just as Freudian psychoanalysis found its origins in Europe and its culmination in America, so too did the European disdain for the popular find its truest elaboration in the culture of the United States.

James Gilbert's argument about the European origins of Wertham's critique of the comic book industry depends on Wertham's association with German émigré critic Theodor Adorno (1984:112). Adorno and the other members of the Institut für Sozialforschung (Institute for Social Research), commonly known as the Frankfurt School, occupy an important place in the American debate about mass culture despite the fact that linguistic and cultural barriers limited their contribution to the debate itself. The Frankfurt School scholars tended to conceive of mass culture as a form of regression that would take the United States down the road toward fascism, as they felt mass culture had done in Germany. This highly pessimistic perspective went hand in hand with an embrace of high culture, or "genuine art," which could show how the world is by showing how it was not. The Frankfurt School position on mass culture can perhaps best be understood through a contrast between the divergent views of one of its members and one of its associates. Adorno had little faith in the working class as agents of revolutionary social change. Adorno's conception of "true" art necessitated a harmonious reconciliation of form and content that was not oriented toward the market (Jay 1973:182).

In contrast, the work of Walter Benjamin, an associate of the Frankfurt School, was much more positive about the potential of the mass media. He held that the loss of a sense of aura around a work of art was a consequence of mechanical reproduction, which held the potential to emancipate art from ritual and aristocratic monopoly. Benjamin disagreed with Adorno's notion of "true" art, arguing in favor of politicized and collectivized art. For Adorno and the Frankfurt School scholars, genuine art and mass culture were irreconcilable entities because art was always singular and unique, whereas mass entertainment lacked this sense of aura. Benjamin, in holding out some hope for politicized art while at the same time generally bemoaning the loss of aura, the sense of wonder that is derived from the unique nature of the art object, was one of the few Marxist thinkers of his period to recognize any affirming value for mass culture.

In his contribution to Bernard Rosenberg and David Manning White's anthology, *Mass Culture,* the Frankfurt School's Leo Lowenthal sought to lay out the institute's departure from more traditionally American conceptions of social science research. Lowenthal suggested that, unlike the politically engaged critical theorists, most social science researchers had abdicated political and ethical responsibility in their work:

> Empirical social science has become a kind of applied asceticism. It stands clear of any entanglements with foreign powers and thrives in an atmosphere of rigidly enforced neutrality. It refuses to enter the sphere of meaning. A study of television, for instance, will go to great heights in analyzing data on the influence of television on family life, but it will leave to poets and dreamers the question of the actual human values of this new institution. Social research takes the phenomena of modern life, including the

mass media, at face value. It rejects the task of placing them in a historical and moral context." (1961:52)

Lowenthal's conclusion that American social science suffered from an "antihistorical allergy" (1961:53) that tended to reinforce the equation of mass communication studies with market research ignored the important ways that a process of intellectual exchange between cultural critics and social science researchers structured the mass culture debates.

In the 1920s and 1930s, social scientists influenced by progressive critiques of mass culture increasingly came to regard the issue of mass entertainment as an urgent question for sociology. Their contribution was not aesthetic but was instead based on whether mass culture was a cause or a product of modern social problems. Growing numbers of studies of American leisure pursuits, such as the Payne Fund studies of the cinema (1929–33), indicate that mass culture was increasingly being cast as a social problem. This perception became increasingly dominant in sociology and anthropology as studies used new methodologies such as ethnography to prove that American culture was losing values associated with nonindustrial ways of life, including a relationship to nature, communal lives, and a spiritual vision. Social science researchers ultimately reformulated cultural scholars' suggestion that mass culture was something imposed on the public from outside, suggesting that this form of culture had become an expected feature of modern life in an industrialized society.

Paul Lazarsfeld, himself a renegade member of the Frankfurt School, summed up the relationship between cultural critics and social scientists at midcentury and noted something of the tensions that existed between the two groups when he suggested that artists and intellectuals unfamiliar with social science methodologies responded to empirical research in a way that resembled the responses of the general public to atonal music—that is, with contempt and scorn (1961:xix).

Nonetheless, despite this tension, social scientists clearly contributed significantly to the general debate on mass culture. For example, in their influential textbook *Mass Culture,* Rosenberg and White included a large number of empirically grounded essays written by anthropologists and sociologists. Many of these articles departed from the general tenor of anti-mass-culture commentaries by problematizing the negative image of mass entertainment and its audiences. In an article on the book reading audience, for instance, Bernard Berelson simultaneously confirmed many intellectuals' suspicions that most Americans did not read quality fiction and suggested that the situation actually remained largely unchanged from any point in the country's literary history (1961:119–22).

Other commentators, however, were more ready to stake out conclusive claims that suggested that social science research overlapped with the commentaries of public intellectuals in demonstrating a shared set of assumptions. Lazarsfeld and Robert Merton outlined a number of traits that they held could be definitively attributed to the mass media, such as the enforcement of social norms and status conferral, and then proceeded to condemn the "appalling lack of esthetic judgment" of women who consumed soap operas. Lazarsfeld and Merton made their argument in such a way that it is difficult to distinguish their ostensibly scientific analysis from those of the nonacademic public intellectuals (1957:466).

Similarly, in an essay on Hollywood's film production techniques, anthropologist Hortense Powdermaker condemned the commercialization of the cinema when she suggested that "art and aesthetic goals have always been less important in society than either business or humanitarian ones" and then went on to suggest in the bluntest terms imaginable that "Hollywood represents totalitarianism" (1957:282, 289). Such comments emphasize the way that empirical social science research relied, perhaps even subconsciously, on the mass culture critique that circulated throughout the twentieth century. They point to the fact that the division between social scientists and independent intellectuals on the question of mass culture was never as clean as Lazarsfeld wanted it to be.

Neil Jumonville argues that questions about mass culture strike close to the heart of the identity of the New York Intellectuals (1991:151). This group of thinkers occupied an unusual position in postwar American culture. For the most part, they were unaffiliated with universities and colleges and sought to maintain an idealized intellectuality that would steer clear of all careers and thereby privilege intellectual autonomy (Biel 1992:32–33). That position ultimately proved untenable, and many of these public intellectuals occupied positions as journalists or editors for small political and cultural magazines. Additionally, with only a few exceptions, these critics were gathered geographically around New York City—specifically Greenwich Village—a spatial location that had an important role in coordinating these intellectuals collectively as a group.

The term *New York Intellectuals,* therefore, can be understood to refer to a group of critics clustered around Greenwich Village through much of the first half of the twentieth century who were affiliated with each other through their association with a small group of journals and magazines. Despite their Marxist roots, the New York Intellectuals had a great deal in common with older conservative critics of the nineteenth century, particularly in the tendency to suspect that the public was to blame for the poor state of American culture. As the most vocal critics of mass culture in the postwar period, therefore, the New York Intellectuals inflected American understandings of mass entertainment with a conservative bias that distanced them from the reformist traditions evident in much of the political landscape of the time.

The two most important midcentury statements on the relationship between high and mass culture originated with writers associated with *Partisan Review.* The first of these statements, Clement Greenberg's 1939 essay, "Avant-Garde and Kitsch," posited avant-garde artists as veritable saviors who could imitate God by creating something that was valid only on its own terms (1957:100–101). If the avant-garde died, he argued, all of culture would also die. At the same time, however, the avant-garde necessarily led to the development of a rear guard, which Greenberg termed *kitsch* and defined as the product of the industrial revolution and universal literacy that had stripped status divisions from leisure pursuits. Kitsch was called vampiric insofar as it drew on and diminished the traditions of high culture and was destructive because its high profits might lure legitimate cultural producers away from the avant-garde (1957:102).

The second key article that helped to define the parameters of the mass culture debate was Dwight MacDonald's "A Theory of Popular Culture," published in 1944 in the introductory volume of his journal, *Politics,* which he had founded after leaving *Partisan Review.* In this article, MacDonald argued a line similar to that of Greenberg, suggesting that mass culture was trying to kill high culture. At the same time, however, MacDonald departed from Greenberg's point of view in citing some approved elements of popular culture, including the comic strips *Krazy Kat* and *Thimble Theater* (1944:20–23).

Nine years later, MacDonald published a revised version of the article under the title "A Theory of Mass Culture." This essay shifted the emphasis of the argument toward a concern with massification and modernization. MacDonald argued that mass culture was increasingly eroding the barriers of class, tradition, and taste to create a new social order governed by the masses, a force he characterized as not entirely human. To prevent the destruction of high culture by the low, MacDonald advocated a return to conservative values espoused by Eliot and Ortega y Gasset. To this end, MacDonald publicly abandoned his Marxism to side with the most conservative of the prewar mass culture critics in calling for a return to cultural stratification and a cultural elite (1957:70–73). These articles by MacDonald and Greenberg, with their privileging of aesthetics as a priority above political improvement and progressive social change, indicated the degree to which the New York Intellectuals occupied a cultural position that was more conservative than radical and that harkened back to centuries-old solutions for perceived postwar social problems. Most strikingly, however, these views not only remained largely unchallenged by scholars from either side of the cultural/empirical divide but actually set the agenda in the postwar debate about mass culture. The only scholar who truly stands out as a legitimate opposing force is Fredric Wertham, whose erasure from the histories is consequently very telling.

When considering Wertham's publishing career, it is necessary to acknowledge that he led two very different lives as a writer. On the one hand, he was a well-known researcher in psychoanalysis and psychiatry, the field in which he was professionally trained, and he published several books and dozens of scholarly articles on subjects related to his expertise in the medical community. On the other hand, Wertham was widely published in nonscholarly magazines and journals on a variety of topics in which he had no professional training. The audience for these works was the general public, and Wertham's efforts in these arenas necessitate regarding him as a sometime public intellectual. In the majority of these cases, Wertham utilized his professional credibility as a psychiatrist to exercise legitimacy in unrelated fields such as culture and politics, bringing him into discursive contact with other critics of mass culture and proponents of competing conceptions of media effects. The ways in which he sought to incorporate psychoanalytic research on artistic productions suggest the nuances contained in his work and helped to lay a foundation for comparison with both his much better known criticisms of mass culture in the 1950s and 1960s and the commentaries of other postwar culture critics.

Throughout his career, Wertham circulated on the outskirts of America's dominant intellectual circles. In the 1920s, for instance, he frequently corresponded with Walter Lippmann, who dispatched Wertham on an unsuccessful effort to persuade Sigmund Freud to author an article for the *Saturday Review*. During his years at Johns Hopkins, Wertham became a member of H. L. Mencken's Saturday Club in Baltimore. Wertham was also a friend of playwright Arthur Miller and served as psychiatrist to both Richard Wright and Zelda Fitzgerald. Wertham's popular writings on crime and criminality were generally well received, and press reviews were mostly positive. *Dark Legend* had particular success, attracting attention from a variety of notable sources, including Thomas Mann, W. Somerset Maugham, and Miller, who wrote to congratulate Wertham on a "profound and to me a deeply significant work" (in Reibman 1990:14). In 1952, Helene Frankel adapted the book into a stage production, and Reuben Mamoulian expressed an interest in turning the book into a film.

Wertham's connection with the arts was lengthy and involved and, although his critical writing in the area of the fine arts remained a minor aspect of his life's work in comparison to his writings on mass culture, his thoughts on the arts significantly illuminate his overall philosophy. Notably, Wertham was a collector of modern art, including a number of pieces by Marc Chagall, Lazlo Moholy-Nagy, Kurt Schwitters, and significant pieces by El Lissitzky, some of which he loaned to the Museum of Modern Art in 1948. Wertham dabbled in theater criticism, writing on the subject of psychodrama and audience participation for the journal *Theater Arts* (1947b). He interviewed Miller for the *New York Times Book Review* after *Death of a Salesman* won the Pulitzer Prize (Wertham 1949e) and exchanged correspondence with novelists as varied as Georges Simenon, Erle Stanley Gardner, and William Styron. Wertham's writings, therefore, can be seen to have crossed a number of disciplinary boundaries, ranging from literary criticism to medical textbooks and from psychiatric analyses of criminality to critiques of the postwar Cold War consensus.

Wertham's most noteworthy early intervention into the arena of literary interpretation occurred in 1941, the same year that he published the criminal case history *Dark Legend*. This is not surprising, given the fact that the clinical case study of Gino, a matricidal Italian American youth, informs Wertham's literary criticism, a psychoanalytic reinterpretation of Shakespeare's *Hamlet*. This research was first presented on 19 April 1940 to the Association for the Advancement of Psychotherapy and was later refined in *Dark Legend*. In that book, Wertham wrote at great length of the matricidal tale of Orestes that marked, he argued, a shift from a matriarchal to a patriarchal code in Greek society. Wertham's evidence for this assumption was that the trial of Orestes was not for murder but for "un-Greek activity," a political rather than criminal question. The acquittal of Orestes in the story was the acknowledgment of a new Greek legal code that was explicitly sanctioned by Athena herself. Wertham, of course, extended this analysis to explicate the actions of his patient, Gino. However, he also extended it to include a critique of Freud's interpretation of *Hamlet*, a critique that also casts doubt on the conception of the Oedipal crisis as an important developmental moment in the lives of individuals.

There is more psychoanalytic work on *Hamlet* than on all of Shakespeare's other plays combined. Almost all of that work centers on the question of why Hamlet hesitates to avenge his father. In *The Interpretation of Dreams* (1914), Freud suggests that Hamlet could not act because his uncle took the action that Hamlet wished he had undertaken, killing his father to become the lover of his mother. Hamlet recognized his Oedipal desire and consequently realized that he was no better than his uncle. Freud supported this suggestion by referring to Hamlet's distaste for his own sexuality, revealed in his conversation with Ophelia, and by reference to the life of Shakespeare, who was said to have written *Hamlet* shortly after the death of his father and who had a son named Hamnet. Thus, Hamlet's hesitation is recognition of his and by extension Shakespeare's Oedipal desires.

Wertham departed from Freud's argument (1941) in six key elements. First, Wertham argued that the ghost of Hamlet's father, in instructing Hamlet to seek vengeance, never explicitly instructed Hamlet to kill Claudius. More importantly, the ghost told Hamlet not to harm his mother. Wertham wondered why the ghost would make such an instruction explicit unless he had some knowledge of Hamlet's desire to do just that. Similarly, later in the play, the ghost warned Gertrude that Hamlet might attempt to harm her. Second, Wertham maintained that the ghost was not a repression, as Freud maintained, but a dream, the self-expression of the patriarch. Third, Wertham suggested that no textual evidence indicated that Hamlet hated his father. Hamlet proclaimed his love for his father, and Wertham concluded that at worst the relationship between the two could be characterized as ambivalent. Wertham's fourth contention was that Freud mistakenly assumed that the murder of Claudius was Hamlet's goal, an assumption that Wertham insisted did not follow logically from the text. Hamlet blamed his mother for the death of his father, so his hatred of Claudius was subordinate to his hatred of his mother. Wertham pointed out that whenever Hamlet spoke of murder, he did so by speaking of his mother's guilt—for example, when he mentioned the "soul of Nero," a classic symbol of matricidal fury. Furthermore, Wertham observed that Hamlet killed Claudius only after his mother was dead and even then only after Laertes exposed his crime. Wertham's fifth disagreement with Freud stemmed from Freud's historical assertion that the play had been written after the death of Shakespeare's father. Drawing on the historical work of George Brandes, Wertham claimed that such timing was very unlikely and that even if it were accurate, the text was not basis enough on which to draw conclusions about the way Shakespeare had reacted to his father's death of his father. With this, Wertham explicitly rejected the possibility that artists or authors could be analyzed through their work. Finally and most importantly, Wertham observed that Freud's contention that Hamlet was working through an Oedipal complex was not a conclusion but a starting point. Wertham went on to suggest that Freud's contention that the Oedipal complex is a "universal, biological, normal, unavoidable inheritance of the human race" was essentially incorrect (1941:115).

Wertham absolutely rejected this ahistorical and aclinical assertion and went on to suggest, by reference to the case of Gino, that a desire to kill one's mother seemed to be every bit as much a clinical reality as the desire to kill one's father: "The basis of Hamlet's hostility against his mother is his over-attachment to her, just as it is in the matricidal patient with whom I have compared him. But this overattachment to the mother need not necessarily lead to hatred against the father or the father-image. It turns into a violent hatred toward the mother, while the image of the father is a friendly one" (119). Wertham concluded, therefore, that Hamlet was more similar to Orestes than Oedipus and further argued that psychiatrists should rethink their understandings of the Oedipal complex's role in personality development.

In his remarks on *Hamlet,* Wertham explicitly rejected the psychoanalytic interpretation of an author by way of his or her work. Wertham reaffirmed this rejection three years later when he published a study of Richard Wright's novel, *Native Son,* that was the result of a series of psychiatric sessions with the author. Wertham claimed that his article, "An Unconscious Determinant in *Native Son*" (1944), was the first published psychoanalytic interpretation done on a novel after therapy sessions with a living author and consequently should occupy an important position in the history of literary criticism. The article suggested that Wright had accounted for elements in his novel in rational as opposed to emotional terms. Wertham suggested that he had brought the affective basis of Wright's novel to the surface after conducting free association with the author based on the novel's symbols and motifs.

The identification between Wright and the protagonist of the novel, Bigger Thomas, ran more deeply than Wright had implied in his autobiographical essay, "How Bigger Was Born." At the root of the identification lay an unconscious memory that analysis had brought to the surface. As a young man, Wright had been employed as a woodcutter for a white family, and his chief job had been to tend the family's fireplace, a job that was obviously related to the furnace in which the body of Mary Dalton was burned in the novel. Wertham suggested that Mary's mother, the blind Mrs. Dalton, who becomes aware that something extraordinary is occurring at the crucial moment of the narrative, corresponded to the matron of the white household for whom Wright worked as a teenager. Moreover, Wright could not account for the reason he chose the name Dalton for the family in the novel. After analysis he recalled that while working in a medical research institute, he had learned that Daltonism was a form of blindness, and Wright concluded that he must have remembered that and associated it with Mrs. Dalton's affliction. Wertham pointed out, however, that Wright had apparently forgotten that Daltonism is actually a technical term for color-blindness, a particularly emotionally charged expression in a novel about American race relations. Wertham concluded, therefore, that psychiatry could be proven to demonstrate the role of the unconscious in creation: "While hitherto it has only been assumed, on the basis of more less valid reasoning, that the unconscious plays an important role in literary creation, the present study gives proof in a scientific instance. The data presented here are sufficient to show that unconscious material enters definitely into a work of art and can be recovered by analytic study" (1944:114).

Wertham's interest in writing for an informed lay public was deep-seated. In 1919 he published his first two articles in *The Quest* on the subject of yoga (Wertham 1919a, b). Over the course of the next decade, his publications would be restricted exclusively to medical and psychiatric journals, but his papers clearly demonstrate his continued interest in writing for the public. In 1928, for example, he submitted an essay, "1828–1928," to *The Outlook.* The essay was rejected with a form letter, but the episode perhaps marks the earliest evidence in Wertham's papers of his attempts to join the cultural elite. The essay examined the historical developments of 1928 in light of those from one hundred years earlier. Many of Wertham's most common concerns surfaced in the article: he focused on the significant crimes, scientific advances, and political developments (including the protosocialism of Bazard) that occurred in that year (Wertham 1928).

Wertham's interest in these questions would, following the success of *Dark Legend,* ultimately lead him to the pages of the *New Republic.* While the vast majority of Wertham's essays and reviews in the *New Republic* covered the areas of politics and psychiatry, he did publish a number of reviews of fiction and literary biography. One of the most significant of these was his 27 January 1947 review of Ernest J. Simmons's biography of Leo Tolstoy (Wertham 1947c). This review demonstrates that to a large degree Wertham saw himself and his concerns reflected in Tolstoy's life and writing. Wertham praised the Russian novelist for his skepticism of science, his disdain of art for art's sake, and his work on behalf of the suffering and oppressed, all traits that Wertham would adopt over the course of his career. Further, this review contained one of his strongest political statements, which would ultimately put him at odds with the New York Intellectuals as their politics drifted toward the political right in the 1950s. Wertham wrote, "We are living in a time when minds are being deliberately poisoned. The people want peace. But when they read the newspapers they are subtly aroused to suspicion by a continuous stream of insinuations against the country of Tolstoy" (39). In hindsight, Wertham's comments about the birth of the Cold War seem eerily prescient, and it is typical of his writings in this period that he would couch his concerns about contemporary geopolitics in the veneer of a literary review.

Wertham's interest in literary biography was also evidenced in the pages of book club mailings. In 1946, for example, he reviewed Matthew Josephson's biography of Stendhal for *Book Find News,* combining three of his interests: literature, social commentary, and psychiatry. Terming Stendhal "the first great psychological novelist," Wertham argued that the birth of the modern novel and psychiatry went almost hand in hand. He compared the focus on individual interiority found in the work of Proust with the psychoanalytic style favored by Freud, criticizing both for their lack of social awareness and their refusal to deal with the most pressing issues facing society.

> Although the gains in psychological insight were tremendous, the whole direction toward individual psychology was an evasion of the concrete social reality which suddenly presented the greatest possible threat to the middle-class mind: CHANGE.
>
> This same threat still exists. That is why the more conservative psychoanalysts go on erecting barriers of profundities against the intrusion of the horrible social problems of our time into the claustrophilic peace of the psychoanalytic office. And that is why our novelists again and again turn to individual problems of abnormal psychology; the chickens come home to Proust. (1946:10)

In contrast to this focus on the individual, Wertham found much to appreciate in Stendhal's strong attention to historical forces, a view much more in tune with Wertham's political orientation in this period. Wertham's renunciation of the individualist orientation of postwar psychiatry and modernist literature would place him very much at odds with the dominant political currents of the intellectuals whom he was most aggressively courting with these reviews.

Despite his insistence that the psychoanalytic interpretation of literature necessitated the participation of the author in analytic sessions, Wertham's most sustained efforts in literary analysis departed from that methodology. In 1947 Wertham provided a series of explanatory and interpretative analyses to a collection of short stories about various mental illnesses and conditions that was edited by Mary Louise Aswell, the literary editor of *Harper's Bazaar.* The resulting book, *The World Within,* was the main selection of the Book of the Month Club for January 1948, and Wertham's introduction was reprinted in the *New Republic* (1947a). Aswell's justification for the book was the furtherance of understanding of what she saw as the relationship between "madness and genius." To this end, she sought to publish the best short fiction of the nineteenth and twentieth centuries related to psychiatric material.

The book overlapped with the New York Intellectuals' concerns insofar as it was a veritable who's who of modernism's literary leading lights, including Dostoevsky, Chekhov, James, Proust, Kafka, and Faulkner alongside contemporary writers such as Edita Morris, Truman Capote, and Conrad Aiken. Each was represented by a single story, with a biographical portrait supplied by Aswell and postscript analysis provided by Wertham. His introduction to the book outlined the reasons for his involvement in such a project. Mentioning Freud's work on *Hamlet,* Wertham contended that psychology had always been influenced by literature and that the two worked well together because each sought to relate the detail to the whole in an organic fashion.

> Psychiatry and literature have to deal with conflict, individual and social. In the period now passing, emphasis on the individual personality was important in psychiatry just as the introspective writing of Proust and Joyce was significant in literature. But most people are not permitted to develop—far less to express—a personality. Society's contradictions are reflected in the troubles of the individual who goes to the psychiatrist and in the subjects clamoring for expression in literature. Bad literature may entertain and bad psychiatry may remove symptoms; but neither leads to the development of independent, socially mature personalities. (xxiii)

Writing here, Wertham touches on the connection between the individual and the social in the realm of the cultural that is so central to *Seduction of the Innocent.* Literature, Wertham maintained, highlighted these relationships because it functioned as a reflection of social life at particular historical moments.

Wertham was fond of quoting various well-known literary figures in his writing, and many of his books contained a literary epigram for every chapter. Wertham's most commonly used sources included Dostoevsky and Goethe, with Shakespeare and the Greeks trailing only slightly behind. Not surprisingly, therefore, Wertham's commentaries on the nineteenth-century material in *The World Within* are both more fully formed and more praise-filled than his analyses of the fiction more contemporaneous with his own writing. Writing on an excerpt from Dostoevsky's *Notes from the Underground,* for instance, Wertham praised the author's "artistic daydreams" and "supreme skill" and cited other critics who agreed with his assessment of Dostoevsky's genius (Aswell 1947:62).

In contrast, Wertham found almost nothing to say about Morris's story, "Caput Mortuum," other than the descriptive comment that it functioned as an "idyll of alcoholic domesticity" (321). This omission was made even stranger by the fact that Wertham regarded alcoholism as a major social problem and addressed the topic at length on a number of other occasions. Nonetheless, Wertham's admiration was directed primarily to classical writers who abstractly addressed psychological issues rather than the contemporaries who were more direct. He praised Henry James's "The Beast in the Jungle" as the best story ever written about neurosis and celebrated the fact that even the style is neurotic. Similarly, Wertham lauded Kafka's "Metamorphosis," suggesting that in the light of Nazi atrocities during the war the tale could be mistaken for reportage rather than allegory. With these comments and others, Wertham for the first time clearly rendered his implicit distinction between art and mass culture. He greatly admired the literature in Aswell's collection because of its ability to generate real insights into mental illness and their relations to society. At the same time, however, he suggested that "bad literature" on this topic, while entertaining, could not lead to the development of a mature personality and consequently was of no use to society as a whole. Wertham's dualistic division between good and bad literature in this instance was clearly reminiscent of common cultural judgments rendered by the New York Intellectuals at this period. This assumption about the negative impact of "bad literature" would be addressed most clearly in relation to Wertham's work on mass culture, which would follow closely on the heels of the publication of *The World Within*. Nonetheless, the basis of his condemnation of certain elements of mass culture was readily apparent in his writing even before he took it up as a serious issue in the 1950s, particularly in his work on violence and aggression.

In much of his writing, Wertham addressed the ways in which he believed that violence had taken a hold on art, especially literature. At the same time, he frequently expressed his belief that art filled an important social and psychological role when it helped to make suffering comprehensible. To this end, he believed that there existed a need for art to harmonize its social and artistic functions. Although he argued that his point of view on this matter should not be read as regarding the role of art in an overly utilitarian fashion, he did indicate his belief that the art-for-art's-sake movements of contemporary modernism had overextended themselves to the point where modernism was no longer productive as a movement. Essentially, however, Wertham held to a conception of a binaristic division of art: that which was proviolence and that which was antiviolence.

For Wertham, good literature and art obviously did not need to contain violence, and when it did contain violence, it should be circumspect. In *A Sign for Cain,* he held up the thirty-two Greek tragedies as positive uses of violence within literature by pointing out that these plays contain no onstage killings. Wertham's other antiviolence artists included painters who explicitly addressed violent themes in their work (such as Goya, Vermeer, and Daumier) as well as abstract painters whose work was well ordered (such as El Lissitzky and Mondrian) because he maintained that violence itself was a form of disorder. The writers praised for exploring a fuller understanding of human violence included Wright, Ernst Sommer, and Alex Comfort. Kafka was also praised as the classic writer of the twentieth century because he most clearly signaled the oncoming culture of violence that Wertham believed dominated the second half of the twentieth century. Finally, Wertham praised American folk art and suggested that its antiviolence qualities demonstrated the idea that violence itself was not a natural component of the American people, an argument that had clear links to dominant tendencies in postwar cultural commentaries that privileged folk arts as an alternative culture for the people and distinct from mass culture (Greenberg 1957:102).

In the category of proviolence art, the targets of Wertham's condemnations ranged from poets such as Rilke, who wrote lyrically about cruelty, to philosophers such as Nietzsche, who laid the groundwork on which the rationalizations for brutality were based. Wertham contended that artists who increased divisions between people or who trivialized war and suffering aided mass violence. In this category he placed the films *The Devils, The Collector,* and *The Americanization of Emily* as well as writers Norman

Mailer and Colin Wilson. Wertham also criticized the works of writers he had previously praised, including Miller for his play *Incident at Vichy* and Capote for *In Cold Blood,* which, he wrote, "represents an attitude about violence which some writers cultivate and which we, as the public, encourage. The measure of its success is the measure of our failure" (353).

Wertham ultimately was content to cast his lot with Plato, Tolstoy, and Engels, each of whom had argued convincingly that literature and art have an effect on the social world in which they are created. For Wertham, all art had a social character and a social value, even if that art was introspective or subjective. This position was, as Martin Jay argues, reminiscent of that of the Frankfurt School insofar as the privileging of social significance reflects the aesthetic Marxism that they supported in opposition to Lenin's conception of partisan literature and Stalinist socialist realism (1973:173). Wertham differed from the Frankfurt School, however, in more strongly emphasizing the psychiatrist's role in the field of artistic production.

In his writings on art and literature, Wertham carefully explicated the relationship between the social world and the individual, whether that individual was the author, character, or reader. In this way, Wertham's views on the arts were remarkably consistent with his general views on the duties and responsibilities of psychiatrists generally as both were to be concerned with providing the foundation on which a progressively oriented reformulation of collective understandings of the relationship between the individual and society could be articulated. At the same time, however, Wertham's focus on the social condition of violence overrode a straightforward fixation on aesthetics and fears of cultural leveling. Thus, while echoes of the concerns of the New York Intellectuals, the Frankfurt School, and other mass culture critics certainly appear in Wertham's writings on culture, these echoes exist only in the background, behind his more prominent arguments about violence and psychiatric theory.

If Wertham's arguments resembled those of any of the mass culture critics wholesale, it would have to be those put forward by the progressives in the 1920s and 1930s. Thus, it seems reasonable to suggest that Wertham's arguments, while clearly influenced by the dominant divide between elite and mass culture in the postwar period, were exceptions to the norms of the time. Wertham's easy dismissal by Fiedler, Warshow, and other writers associated with the New York Intellectuals becomes much more problematic in this light.

In an essay published in *Dissent* in 1956, Henry Rabassiere wrote that the intellectual's concerns about mass entertainment had become the newest form of mass culture. Members of the political left and right, Rabassiere argued, competed to outdo each other in denouncing the tastes of the general public: "Members of their bi-partisan club display in their home a copy of *Partisan Review* together with a painting conceived in an advanced style (as to records, progressives favor Bach while new-conservatives may boast a Shostakovitch concerto played by Oistrakh), and are conversant with words such as alienation, popular culture, pseudo-whatever-fashion-is, anxiety, crowd, absurd and a few others, judicious use of which will silence the uninitiated and bring recognition from those who belong; many will grant you such recognition to be recognized themselves" (1957:373). Rabassiere's notion that the mass culture critique constituted little more than a game of culture for the educated elite indicates how the debate had become narrowly limited and open only to those the intellectuals deemed qualified.

H. Stuart Hughes pointed out in 1961 that the idea of mass culture itself depended on cultural elitism because the cultural elites had first noticed—and made an issue of—mass culture (142). Hughes's suggestion that mass culture did not corrupt the taste of mass audiences but rather that intellectuals had consistently misread mass tastes and mistakenly condemned them as corrupt echoed Gilbert Seldes's earlier suggestions that the popular arts always worried cultural moralists and aesthetes, who regarded those arts as vulgar (1975:75). Seldes went on to suggest that most theories of mass culture should be recognized as extensions of political arguments that have relevance not only in the cultural domain but also for society as a whole (1957:79). While these political arguments can be easily characterized in a shorthand way—conservatives condemn the audience for mass culture because they fear the masses; progressives and Marxists condemn the marketplace for mass culture because they are disappointed with the masses—this belief in the myth of continuing cultural decline indicates that mass culture was held to pose a serious political problem in the postwar period. More to the point, it is necessary to come to terms with how that conception of a shift in social organization influenced the specific critique of mass culture by promoting the perceived crisis of individualism to center stage in the ongoing discussions about the nature of social life, just at the time when the media-effects paradigm began to emerge in its fullest form.

CHAPTER THREE

AMERICAN CONCERNS ABOUT A MASS SOCIETY

The increasingly important but constantly changing status of the American intellectual in the postwar period was highlighted by the cover of *Time*'s 11 June 1956 issue, which carried a photo of Jacques Barzun captioned, "America and the Intellectual: The Reconciliation." Fredric Wertham's papers at the Library of Congress Rare Book and Special Collections Division contain a well-underlined copy of this issue. The cover article laid out the central question intellectuals were asking as the 1950s advanced: "What does it mean to be an intellectual in the United States? Is he really in such an unhappy plight as he sometimes thinks—the ridiculed double-dome, the egghead, the wild-eyed absent-minded man who is made to feel an alien in his own country?" ("Parnassus" 1956:65). For the *Time* writer—following the lead of Barzun—the answer was quite simply that any problems hindering the intellectual were the fault of the intellectual. For those who were willing to reconcile themselves to the new American Cold War consensus, however, intellectual life was potentially quite rewarding. *Time*'s argument, in its simplest terms, was that the American "Man of Protest" who had come of age in the Depression of the 1930s had no role in the new reality. He was being replaced by the "Man of Affirmation"—the intellectual—who, like Thomas Jefferson and Benjamin Franklin in the eighteenth century, wanted America to set a leadership example for the entire world (65).

In support of this point of view, *Time* quoted a number of the New York Intellectuals—among them Sidney Hook, Leslie Fiedler, Walter Lippmann, and Daniel Boorstin—who had renounced pasts rooted in dissatisfaction and protest to support America's increasingly conservative Cold War orthodoxies in both domestic and foreign affairs. Perhaps the most straightforward example of the changing philosophy on the part of the New York Intellectuals came from Lionel Trilling when he pronounced the end of intellectual anti-Americanism: "An avowed aloofness from national feeling is no longer the first ceremonial step into a life of thought. . . . For the first time in the history of the modern American intellectual, America is not to be conceived of as *a priori* the vulgarest and stupidest nation of the world" (67). Understanding the changing attitude that Trilling expressed and *Time* reported is crucial to coming to terms with the shifting status of intellectual labor in the postwar period. More importantly, an examination of this attitude plays a crucial role in illustrating how the progressive social thought of a critic such as Wertham fell completely beyond the narrow confines of the New York Intellectual circles.

Andrew Ross has pointed to the fact that in 1950s America, intellectuals increasingly championed a national culture that was defined against a series of perceived foreign threats (1989:43), chief among them the possibility that an American mass society might be converted to fascism or totalitarianism. The Cold War assumption that totalitarianism could befall any industrialized nation—even the United States—dominated a good deal of the public debate throughout the postwar period. The intellectuals' dismissal of any form of social organization that might conceivably lead down the road to increased levels of social coordination at the macrolevel obliged these men to champion a series of positions that easily fit into the growing Cold War consensus. The positions embraced included individualism, democracy, and cultural pluralism. The classical position established the links between high culture and antidemocratic social institutions that would define the aristocratic approach to culture well into the beginning of the twentieth century (Brantlinger 1983:60). Interestingly, postwar critics sought to reverse that particular association to claim both democratic social organization and high art in the cultural realm.

The New York Intellectuals' effort to define the twin bases of American virtue in democracy and high art can best be seen in the three-part 1952 *Partisan Review* seminar, "Our Country and Our Culture," that placed a new emphasis on the United States as culturally homogeneous. The editorial statement called on the collected respondents to address whether the relationship between America and its intellectuals had changed. Intellectuals, the editors argued, now felt closer to the nation than at any time in its history because, following the economic and cultural devastation wrought by the war, the United States had supplanted Europe as the guardian of Western civilization (*Partisan Review* 1952:282–84).

This new closeness with the nation could be seen in the editors' uncomplicated and unwavering embrace of American democracy: "Politically, there is a recognition that the kind of democracy that exists in America has an intrinsic and positive value" (284). This position was further extended in the explicitly stated rejection of the extreme aristocratic views previously pronounced by José Ortega y Gasset, views that had been published by the same journal (285). For the *Partisan Review* editors, the democratic values that America "either embodies or promises" constitute "necessary conditions for civilization and represent the only immediate alternative as long as Russian totalitarianism threatens world domination" (285). A few of the invited commentators, such as Norman Mailer, C. Wright Mills, and Irving Howe, rejected the editorial point of view for its conservative bias.

Nonetheless, the vast majority concurred with this new Cold War take on the relationship between culture and democracy. James Burnham, for instance, argued that the intellectual's new response to American society was justified both militarily and politically (1952:290), while Philip Rahv suggested that the reconciliation of America and its intellectuals rested on the exposure of Soviet myths and the consequent realization that American democracy "looks like the real thing" (1952:304). Sidney Hook stated that "the task of the intellectual is still to lead an intellectual life, to criticize what needs to be criticized in America, without forgetting for a moment the total threat that Communism poses to the life of the free mind" (1952:574). These responses, along with a number of similar sentiments expressed by other contributors to the seminar, sent out a very clear signal that the New York Intellectuals had, as Mills commented at the time, adopted "a shrinking deference to the status quo; often to a soft and anxious compliance, and always a synthetic, feeble search to justify this intellectual conduct, without searching for alternatives, and sometimes without even political good sense" (1952:446). The intellectual embrace of Americanism as the pinnacle of democratic values in the postwar period was the starting point for a serious retreat from the critical perspectives that had characterized the intellectual activity of previous decades. At the same time, this change helped to close off avenues for domestic social reform by directing attention away from the social problems facing the country and toward perceived or imagined foreign threats to the American way of life.

This postwar conservative political consensus existed in stark contrast to Wertham's conception of a socially engaged politics dedicated to progressive change. To this end, Wertham's political positions on issues such as civil rights and anticommunism were almost diametrically opposed to those of the New York Intellectuals. Further, Wertham's specific political goals and the foundational beliefs that structured his subsequent writings on psychiatry, mass culture, and media effects differed sharply from the orthodox consensus. These oppositional positions go some way toward explicating how Wertham was dismissed on terms that were ostensibly intellectual—such as method, polemic, and expertise—but were in fact far more deeply rooted in political bias. Essentially, the primary distinction between Wertham and postwar mass communication researchers lay in the area of the current state of American society, particularly insofar as political questions structured Wertham's particularistic approach to the study of mass culture through psychiatry and informed his rejection of empiricist methodologies that would ultimately come to dominate the study of media effects.

Warren Sussman argues that the problem at the heart of postwar American anxieties was the fact that the country had become, by the end of the Second World War, a "success" (1989:19). He suggested that the ideal nation that intellectuals had championed in the first half of the twentieth century—a democratic and inclusionary state that guarded the general welfare of the populace through a managed economy—had come to pass during the Truman administration. Yet ironically, just as Truman made intellectuals' dreams into reality through the affirmation of Keynesian economic theories in the 1946 Full Employment Act and the development of new agencies such as the Central Intelligence Agency to monitor foreign threats to the nation, an "age of anxiety" began to arise (20–21). The source of this anxiety resided in a growing sense that the large governments that had once seemed desirable were now seen as potentially totalitarian and that the mass involvement in the political process that had been an early progressive goal was now regarded as a problem. Insofar as old ideals had manifest themselves as new threats, the American dream had not worked in the way that the intellectuals had predicted.

The New York Intellectuals' shifting political interests can be seen in their decisions to support Truman's conservative consensus politics in the first major election following the end of the war. As Richard Pells points out, American postwar power grew quickly because the United States as a nation had escaped the destruction of the war and consequently could march toward the suburbs, while Europe was concerned with rebuilding its cities (1985:5–7). If the fact that America was relatively untouched by the war led many observers to perceive it as the "ultimate country" (30), this phenomenon also made for great difficulties in organizing for broad social change at the domestic level.

This difficulty can be seen, for example, in the failure of Henry Wallace's 1948 bid for the presidency and the subsequent consolidation of Cold War antagonism toward the Soviet Union in particular and toward communism in general. In 1947, Wallace formed the Progressive Citizens of America, a collection of "dissident liberals, trade unionists, veteran Communists, and Hollywood artists" pledged to an "impeccably reformist agenda" that included an end to racial segregation and the Red Scare as well as greater economic planning and labor rights (Pells 1985:69). The New York Intellectuals, who had welcomed Wallace as the editor of the *New Republic* the previous year, quickly turned on the new group. James Burnham opined that "a vote for Wallace is a vote for Stalin" (Pells 1985:116). With that, the intellectuals began their embrace of Cold War thinking. By 1949 the Soviets had developed the bomb, and 1950's Korean War cemented anti-Soviet feelings within New York's intellectual circles. This changing relationship to American foreign policy formed the backdrop against which intellectuals would outline their equation of mass culture and totalitarianism—an equation that would help to define critical thinking in the postwar period.

Among the key texts that sought to explicate the new consensus politics of the postwar era were William Kornhauser's *The Politics of Mass Society* (1959) and Hannah Arendt's *The Origins of Totalitarianism* (1951). Kornhauser was one of many postwar writers who equated fascism and communism under the common rubric of totalitarianism, which was held to be the natural enemy of democracy. Kornhauser struggled to bridge the philosophies of aristocratic critics of mass culture with the work of writers who had more democratic tendencies by suggesting that both arguments were correct up to a point. He argued that mass society was a nonaristocratic system in which elites were not isolated and were consequently prone to influence from the masses and in which the masses were available for mobilization by the social elites into pseudo-communities (39–73). The direct exposure of mass and elite to each other led to the possibility of creeping totalitarianism (74). Culturally, the result of this situation was the creation of atomized individuals with uniform tastes that ultimately separated them from their true selves, a type of alienation that enabled "totalitarian man," or the individual who was both self-alienated and group-centered (111). To this end, then, mass culture could be seen as the thin edge of the wedge that would lead to a mass society and even totalitarianism.

The Cold War equation of Nazism and communism through the use of the term *totalitarianism* to represent both—an equation that can be seen in Kornhauser's work—owed a great deal to Arendt's writing. *The Origins of Totalitarianism* has been termed the "political masterpiece of the postwar era" (Pells 1985:84). It defined the New York Intellectuals' concern with the problems of mass society as relating to the perils of conformity. Arendt argued that three nineteenth-century movements had converged to construct the totalitarian mind: the rise of anti-Semitism, overseas imperialism, and tribal nationalism. For Arendt, the primary concern about mass societies was the fact that the masses comprised superfluous individuals who sought to combine with a force greater than themselves to make sense of their lives. Arendt defined totalitarian movements as "mass organizations of atomized, isolated individuals. Compared with all other parties and movements, their most conspicuous external characteristic is their demand for total, unrestricted, unconditional, and unalterable loyalty of the individual member" (1951:316). The mobilization of the atomized individual as a force external to a democratic and pluralist society was potentially totalitarian. Arendt's contribution to the postwar discussions of mass society and totalitarianism, therefore, convinced American intellectuals that merit existed in returning to nineteenth-century conservative values to repair the decomposition of society. On questions of foreign policy, therefore, intellectuals felt a new urgency to join with the new American consensus, which sought to oppose the spread of communism abroad and curtail it at home, by challenging the components of the mass society.

Critics such as David Riesman and William Whyte led the postwar reexamination of the social character of the average American, together providing a foundational critique of postwar American social character. Both Riesman's *The Lonely Crowd* and Whyte's *The Organization Man* investigated the issue of personal freedom within what was seen as an increasingly restrictive and coercive social order. In *The Lonely Crowd,* for example, Riesman argued that "man is made by his society" and that an explicit and definable relationship existed between a society and the types of character that society produces (1950:4–6). Riesman's definition of the three types of society producing three types of character—which he termed tradition-directed, inner-directed, and other-directed—subtly condemned postwar America for its growing reliance on other-directed individuals. For other-directed types, as Riesman defined them, relations with the world were mediated by mass communications, while contemporaries and colleagues became the source of social orientations and direction in personal behavior (21–25). The change from the self-orienting inner direction to the group-orienting other-directed personality type resulted, Riesman suggested, in part from the fact that postwar America was increasingly consumption oriented. With additional leisure time and disposable income, Americans had witnessed the quickening rise of mass culture entertainments to fill that time, and conspicuous consumption had been socialized (1954:228).

Whyte similarly sounded the alarm about the potentially negative impact of the group on the individual in *The Organization Man*. He argued that the collectivization of the corporation had led to the development of a new form of organizational life that conflicted with the American heritage rooted in the Protestant ethic. Whyte termed this new form of organization the social ethic and identified its major tenets as belief in the group as the source of creativity, belief in "belongingness" as the ultimate need of the individual, and belief that science has the tools to achieve belongingness (1956:7). The social ethic that was the new orthodoxy of the American corporation stressed togetherness and group work at the expense of the individual and promoted a harmonious atmosphere through the complete elimination of individualism. The apotheosis of this type of false collectivization could be found in the new living arrangements in the suburbs (392–94). Whyte saw all of these changes as negative. Like so many intellectuals in the postwar period, he stressed the importance of personal liberty in opposition to the group. Similarly, Riesman believed that the optimal position was with the autonomous individual who manifested the ability to choose. Both of these texts argued in favor of a reform of individual patterns of behavior rather of broad-based social change at the institutional or social level. Progressive reform of the type that Wertham advocated had no currency in this discourse.

The combination of Cold War anticommunism on matters relating to foreign affairs and domestic anxiety over the effects of group-mindedness, bureaucracy, and mass culture on the domestic front ultimately came to be known as the "consensus perspective" in postwar American thought. Notably, *Time* profiled these consensus intellectuals for its 1956 cover story, and this group dominated intellectual discussions through the 1950s as the media-effects paradigm was beginning to gain momentum. What William Graebner identifies as the postwar intellectual's loss of faith in history and abandonment of the progress model of human development (1991:48) formed the backdrop against which Wertham's discussion of comic books, the mass media, and the nature of human violence was juxtaposed.

Wertham's concerns about racism and poverty simply could not be acknowledged within the new consensus orthodoxies. The new consensus notion that America's lasting heritage was one of pragmatism and unfettered economic growth was foregrounded by writers such as Daniel Bell who suggested that the combination of social science and modern technology would allow the United States to realize a frontier of abundance and end competition for scarce resources. The increasingly conservative tone of postwar intellectualism appeared in the journals and organizations that had their start in the 1950s, such as the Committee for Cultural Freedom and its journal, *Encounter*. Subsequently revealed as funded by the Central Intelligence Agency, the committee formed a nucleus of anticommunist intellectuals in the 1950s and included David Riesman, Daniel Bell, and Sidney Hook as well as other prominent New York Intellectuals (Pells 1985:130). As these writers increasingly turned away from economic explanations for problems in postwar American life, they increasingly took up discussions rooted in philosophy, psychology, and morality. The critique of mass culture that reached a fevered pitch during this era and found its fullest expression in the writings of many of the consensus intellectuals can be seen in this light as a strategy to continue a facade of political critique while arguing in favor of the pluralistic status quo.

These attitudes represent the great divide between the New York Intellectuals and Fredric Wertham. Wertham's aesthetic critique of mass culture was broadly influenced by the ongoing criticism of mass culture that dominated American cultural thought in the twentieth century. However, his conclusions on questions of politics and the prospects for wide-scale social change were almost completely at odds with the new consensus in the 1950s. Wertham's writings in this period, including his condemnations of mass culture, did not seek to foster a new individualism but instead argued for a greater connection between the individual and society. His conception of a social psychiatry that would examine the individual as a member of various forms of social organization, from the family to the community, was the fundamental reason why he did not fit within a discursive framework dominated by intellectuals whose primary concern was a fear of institutional bureaucracies. While the dominant intellectuals of the period attempted to obscure the relationship between social structures and personal problems, Wertham made a point of constantly stressing that connection.

Wertham was not simply a failed New York Intellectual; rather, he was working within a framework for the critique of mass culture that should be regarded as existing in opposition to prevailing orthodoxies. Thus, it is necessary to pay attention to the ways in which he departed from the postwar consensus on the major political issues of the day. To this end, therefore, Wertham's involvement with two of the most controversial political issues of the era can shed light on his antagonistic relationship to the dominant discourse of postwar intellectuals. Wertham acted as a psychiatric witness on behalf of Ethel Rosenberg in 1953. One year later, his expertise was cited in the landmark *Brown v. Board of Education* Supreme Court decision regarding racial segregation. These two issues—one relating to foreign policy, the other to domestic policy—helped to lay the groundwork for his critique of mass culture, which was rooted in a waning form of progressive liberalism. Similarly, two books by Wertham marked his clear departure from the postwar consensus: *Circle of Guilt,* a book-length study of racism and its role in fostering juvenile crime, and his major statement on the nature of human violence and the prospects for widespread social reform, *A Sign for Cain.*

One of the most important touchstones of the postwar debates about American domestic and foreign policy was certainly the case of Julius and Ethel Rosenberg, sentenced to death for espionage in 1951 and executed on

19 June 1953. Throughout the 1940s and into the 1950s, the Truman administration had made the persecution of communists and suspected communists a hallmark of its foreign policy. In March 1947, for instance, Truman authorized the Federal Bureau of Investigation to check the loyalty of all federal employees, a move that was endorsed by a number of prominent intellectuals, including Bell, Hook, and Fiedler (Pells 1985:269). In July 1948, twelve Communist Party leaders were convicted under the Smith Act of 1940, which made it a crime to advocate the violent overthrow of the U.S. government. The Supreme Court upheld the convictions in 1951. In 1948 Alger Hiss was tried for treason and, after a mistrial, was convicted at a second trial in 1950. By 1949 twenty-two states required loyalty oaths for teachers. The Rosenbergs would be judged within this climate of persecution and hysteria, first by a jury and second by the intellectuals who had made anticommunism the driving force of American thought in the 1950s.

The Rosenbergs were arrested in 1950 on information provided to the government by David Greenglass, a coconspirator and Ethel Rosenberg's brother. The couple was convicted in 1951 at the height of the Korean War and of Cold War hysteria. At the sentencing, the presiding judge argued that by providing the Soviet Union with the secrets to the atomic bomb, the Rosenbergs should be held personally responsible for the fifty thousand American casualties in the Korean conflict. The pair were separated and sentenced to death, able to see each other only when meeting with their lawyers. In the years between their conviction and their execution, the couple corresponded by letter and an edited selection of 187 of these letters were published in June 1953, the month of the execution, as *The Death House Letters*. This volume attracted critical commentary from Fiedler and Robert Warshow, spotlighting the position of the New York Intellectuals with regard to the Rosenbergs.

Fiedler's essay, originally published in the first issue of *Encounter*, argued that there were two Rosenberg cases: the legal trial of March 1951 and the symbolic trial that had begun subsequent to the conviction. While the Rosenbergs' legal guilt had been established in the court of law, they had won the symbolic case because many liberals and fellow travelers had been swayed by the humane plea that had been launched on their behalf by friends and supporters (1952:27–33). Fiedler, however, was unmoved. Reading their letters, he rejected the Rosenbergs for their tendency to see themselves as clichés, suggesting that the letters were "too absurd to be tragic" (38). For Fiedler, the Rosenbergs' biggest crime was the fact that even after the conviction they did not confess, even to each other. Thus, he condemned them for the fact that "they failed in the end to become martyrs or heroes, or even men" (45).

Fiedler stripped the couple even of their humanity, and Warshow felt that they deserved no better. He condemned the Rosenbergs for the fact that they had no internal sense of their own being, as was evidenced, Warshow argued, by their false and awkward relationship to culture, which marked them as inextricably middlebrow and insincere (1962:37–40). The Rosenbergs' inauthenticity stemmed, Warshow argued, from the fact that the couple believed whatever their politics required them to think. In this sense, the Rosenbergs were indicative of the new personality types found in a mass society, "people of no eloquence and little imagination" (43). For the New York Intellectuals, therefore, the Rosenbergs were conveniently dismissed through an appeal to existing ways of conceptualizing American society and its culture. Their letters written while imprisoned bore all the marks of the middlebrow, and their middleness, rather than their alleged treason, was cast as their ultimate crime against the Cold War consensus.

In an essay on the relationship between the Rosenbergs and the New York Intellectuals, David Suchoff justifies Arendt's silence on the Rosenberg question despite her condemnations of the growing anticommunist hysteria of the period by suggesting that she "would indeed have been courageous to support them publicly" because to do so would have meant risking irreparable harm to her career as a postwar intellectual (1995:160). In that light, Wertham was extremely courageous not only to support the couple publicly but also to actively work on behalf of them and their two young sons. In 1951, Wertham was asked to examine the imprisoned Ethel Rosenberg because it was feared that her solitary confinement as the sole female death row inmate at Sing Sing might contribute to a nervous breakdown. The presiding judge in the case refused to permit Wertham to meet with Rosenberg, and Wertham was forced to make his evaluation of her based on information passed to him by her lawyer, Emanuel Bloch. Wertham evaluated her case in this unusual way through reference to his extensive experience with prison psychoses. As her sons later recalled in their memoir, *We Are Your Sons,*

There was no doubt that she was in a bad way. She was evidently a courageous woman, but the strain of being isolated in the Death House was
becoming too much for her. Except for a guard she was kept all alone in an
entire building and could not see or speak to any other person from morning
to night. . . . Aggravating her emotional state was the mental torture she was
exposed to. The electric chair was used as psychological pressure: it was a
matter of talk or die; if you'd only "name names" their lives could be spared
and she could save her husband's life. . . . In my testimony . . . I stated that
if the absolute separation of husband and wife were to continue so that
Mrs. Rosenberg could not confer with her husband there was a definite
and strong probability that she would break down and develop a prison
psychosis. . . . [W]ithin a few days after my testimony Washington reversed
itself. Mr. Rosenberg was transferred . . . to the Death House in Sing Sing.
After visiting with her husband, Mrs. Rosenberg's depression lifted and her
spirits revived. (Meeropol 1975:59)

Wertham's conception of Rosenberg as a "courageous woman" tortured by
the state could not be further removed from the condemnations of her as
the quintessentially inauthentic middlebrow voiced by Warshow and Fiedler.
There can be no question that Wertham placed his career in the public
health sector in jeopardy through his willingness to work with Rosenberg.
The scandalmongering press swirling around the case pilloried him relent-
lessly. "Denies Favoring Soviet" was the headline reporting Wertham's testimony in the staid *New York Times*. Later in life, he wrote, "Never in my life
have I been blamed so much for anything I did as I have been for testifying
for Mrs. Rosenberg. This happened not only with uneducated people but
also with those who think of themselves as informed and liberal-minded.
Some people even stopped talking to me! " (Reibman 1990:16–17).

Wertham's support for the Rosenbergs went beyond simply testifying on
behalf of Ethel, however. In 1953, Wertham also examined the Rosenbergs'
children, then aged six and ten, at the Lafargue Clinic. They recalled him
fondly as one of a few stable elements at a time of tremendous personal
tragedy. Michael and Robert Rosenberg were shuttled among numerous
state-run institutions and foster homes after the execution of their parents,
and Wertham concluded that both boys had been "severely traumatized"
but had "positive emotional resources that warranted a good long-range

prognosis" if they were treated aggressively (Meeropol 1975:253). The Rosenberg sons continued to see Wertham on a weekly basis for a few years, and he ultimately recommended that the boys be adopted, have their names changed, and be placed in private schools to give them the best chance for normal lives (Meeropol 1975:254). These suggestions, like Wertham's recommendation regarding Rosenberg's treatment, were fully adopted by the boys' guardians, Abel and Anne Meeropol.

While Wertham did not publish any articles specifically on his work with Ethel Rosenberg and her sons, he nonetheless did not shy away from publicly discussing his participation in the cases altogether. In *A Sign for Cain,* for instance, Wertham's discussion of the ethics and morality of the death penalty touched on his involvement with the case. While arguing that the death penalty had to be abolished because it was inhumane and immoral, Wertham noted that "capital punishment is particularly cruel when the law plays with the life of a prisoner, much like a cat playing with a mouse" (1966b:304). He claimed that this form of game playing occurred when federal officials told Rosenberg that her life and that of their husband would be spared if she were to cooperate with the government. Wertham saw this offer as indicating the sorry state of American culture: "That two otherwise respected federal government officials should lend themselves to a you-talk-or-we-will-kill-you maneuver is understandable only if we realize how deeply violence as a method is entrenched in our society" (304). Similarly, the state's decision to execute the mother of two young boys displayed the cruelty of the American legal system: "We have closed-season hunting laws for animals while they bring up their young. This principle should be extended to humans" (304).

This position was, of course, totally at odds with the casual indifference to the executions found in Fiedler's and Warshow's coldhearted and condemning literary analyses. Furthermore, both Fiedler and Warshow subsequently explicitly rejected Wertham's work on comic books in the harshest possible terms. While likening the death penalty to the comic book controversy may appear glib, recalling Warshow's argument that the Rosenbergs deserved death because of their debased cultural attitudes gives some indication of how social issues were ultimately debated at the level of aesthetics in the 1950s. Thus, a clear link apparently existed between the strident and unfeeling anticommunism of the New York Intellectuals and their particular condemnations of the middlebrow mass culture that spurned the humanitarian sentiments of Wertham and his idiosyncratic take on the problems presented by mass culture. This sort of opposition would reappear two years later in the differing responses of the New York Intellectuals and Wertham to the question of civil rights.

In the *Partisan Review*'s 1952 "Our Country and Our Culture" seminar, Max Lerner argued against pronouncements by the New York Intellectuals that America was moving toward becoming an increasingly classless society.

> The image of an American "classless society" which crops up in the more lyric business pronouncements such as William H. Whyte, Jr. has so delightfully gathered, is largely NAM [National Association of Manufacturers] ammunition. What we have roughly is an open-class system, with a high degree of mobility still left in it despite its recent rigidities on top and bottom, and (as Riesman documents in *Faces in the Crowd*) with vast stores of new experience opened for all classes, especially the middle. We have a "democratic class struggle" still operative, in which the working class and its allies use every economic and political means to better their own position and the nation's welfare. Finally—and worst of all— how about our Negro population, whose treatment is the ugliest scar we bear? (1952:583)

That Lerner brought "our Negro population" into the question was remarkable, for he was the only writer included in the seminar to acknowledge the possibility that the new classless American society and the new consensus might be in any way racially based. While Lerner had faith that American democracy would be able to overcome the country's racial divisions, his certainty was not universal.

Pells suggests that after 1955, the American Cold War consensus began a long process of unraveling and that one of the keys to the dissolution of the consensus lay with the fight for civil rights in the South. By 1955, for instance, the Montgomery bus boycott had called into question the idea that African Americans in the southern states participated as equals in American democracy (Pells 1985:346). However, as the absence of discussion about race in "Our Country and Our Culture" demonstrated, few New York Intellectuals seemed interested in questions pertaining to race or willing to acknowledge the fact that the new "white collar" collectivity that was seen to dominate the 1950s was a particularly racialized form of social organization. Writing on Ralph Ellison's classic novel of racial alienation, *Invisible Man,* Andrew Hoberek argues that he essentially agreed with Whyte, Riesman, Mills, and other postwar intellectuals who regarded with suspicion the deindividualizing power of the organization (1998:106). However, by 1961 a U.S. Bureau of Labor Statistics survey noted that "nonwhite workers" made up a scant 3.7 percent of the white-collar workforce, concluding that "white-collar culture did not simply reflect but helped generate the white-black racial schism in the postwar United States" (107–8). The intellectuals' role in perpetuating a U.S. social crisis that denied black Americans their fundamental civil rights can be brought to light by examining the social position occupied by African Americans outside of the postwar consensus.

Despite the fact that black Americans overwhelmingly endorsed the Truman government in the 1948 election, they did not clearly benefit from the government's policies, particularly as they related to the Cold War. Manning Marable suggests that "the impact of the Cold War, the anti-Communist purges and near-totalitarian social environment, had a devastating effect upon the cause of blacks' civil rights and civil liberties" (1991:18). As American business interests attempted to bolster their incomes by expanding global markets and curtailing labor costs at home, they discovered that the Red Scare accomplished both. In 1947, the Truman administration spent $400 million to halt the spread of the political left in Turkey and Greece, and at the same time began to investigate the federal bureaucracy for suspected communists. As individual states began to outlaw the Communist Party, one effect was to oust individuals who had been the most dedicated proponents of civil rights and desegregation (Marable 1991:18–20). Antiracist unions were accused of being infiltrated by communists, forcing the Congress of Industrial Organizations to expel more than 1 million members, thereby weakening both the drive for civil rights and the potential of American labor power (Plummer 1996:193).

At the same time, the Cold War enabled proponents of the status quo to argue that the possibility of rapid change endangered the American way of life in light of the ongoing foreign policy interests in the promotion of that way of life abroad. The foreign policy dictates of the Cold War so aggressively endorsed by the New York Intellectuals, therefore, were instrumental in stalling the passage of meaningful civil rights legislation for more than a decade until the Civil Rights Act of 1957. Thus, by embracing the Cold War status quo on the foreign and domestic front and espousing the virtues of American pluralism as a curative for every institutional social problem in the United States, the leading postwar intellectuals obviously turned a blind eye to the specific problems facing America's black population, which remained outside of the promises of American democracy.

In Wertham's writings, questions about race were inextricably linked to questions of violence, the overwhelming concern that runs through all of his work. Wertham's emphasis on questions of human violence formed the backbone of both his political and social thinking as well as his critique of mass culture, and he dedicated much of his working life as a psychiatrist to the elimination of violence from human relations. To address the practical question of violence in the community, Wertham founded the Lafargue Clinic in Harlem in 1946 and the Quaker Emergency Service Readjustment Center, a pioneering clinic for the treatment of sex offenders, in New York in 1947. These clinics were symptomatic of Wertham's desire to bring psychiatry into the community to counteract the threat of violence and exemplify Wertham's involvement with grassroots organizations.

Wertham had tried unsuccessfully since the 1930s to generate funding for a clinic that could meet the psychiatric needs of New York's black community, members of which were often denied access to treatment in hospitals. In 1946, with the encouragement and advice of Earl Brown, Paul Robeson, Richard Wright, and Ralph Ellison, Wertham opened his clinic without governmental or philanthropic support in the basement of Harlem's influential St. Philips Episcopal Church. There, a multiracial volunteer staff of fourteen psychiatrists and twelve social workers sought to alleviate hostility in the community and to better understand the reality of black life in urban America. Named in honor of Paul Lafargue, a Cuban-born black French physician who married Karl Marx's daughter, the clinic became a leading New York center for the promotion of civil rights.

The press in New York and nationwide widely celebrated the Lafargue Clinic during the late 1940s for its contribution to improving race relations. Ellison called the clinic one of Harlem's most important institutions and "an underground extension of democracy" (1953:295). He praised its approach to psychiatry, which was at odds with dominant intellectual conceptions of postwar America:

> [T]he Lafargue Clinic rejects all stereotypes, and may be said to concern itself with any possible variations between the three basic social factors shaping an American Negro's personality: he is viewed as a member of a racial and cultural minority; as an American citizen caught in certain political and economic relationships; and as a modern man living in a revolutionary world. Accordingly, each patient, whether white or black, is approached dynamically as a being possessing a cultural and biological past who seeks to make his way toward the future in a world wherein each discovery about himself must be made in the here and now at the expense of hope, pain and fear—a being who in responding to the complex forces of America has become confused. (1953:295)

This approach to a mode of psychiatry that equally emphasized the individual and the social world was far removed from the mainstream of both psychiatric and general intellectual thought in the postwar period. The *New Republic* observed that Wertham and his associates at the clinic termed their approach "social psychiatry" to denote the need to come to terms with a patient's economic and community life as well as his or her interior or psychological life (Martin 1946:798). Indeed, the magazine stressed the uniqueness in the United States not only of the approach but even of the desire to treat black patients at that time, when the entire country had only eight black psychiatrists (Martin 1946:798) and when, according to *Time,* Harlem accounted for more than half of New York City's juvenile delinquency cases ("Psychiatry in Harlem" 1947:50). These facts made the decision to move to the area with the greatest need seem both logical and necessary. Individuals from the community could receive psychiatric counseling without an appointment and for only a quarter (fifty cents if a psychiatrist was required to testify in court). The Lafargue Clinic clearly sought to spark genuine social change.

The coupling of progressive politics and science was a hallmark of Wertham's writings generally but never more so than when he concerned himself with the status of blacks in postwar America. Wertham's name appeared frequently in the New York press as he chastised complacency on civil rights throughout the 1950s. In 1951, for instance, Wertham testified that "segregation by custom"—or segregation brought about by administrative decisions fixing school boundaries—was as significant a problem in New York as was legally mandated school segregation in the South (Dale 1951:23), and he repeated the charges at the end of the decade, when he accused the city of promoting segregated classrooms in its integrated schools (Kihss 1958:12). Similarly, Wertham regularly derided the hypocrisy and posturing that many intellectuals and critics substituted for concrete action on social change. A 1949 *Saturday Review of Literature* portrait of Wertham rendered explicit the connections among race, democracy, intellectual posturing, anticommunism, and the question of human violence:

> At the recent Middlebury, Vt., conference to consider "a positive program for a democratic society" among many splendid observations "a spiritual ground swell" was noted. Typically, Dr. Fredric Wertham took out a box of brass tacks when his turn came to speak. What, he demanded, about the six innocent Negroes sentenced to death in Trenton? "If I were to go to them and say, 'There is a spiritual ground swell around you,' it wouldn't do much good. It's a problem of democracy to solve that! It isn't possible to discuss any program of democracy or peace on earth without discussion of violence. At present there is a condemnation of people who advocate the overthrow of the Government by violence. What the powers that be are really worried about are the people who advocate the overthrow of violence by government." (R.G. 1949:10)

Wertham's connection in this instance of racism and the legal system would find a fuller expression in his 1956 book, *The Circle of Guilt.*

Circle of Guilt closely resembled Wertham's previous criminal case histories, *Dark Legend* (1941) and *The Show of Violence* (1949), insofar as it was a case study of a murder wherein he had served as the psychiatrist for the accused. *Circle of Guilt* differed from its predecessors, however, in the way in which it treated the crime not so much from a psychiatric perspective as from a social perspective. The case under review was that of Frank Santana, a young Puerto Rican boy living in New York who was accused of killing a white boy, William Blankenship. The case was notorious in New York for its "senseless" nature, and, as Wertham noted, the press coverage leading up to the trial drew on a number of racist preconceptions.

In *Circle of Guilt,* Wertham first mentioned his structuring belief that violence and communication are opposites. He did so by noting that Santana was "not accustomed to communicating" and that he had consequently become involved with a local Puerto Rican gang, the Navahos. According to Wertham, Santana's lack of communication skills resulted from his shyness and his inward emotional life. Denied opportunities at school because of institutional racism, Santana had largely stopped attending, choosing instead to go to the movies all day, every day. Wertham suggested that Santana used these movies to fill the gaps in his emotional life and make up for his feelings of inferiority, which should have been addressed professionally early in his life. The lack of attention paid to Santana was indicative of a larger ethical problem in American society. Wertham contended that those individuals who had the least support from family, social networks, and authorities were most prone to juvenile delinquency. By abandoning Santana, the schools and other social institutions had violated the boy's basic human rights to education, health, and protection from harm, which Wertham held as the most fundamental rights of every child.

Circle of Guilt was published only two years after *Seduction of the Innocent,* his most sustained critique of mass culture, so it is perhaps little surprise that Wertham dedicated an entire chapter of *Circle of Guilt* to Frank Santana's relationship with comic books. Yet comic books were only one of the extrinsic factors Wertham addressed and, judging by the page count, the least important. Whereas the New York Intellectuals and other critics of mass culture in the new consensus typically would assign moral responsibility for criminality to mass culture, Wertham stressed a series of social factors that he found more pressing. Significantly, he dedicated a much larger chapter of the book to the history of Puerto Rico and its not-quite-colonial relationship to the United States in the twentieth century.

Beginning with Columbus's 1493 discovery of the island, Wertham traced its history through its annexation by the United States during the Spanish-American war and its ongoing economic enslavement by the United States. Wertham noted, for instance, that half of Puerto Ricans were unemployed or underemployed, leading to serious social ills. Puerto Ricans in the continental United States, Wertham continued, highlighted social inequalities: "If one views the evils in the living conditions of the vast poorer section of Puerto Ricans in the United States, one incontestable fact stands out: the Puerto Ricans have not caused these evils. Their presence has merely highlighted already existing shortcomings. These evils are the result of neglect, greed, maladministration and prejudice" (122).

Wertham ultimately concluded that Puerto Ricans in the United States had been ignored and disdained by social service agencies, abused by the courts, and wrongly diagnosed by psychiatrists unable to see beyond their prejudices. He further suggested that such blatant anti–Puerto Rican racism lay at the root of gang activities. In this particular case, he was sure of that fact. Moreover, he reported that the murder victim, Blankenship, widely portrayed in the media as an angelic boy minding his own business who had been murdered for no reason while on his way to the movies, was actually a member of the Red Wings, an anti–Puerto Rican gang. Santana, Wertham argued, had been defending himself from a tormentor when his gun went off, killing Blankenship, an action that the psychiatrist diagnosed as a "short-circuit reaction" rooted in his double orientation in both violence and the fear of violence (183–85). Wertham concluded that "the boy, although not legally insane, was a mentally abnormal boy who had a disturbed sense of right and wrong" (190) that should supply background for clemency in his sentencing. Before the trial, however, Santana pled guilty to second-degree murder and received a sentence of twenty-five years to life rather than face a potential death penalty for a conviction on a first-degree charge. After the trial, the district attorney attempted to clarify the facts about Blankenship's status in a gang, a move that Wertham criticized as the heaping of abuse on the victim after the drive to execute Santana had failed. Blankenship, Wertham argued, was no more at fault than was Santana. The driving force behind the entire incident had been anti–Puerto Rican racism: "From this larger perspective we can see what set these children against each other and led them to find such outlets. The adult community's attitude against Puerto Ricans was the most potent, the most traumatic factor in Santana's dislocation. As reflected in his mind, it affected all the common relationships of his life. What would be the best method to confuse a boy? Ask him to adjust to a society and at the same time make him feel that he is not really part of it" (199–200).

Wertham wrote his book on the case because he was unable to testify on Santana's behalf and therefore was unable to attempt to resolve in the courts the causes of this violence. He took the story to the public realm in the hope that the underlying basis for this tragedy could be addressed somewhere. Wertham felt so strongly about this case that when his publisher, Rinehart, refused to promote the book to his satisfaction, he personally bought advertising space in the *New York Times*. Wertham's tendency to intrude into the space between the legal realm and public consciousness in this and other cases can be better seen in his intervention into the pressing question of school segregation and his important role in the fight to end that injustice.

Wertham's single most important contribution to the lives of American blacks in the postwar era was his participation in the landmark 1954 Supreme Court decision, *Brown v. Board of Education*. As early as 1948, Wertham had decried the lack of substantive psychiatric work on the question of racism: "If one reads many psychiatric and psychoanalytic case histories one cannot fail to notice the absence of any proper evaluation of race hatred, prejudice, discrimination and segregation in the emotional development of the patient. And yet many years of careful analytic studies have convinced me that exposure to racial hatred from early childhood is in our historical epoch as important a pathogenic factor as sexual difficulties" (1948f:497). Further underscoring Wertham's interest in this topic was his belief that racism was motivated by social and economic factors that could be understood only historically. Consequently, the study of racism provided an exceptional opportunity to promote the type of social psychiatry he had long advocated.

In 1951, the Delaware chapter of the National Association for the Advancement of Colored People (NAACP) contacted Wertham and asked if he would undertake a psychological study of the effects of school segregation on children. Wertham agreed, and thirteen Delaware schoolchildren from four locations in the state were brought five times to the Lafargue Clinic, where psychiatrists and social workers took individual clinical case histories, conducted interviews, and administered standardized tests. Wertham presented the results of the findings in October 1951 at Delaware desegregation trial. The NAACP considered Delaware, a border state with entirely segregated schools, a key in the battle against segregation. More importantly, the basis for the legal argument in the Delaware case differed from the arguments in four other segregation cases being heard simultaneously in other states. In the other cases, the plaintiffs alleged that the *Plessy*-derived separate-but-equal policy could not legitimately be called a form of equality and was therefore illegal. The Delaware case argued instead that segregation constituted a public health problem.

Wertham's participation in the Delaware case came about because his work at the Lafargue Clinic made him extremely qualified to speak to the question of segregation as a public health crisis. Jack Greenberg, the lead lawyer for the Delaware case, later described Wertham as a "famous psychiatrist" who "cared deeply about discrimination," even if he had a tendency to wander into complaints about comic books (1994:136). Wertham was one of several social scientists who agreed to testify on behalf of the plaintiffs in the case. Greenberg described the testimony of Otto Klineburg, Jerome Bruner, and Kenneth Clark as having been reasonably routine but noted, "only Wertham's testimony was different than expected—he captivated the courtroom. The Viennese accent helped, but the impact came from what he had to say" (137). Wertham's complete testimony regarding the psychological effects of school segregation circulated in an NAACP press release (NAACP 1951), and Wertham published his findings as an article in the *American Journal of Psychotherapy* in 1952.

In his testimony, Wertham asserted that three distinct factors could injure a child's life: personal factors, such as the family; infrapersonal factors, those related to the physical constitution, such as epilepsy; and suprapersonal, or social factors, of which racism represented a particularly striking example. Wertham argued, based on his specific observations of the Delaware students, that children who attended segregated schools developed a neurosis because they were unable to rationalize the fact of segregation. This inability stemmed from the fact that the adults around them were unable to provide a sensible justification for the ongoing disparity of treatment under the law. Therefore, not the physical aspects of the school (such as the poor conditions in schools for blacks) but the fact of segregation itself caused emotional harm. Wertham reinforced this idea with his testimony that the quality of the instruction and the quality of the institutions had no bearing on the case of segregation—the law itself did the harm: "I have come to the conclusion that the physical differences in these schools are not at all really material, to my opinion. In other words, if I may express it graphically, if the State of Delaware would employ Professor Einstein to teach Physics in marble halls to these children, I would still say everything I have said goes. It is the fact of segregation in general and the problems that come out of it that to my mind are anti-educational" (NAACP 1951:7).

Moreover, because segregation was governmental policy, children experienced it as a moral practice and were therefore unable to resist through appeal to the sense that someone bad was perpetrating a wrong because they had been led to understand that the government could not act immorally. Children, therefore, interpreted segregation as government-imposed punishment. When they realized that they had done nothing to deserve this punishment, they rationalized that the fault must lie with the adults, their parents. This led to the development of chronic self-esteem problems within the community, particularly insofar as the problem of segregation was not episodic but was continuous and of long duration (Wertham 1952). Wertham's argument was supported, he argued a year later in the *Journal of Educational Sociology* (1953d), by studying children from the newly desegregated Delaware schools.

In the second study, Wertham and his colleagues examined twenty-two children, including ten from the original study, and concluded not only that the children performed better at school but also that the essential psychological conflict from which they suffered had been removed. This, Wertham concluded in *The Nation,* proved that it was possible to "single out one force from a complex structure of a child's emotional health" (1954g:97). Wertham concluded his trial testimony with precisely that argument: "Segregation in schools legally decreed by statute, as in the State of Delaware, interferes with the healthy development of children. It doesn't necessarily cause an emotional disorder in every child. I compare that with the disease of tuberculosis. In New York thousands of people have tubercle bacilli in their lungs—hundreds of thousands—and they don't get tuberculosis. But they do have the germ of illness in them at one time or another, and the fact that hundreds of them don't develop tuberculosis doesn't make me say, 'never mind the tubercle bacillus; it doesn't harm people, so let it go' " (Greenberg 1994:139).

Handing down its decision in the Delaware case on 1 April 1952, the court cited Wertham in ruling in favor of desegregating the state's schools, accepting and repeating his testimony to the effect that "State enforced segregation is important, because it is 'clear cut' and gives legal sanction to the differences, and is of continuous duration" (Greenberg 1994:150).

Greenberg recounts that NAACP legal strategist Thurgood Marshall termed Delaware "our best case" and suggested that its importance lay in the fact that because it was a victory at the state level, it drove a wedge into the solid foundation of segregation that might persuade the Supreme Court to follow the state court's lead (151). When consolidated with the losing 1953 cases from Kansas, South Carolina, Virginia, and Washington, D.C., into what resulted in the *Brown* decision, the Delaware decision became the template on which American school segregation—and, by extension, the legal basis for the *Plessy v. Ferguson* separate-but-equal doctrine in all matters of public life in America—was thrown out.

Despite the fact that the Court's ruling that schools should be desegregated "with all deliberate speed" allowed for a great deal of stalling at the state level—in 1956–57 more than three thousand school districts remained segregated (Marable 1991:41)—the *Brown v. Board of Education* ruling was one of the most important moments in the postwar drive toward civil rights. Years later, Wertham recalled his participation in the desegregation efforts and praised *Brown* as "one of the most momentous decisions of the high court in this century." Nonetheless, he decried the fact that so many liberals of the day had refused to get involved or to testify that school segregation harmed children (1976:508). Around this case, therefore, the distinctions between Wertham and other intellectuals of the postwar period can be most clearly drawn. Wertham's commitment to ending segregation was intensely deep and ongoing. On 23 March 1953 he gave a short speech as part of the second annual Big Night of NAACP fundraiser at New York's Madison Square Garden, reiterating many of the points made in his testimony. The degree to which Wertham's position on desegregation was not simply an aberrational difference between himself and the New York Intellectuals but was symptomatic of a much wider divide that can be seen by turning to the fullest statement of Wertham's social philosophy, his 1966 book, *A Sign for Cain*.

In many ways, *A Sign for Cain* represented the culmination of Wertham's thinking. Whereas his earlier books dealt with either psychiatry and the legal system or the relationship between mass culture and juvenile delinquency, this particular volume incorporated and then expanded on all of his previous work to present a unified thesis on the nature of human violence and the potential for its eradication through social psychiatry. In a

1954 letter to Ida McAlpine, Wertham had indicated that his long-term plans including authoring a magnum opus on the relationship of the thinking of Karl Marx and of Sigmund Freud (1954e). *A Sign for Cain* was as close as he would come to that goal.

The book was widely reviewed in the fall of 1966, with the reviews generally falling into two categories, extremely positive and extremely negative. The positive reviews included short pieces from the *Christian Century*, which called the book "disturbing" and "well-documented" ("This Week" 1966:1116); *Publisher's Weekly*, which suggested that Wertham's work would be of wide interest to community leaders ("October 26" 1966:87–88); and the *Library Journal*, which suggested that *A Sign for Cain* "should be recommended to every person who can read" (De Rosis 1966:4678). The *American Journal of Psychotherapy*, on the editorial board of which Wertham served at the time, predicted that the book would become "a classic in this field" (Meerloo 1968:116), comparing it to Konrad Lorenz's *On Aggression* for its timely comments on violence.

A number of other reviewers and critics reiterated the comparison to Lorenz's work, though far less favorably. The *New York Times*, for instance, reviewed the book alongside Robert Ardrey's *The Territorial Imperative*, which drew on Lorenz's research to suggest that aggression was an innate factor in biology. The *Times* suggested that in light of the newer arguments from Lorenz and Ardrey, Wertham's contributions to the field seemed "hopelessly dated" (Fremont-Smith 1966:41). Similarly, the *Wall Street Journal* compared *A Sign for Cain* to Ardrey's book and flatly rejected Wertham's thesis, pessimistically remarking, "We believe the seed of violence to be ineradicable from man's nature, and therefore its flow to be ineradicable from society" (Fuller 1966:18). In a lengthy piece, the *Saturday Review of Literature* adopted the same line, suggesting that Wertham overstated the cultural factors involved in human violence by rejecting the thesis that aggression was innate (Fox 1966:40). Norbert Muhlen, a leading New York Intellectual, chastised Wertham for failing to promote the Cold War agenda by criticizing the Soviet Union and China, ultimately concluding that his book displayed the "slapdash staccato of a hysterical Sunday supplement crusade" (1966:353). The polarized reactions to Wertham's book were atypical given the fact that critics had enthusiastically received his previous efforts. These reactions thus point to the fact that his views were, as the *New Statesman* pointed out, "unfashionable" in the postwar period and at odds with the dominant thinking about the possibilities of widespread social reform (Lethbridge 1967:688).

A Sign for Cain was essentially a sociological history of violence in Western culture; as such, the book focused on the effect of political tyrannies on the shaping of human relations, the medical and legal legitimization of violence, and its acceptance as a human value. Wertham opened the book by suggesting that postwar America had become an age of violence: "Force and violence are deeply embedded in our whole economic process. A very substantial part of production, employment, economic planning, and research is devoted to the means of violence. We live in a violence economy" (1966b:12). Throughout the volume, the constant background was Wertham's double thesis that the postwar era had more violence than any preceding time in human history and that that violence could be ended. Wertham's fundamental belief in humanity's educability structured this twin argument and formed the basis for his rejection of Lorenz's and others' contention that human violence was innate or natural (17).

In a 1971 article bluntly titled "Human Violence Can Be Abolished," Wertham rejected the innate-violence thesis by pointing to social causes that Lorenz and his associates had neglected: "Have we really tried to eliminate violence? Have we tried with any consistency and fervor to stamp out some of the potent and concrete conditions behind it, such as race prejudice, national rivalries, . . . hunger, hate, clinging to power and privilege, cold war vilification of people, needlessly frustrated lives, justified remonstrance of the oppressed, brutalizing prison conditions, and teaching of sadistic thrills in the mass media?" (1971a:37).

On the question of innate human violence, Wertham rejected all arguments by theorists rooted in neuropathology that suggested, following evidence from animal psychology, that the natural mental state for humanity was aggression. In a letter to *The Sciences,* he pointed out that Lorenz had advocated the "extermination" of humans as a consequence of his belief in the innate nature of human violence: "it would be most hazardous to assume that Lorenz' theory about human violence and his advocacy of mass human extermination are entirely unrelated" (Wertham 1974b:3). Similarly, Wertham rejected the anthropological notion that a golden age of nonviolence existed in human prehistory. Wertham refused to romanticize a mythological past, instead choosing to draw readers' attention to a history of mutilation, torture, infanticide, slavery, and human sacrifice, all of which grew out of the social conditions and institutions of the past. Wertham did not believe in a romantic past to be held up as utopian and from which humanity could be seen to have fallen from grace. Rather, the era of nonviolence was always located in a scientifically producible future (1966b:26).

In *A Sign for Cain* more than in any of his other works, Wertham dealt directly with what he considered to be the social causes of violence, among them the political climates of fascism and colonialism, which were, in his estimation, political systems utterly dependent on violence and the threat of violence. He argued that each found its basis not in the psychology of individual leaders—a common assertion that Wertham found absurd—but in the fundamental logic of capitalism. He therefore made great efforts to enumerate, for instance, the economic underpinnings of Nazism. He described racism as a form of potential violence closely akin to colonialism. Furthermore, racism was generally the primary rationalization in the psychological preparation for administrative mass killings such as in the Holocaust. Complacence about racism, Wertham suggested, was fundamentally a complacence about violence: "Not only may race discrimination lead to violence; it is in itself latent violence. If we exclude an individual from significant human relationships because of race—that is to say, for biological or alleged biological reasons—we deprive him of his identity. We deprive him of his right to be an individual" (1966b:85).

The concept of the administrative mass murder drove the logic of a great deal of Wertham's theory. He suggested, for instance, that the euthanasia project undertaken during the Second World War by German psychiatrists, in which as many as 275,000 patients were put to death, constituted a new and completely unforeseen era of human cruelty and disregard for human life. At the ideological base of this type of atrocity lay Malthusianism, a nineteenth-century philosophy of eugenics and population control that Wertham regarded as deeply dangerous because of its casual disregard for the sanctity of life and the ease with which it could be tied into racist and genocidal thinking.

At the end of the volume, Wertham discussed what could be done to end the culture of violence, at this point bringing his particular politics into sharpest relief. Wertham traced the history of the death penalty back to its origins as a form of exorcism or purification through to what he held to be its contemporary function as a weapon held in reserve for opponents of society's contemporary political or economic organization. Wertham suggested that the act of political murder and the use of capital punishment were only narrowly divided; therefore, it was incumbent on society to abolish the death penalty. At the same time, he acknowledged that the death penalty indeed functioned as a deterrent, as its proponents claimed, but he saw this deterrent as a mode of institutionalized terrorism: "Those who claim that the death penalty has no deterrent effect whatsoever leave out its use as a terror method, both in peace, where this purpose is not openly acknowledged, and in war, where it is almost routine" (302–3).

On the question of nonviolent resistance, Wertham's liberalism was at odds with many of the orthodoxies of the 1960s. In tracing the history of nonviolence from Etienne de la Boétie through to Gandhi, Wertham departed from popularly held philosophies of nonviolence, particularly those of Gandhi, Tolstoy, and Lao Tse located in a disdain for technology and science. Instead, Wertham suggested that the role of nonviolence was limited and historically determined, that it could never function as a panacea, and that the elevation of nonviolence to an absolute moral position only served the interests of oppression: "Making a universal fetish out of nonviolence may perpetuate potential violence. It may mislead people and lull them into the belief that the age of violence is already past" (1966b:319). To this end Wertham suggested, for instance, that the Spanish Civil War constituted a legitimate response to Spanish fascism. His conditional endorsement of nonviolence was rooted in his belief that a link between violence and the social and institutional life of a society was required to eliminate the causes of violence, a goal that Wertham held to be reachable in the long run because he fundamentally believed in the power of human progress. To accomplish this, however, society needed to look in detail at the general influences and specific agencies of violence.

Wertham concluded *A Sign for Cain* by suggesting that two paths led toward the cessation of violence. The peace movement sought to stop wars at all cost, while the social justice movement sought to alter social and economic conditions on a global scale. Wertham suggested that the end of wars should be the result rather than the aim of progressive activists and that the two paths must somehow meet.

The struggles for peace and for social betterment cannot be separated. No isolated solution is possible. We cannot have war abolished without very many other things having been changed too. This is why the call for a "world government," a "supernational authority," and so on, cannot be successful if raised without that. In the struggle against war, if it is seriously pursued, we inevitably learn about power conditions within our society; and in the struggle to improve social-economic conditions for all, we learn about the subsoil of war. In a thoroughly democratic society where "the thousand voices of democracy" *are* fully heard, the people do not want war. The objective situation is this: if we want to abolish war, we must bring about more democracy; and if we want to increase democracy, we must do away with war. Under the present world threat of armed conflict, democracy cannot fully flourish anywhere. Therefore it is necessary to perform both tasks with out preconceived priorities. (1966b:373)

Importantly, Wertham insisted that there was no panacea or master plan, such as Marxism, that would ensure the triumph of a nonviolent world. What was required, he insisted, was a scientific disinterestedness to resist both the hyperindividualization that had undermined social institutions, including psychiatry, and the hypernationalism that had erected artificial barriers between people. Thus, Wertham's politics can best be seen as a near-total rejection of the thinking of the New York Intellectuals at the point where questions of politics and social change entered into the picture. That rejection did not, however, extend to his view of mass culture.

Wertham's disdain for individualistic conceptions of human interaction and his call for a more thoroughgoing understanding of the interaction between individuals and the social structure were not simply out of fashion with the New York Intellectuals in the postwar period but were actually in opposition to their way of conceptualizing postwar American society and the individual's place within it. Crucially in *A Sign for Cain*, Wertham condemned the culture of "getting ahead" individualism and the acquisitive society fetishized by postwar intellectuals as the key to all of America's social problems. Wertham's work with Ethel Rosenberg demonstrated that he was not afraid to take principled positions in the face of Red-baiting. Indeed, Wertham refused to indulge in Cold War condemnations of countries perceived to be America's enemies but, like Wallace, criticized the U.S.

failure to communicate with those nations. In *A Sign for Cain,* for instance, Wertham suggested that when the Soviet Union sent the first woman into space, the United States unnecessarily derided an accomplishment that should have been seen as an emancipatory moment for all women (1966b:53). Wertham's refusal to condemn the Soviets was just one way that his politics were at odds with the norms of his day.

Furthermore, those political differences suggest the reasons why the New York Intellectuals were so quick to dismiss his work on mass culture, to which—on the surface at least—they might otherwise have been sympathetic. Despite the fact that Wertham and the postwar critics shared an aesthetic disdain for mass culture, they could find no point of agreement on the larger question of why mass culture was a particular social danger. For the New York Intellectuals, the problem was that mass culture could lead the United States toward totalitarianism. For Wertham, the problem had much more to do with the psychological interrelationship between the individual and society, a relationship that is best understood through reference to his personal brand of social psychiatry.

CHAPTER FOUR

WERTHAM AND THE CRITIQUE OF COMIC BOOKS

By 1957, Fredric Wertham's critique of comic books was well enough known that he was the specific target of *Mad,* a legendary American satire magazine. In his office, Wertham kept a framed copy of a mock article, "Baseball Is Ruining Our Children," that appeared under the byline Frederick Werthless, M.D. ("Baseball" 1957). Alongside a dozen Wally Wood illustrations depicting leering, aggressive baseball players, the text of the article ridiculed psychological and monocausationist beliefs regarding juvenile delinquency by exaggerating the rhetoric of traditional critics of mass culture:

> For many years, I worked closely with "juvenile delinquents." Then my hair turned gray, and they kicked me out of their gang. But while I was with them, I studied them. I questioned them, probed their minds, uncovered their ids, examined their egos, and rifled their pockets. And in every single case I examined, I repeatedly came up with the same shocking fact: *At one time or another, every one of those poor misguided children had been exposed to the game of "Baseball"!* They had either *played* it themselves, or *watched* it being played . . . not to mention the countless other indirect exposures such as *"Baseball Magazines," "Baseball Record Books,"* and the worst offender of all, *"Baseball Bubble-Gum Cards."*
>
> Yes, the game of "Baseball" is souring the soil of society's garden, rotting our flowering youth. ("Baseball" 1957)

104

The satire continued in this vein, citing specific examples of the values that children were supposed to be learning from the game: pitchers teach deceptive practices, batters encourage the use of force, arguing with the umpire leads to lack of respect for authority, and so on. Yet what was most noticeable about this parody was the precision with which Wertham's rhetorical style was mocked. The garden metaphor, for instance, was a particular favorite of Wertham's and appeared on more than one occasion in *Seduction of the Innocent*. The reason for this fidelity lay in the identity of the players involved. By that time, *Mad* was the only comic book left in the EC stable of titles. EC had been hard hit by the mid-1950s furor over comic books, and the *New York Times* had used its front page to chastise EC's publisher, William Gaines, for publishing salacious works. Gaines vocally defended the types of comic books that Wertham criticized in his articles and in his book, and the testimony of the two men before the Senate Subcommittee Investigating Juvenile Delinquency on 21 April 1954 came to define the pro- and anticomics camps in the mid-1950s. Thus, the *Mad* article can be seen as a sort of last gasp from a comics publisher who largely felt that Wertham and other crusaders against mass culture had undermined his credibility and destroyed his company.

Comics publishers like Gaines had lost the battle for public opinion in the 1950s largely because comics were successfully positioned as a part of an allegedly degrading postwar mass culture. In *The Lonely Crowd*, David Riesman decried the child market for mass media because "the child begins to be bombarded by radio and comics from the moment he can listen and just barely read," and these media "train the young for the frontiers of consumption" (1950:101–2). Riesman compared other-directed comics-reading children whom he saw "lying on the bed or floor, reading and trading comics and preferences among comics" (102) unfavorably with the inner-directed and solitary readers of the past. In this way, he brought comic books fully into the critiques of mass culture that were gaining momentum. Commentaries on comics, which originated with social scientists, educators, librarians, parents, and literary critics, can be roughly broken down into three historical periods: prewar and wartime accounts, immediate postwar commentaries, and writings from the 1950s.

An 18 April 1942 *Business Week* article was among the first magazines to note the popularity of the comic book. That article suggested that in

December 1941, 148 comic book titles had been for sale on New York news-stands and that total national sales of all comic books had climbed to more than 15 million copies per month. *Business Week* also noted two factors that would soon change about comics in the United States. First, advertisers had not yet caught onto this new trend; second, at that point, no organized opposition existed to the comic book as a mass cultural form ("Superman Scores" 1942:54–56). An article in *Recreation* from later that year began to sound an alarmist tone when it noted that 75 percent of the leisure reading of American children was comic books ("Regarding Comics Magazines" 1942:689). Further readership surveys demonstrated that by the end of 1943, 95 percent of children aged eight to eleven and 84 percent of children aged twelve to seventeen read comics, while 35 percent of adults aged eighteen to thirty did the same ("Escapist Paydirt" 1943:55). At the height of the Second World War, therefore, comic books had clearly emerged as a significant American leisure-time activity with particular appeal to children. The stage was consequently set for a rash of articles from a variety of sources that would alternately condemn and condone comic books.

The most vocal participants in the wartime debate about comic books included American librarians and public school teachers. This is not surprising given the fact that the former viewed themselves as charged with protecting the nation's literary heritage and the latter saw themselves as at least partially responsible for the safeguarding of American children. During the war, librarians generally had two reactions to comic books: one group saw them as essentially harmless diversions, while the other viewed them as a legitimate threat to literacy. Gweneira Williams and Jane Wilson were emblematic of the point of view that comics were generally harmless. Arguing that it was time to "cease being Victorian about comics" (1942a:204), they suggested that comics were a form of "mental candy bars" that satisfied particular needs of children that books could not (1942b:1490). Williams and Wilson suggested that comic books' popularity stemmed from the harmless thrill they imparted to children and argued that librarians who were genuinely concerned about comics should find books that provided the same sorts of enjoyment that children found in comic books (1496).

Opponents of the comics generally also embraced the suggestion to replace "the highly colored enemy" (S.J.K. 1941a:846) with books. Arguing the anti-mass-culture line when she suggested that comic books represented a "pseudo-culture," Eva Anttonen suggested in the *Wilson Library Bulletin* that comics were ruining the library experience for youngsters by convincing lower-class "'Dead End' kids" that "the library is a 'sissy place'" (1941:567). She concluded that the only solution to the problem posed by comics was to "bring out all our dragons" (595) and expose children to high-quality adventure literature. This sentiment was echoed in the same journal the following month. Brushing off the suggestion that bad comics could be combated by the substitution of good comics, columnist S.J.K. wrote, "what we have is still an aesthetic monstrosity, a monument to bad taste in color and design, a disconcerting surrender to sensationalism" (1941b:670). Librarians, it was suggested, bore responsibility for training children away from things like comic books and toward an appreciation of superior literature. In this way, wartime librarians, whether generally favoring or opposing comic books, relied on and reified a series of high-culture assumptions about the relative merits of mass and elite culture for children. In fact, these assumptions defined the wartime and postwar consensus about comic books and were shared by critics and defenders alike.

Education journals, such as library publications, paid great attention to the problem posed by comic books in the midcentury era, although these education works tended to do so through reference to classroom-based research. In one of the first articles dedicated to comics in an education journal, Roger Gay concluded on the basis of his own reading of newspaper comic strips that while some children seemed to imitate the actions of comic strip heroes such as Tarzan, most comics were "harmless enough" (1937:208). Later studies, however, attempted to approach the question from a more scientific perspective than could be found by simply reading and classifying strips. Specifically, education researchers sought to determine children's preferences for various comic books and comic strips. Katharine McCarthy and Marion Smith, for instance, argued that comic books constituted a new form of children's literature when they surveyed eighty-six hundred school-aged children in Duluth, Minnesota, and found that they had read twenty-five thousand comic books in the previous week (1943:98). In drawing conclusions from these findings, McCarthy and Smith shifted from dispassionate researchers to moral crusaders, noting that the findings were "disconcerting" because "lurid" comic books could harm the "maladjusted child" (98–100). Other researchers, however, were less prone to condemnations.

Following a survey of 121 Phoenix, Arizona, children, Flida Cooper Kinneman praised comic books because "even the poorer readers can scan these rapidly," but she agreed with the librarians when she suggested that wherever possible, good books should be substituted for comics in a child's reading (1943:332).

The importance of value judgments in shaping the conclusions of educational researchers can be seen clearly in the work of George Hill. In a 1940 study of 240 children in Philadelphia, Hill and Estelle Trent concluded simply that boys and girls preferred different types of comic strips, that white children read more strips than black children, and that all children liked strips featuring action, adventure, and humor (1940:32–36). A year later, however, following the burgeoning public outcry about comics at the end of 1940, Hill's position shifted, and he condemned comics for their poor language and morals and their tendency to teach bad habits while suggesting that parents needed to guide children away from comics and toward edifying literature (1941:413–14). To this end, then, the moral and aesthetic condemnations of comics and mass culture in the 1940s impinged on ostensibly dispassionate research and led researchers to negatively associate the reading of comics with a host of social ills.

This is not to say, however, that comics were without defenders during the war—far from it. Ruth Strang, for instance, argued that comic books met certain needs of children at certain moments in their development. She suggested that children eventually would outgrow their fascination with comics and that responsible parents should advocate moderation rather than abstinence (1943:342). The leading researcher on children's preferences in comic books during the war was Paul Witty, who published a series of articles on the topic in 1941 and 1942. Witty's conclusions help to illustrate the high degree of confusion and ambivalence about comic books that surrounded their defenders at this time. His most significant contribution to the study of comics came with the publication of a series of articles about reading preferences of children that appeared in the *Journal of Experimental Education,* the *Journal of Educational Psychology,* and *Educational Administration and Supervision.* These articles were remarkably similar, surveying the reading preferences of children in grades 4–6, 7–8, and 9–12 (Witty 1941a; Witty, Smith, and Coomer 1942; Witty and Coomer 1942). The influence of these studies widened when, in response to suggestions in *National Parent-Teacher* that comic books were entirely without merit, he summarized his findings in an article in that journal (Witty 1942).

In these studies, Witty and his associates concluded that comic books were among the most popular of all children's leisure activities but that interest in comics declined as children aged. In a related study, Witty concluded that the amount of comic book reading done by a child did not seriously impact other types of reading. In terms of intelligence, academic achievement, and social adjustment, no differences existed between heavy readers and nonreaders of comic books (Witty 1941b:109). Yet at the same time as he was defending comics against charges that they were harmful and that their reading should be discouraged, Witty undercut the significance of his conclusions by suggesting that "excessive reading in this area may lead to a decline in artistic appreciation, and a taste for shoddy, distorted presentations" (Witty, Smith, and Coomer 1942:181). The solution, he suggested—in accordance with so many other critics of the period—was to provide children with good literature in the place of comics, despite the fact that his research indicated no significant differences between avid readers and nonreaders of comic books. Thus, even defenders of mass culture in this period were susceptible to the suasion of anti-mass-culture charges.

While most librarians and educators insisted on the substitution of good literature for bad comics in children's literary diets, another option presented itself during the war. In 1941 the Parents' Institute, the publishers of *Parents' Magazine,* entered the anti-comic-book fray with an effort to combat bad comics through the substitution of good comics. The institute's initial effort was called *True Comics,* and its launch was widely reported in educational journals ("Tis True" 1941:598). Within a few months, the Parents' Institute line had grown to three comics, whose goal, according to publisher George Hecht, was "sublimating and redirecting a powerful and now deeply-seated childhood interest" ("How Much" 1941:436). Many people found these efforts to fight comics with comics appealing because it seemed unlikely that the mass culture tide could be entirely diverted. Louise Seaman Bechtel noted in 1941 that comic books' monthly circulation of 10 million was five times the annual circulation of children's books (297). Bechtel suggested that with its circulation already at half a million copies per issue, *True Comics* could begin to turn the tide on bad comics.

Other advocates of good comics, like Josette Frank of the Children's Bureau, suggested that good comics far outweighed the bad nationally and that publishers such as National who had their own advisory boards were dedicated to cleaning up the industry and working with parents for the protection of the nation's children. Frank, who received three hundred dollars per month from National to serve as a consultant, became one of the leading wartime voices in favor of comic books as social scientists employed by the comic book industry attempted to shift the terms of the debate without letting go of deep-seated aesthetic biases.

The strongest wartime defense of comic books came in December 1944 with the publication of a special issue of the *Journal of Educational Sociology*. In his opening editorial, Harvey Zorbaugh suggested that "it is time the amazing cultural phenomenon of the growth of the comics is subjected to dispassionate scrutiny" (1944b:194), but he failed to suggest that dispassionate scrutiny should also imply disinterested research. The issue contained seven articles, six of which were written by researchers or critics employed directly by comic book publishers. Advisory boards for comics publishers had come into fashion in the early 1940s, when comic books first came under attack for degrading the act of reading and contributing to the corruption of minors. National, the publisher of comics featuring Superman and Batman, established a large advisory board that included Josette Frank, Roger Thorndike, W. W. D. Sones, C. Bowie Millican, Gene Tunney, and Pearl S. Buck ("Comics and Their Audience" 1942:1479). In later years, National added Lauretta Bender and Harcourt Peppard to its board (Ellsworth 1949:294). The Fawcett board included Sidonie M. Gruenberg, Ernest G. Osborne, Al Williams, and Zorbaugh (Nyberg 1998:15).

The December 1944 issue of the *Journal of Educational Sociology* opened with a celebratory essay by Zorbaugh (1944a), the chair of the Department of Educational Sociology at New York University, asserting that comics had emerged as major medium of communication and a favorite form of literature that was influencing American culture. The essay contained little argument and no original research, although it ended with a call for such (203). Ironically, given its complete lack of original scientific research, this piece received wider circulation when it was condensed and published in *Science Digest* under the provocative title "Comics—Food for Half-Wits?" (Zorbaugh 1945). Similarly, the essay by Gruenberg, director of the Child Study

Association of America, contained no research and instead settled for an argument that cited a number of comics that she felt were good for children—including comics from Fawcett, on whose advisory board she sat—and suggested that comics required an undefined amount of time to develop as a legitimate art form and should remain unhampered until that time (1944:206–11).

Frank adopted a similar position, suggesting that some comics were good for children while others were not quite as good. It was the duty of parents and educators, Frank argued, to take notice of comic books, but she also assured readers that there was nothing serious to take notice of. Frank insisted, for instance, that "comics always end well" and that there was absolutely no evidence that the reading of comics could be linked to rising crime rates (1944:216–17). Frank reiterated these claims in a booklet published five years later by the Public Affairs Committee in which she promoted the most popular character of the publisher on whose staff she served: "Superman strikes at the roots of juvenile delinquency" (1949a:4). The essays of Frank, Gruenberg, and Zorbaugh were united by the fact that all presented comic books in a generally positive light while allowing that some comic book publishers—but not the ones with whom they themselves worked—produced questionable work. Further, none of the three authors presented research findings that could in any way be termed scientific, relying instead on positive rhetoric supported only by their own claims to expertise by virtue of their status in the Child Study Association or employment at New York University.

The same cannot be said for the work of other contributors to the special issue of the *Journal*. The essay by Bender, "The Psychology of Children's Reading and the Comics," drew on her research as a psychiatrist at Bellevue and a professor at New York University's medical school. Bender's essay opened with her theory of fantasy as an integral part of childhood development and her understanding of the ways in which fantasy worked in art. Bender argued that comics benefited children by stimulating fantasies: "We concluded that the comics (dealing with universal problems of relationship of the self to physical and social reality; replete with rapid action and repetition; given continuity by a central character who, like Caspar, invites identification; free to experiment with fantastic solutions, but with good ultimately triumphing over evil), like the folklore of other times, serve as a means to stimulate the child's fantasy life and so help him solve the individual and soci-ological problems inherent in his living" (1944:226). Bender went on to suggest that the so-called good comics, such as those published by the Parents' Institute, were more threatening to children than the bad because such comics "offer no solution to the problem of aggression in the world" (227).

Bender's argument here represented an extension of her previous work on this topic (Bender and Lourie 1941), which had been widely reported and cited. That work had suggested that "normal, well-balanced children are not upset by even the more horrible scenes in the comics as long as the reason for the threat is clear and the issues are well stated" ("Let Children Read" 1941:124). Bender's conclusion that comic books did not harm children was an extreme version of the "blame the child" school of media effects, and it echoed her earlier findings about the impact of incest on children: "The history of the relationship in our cases usually suggested at least some coopera-tion of the child in the activity. . . . Even in cases in which physical force may have been applied by the adult, this did not wholly account for the frequent repetition of the practice. . . . [A] most striking feature was that these children were distinguished as unusually charming and attractive in their outward personalities. Thus, it is not remarkable that frequently we considered the possibility that the child might have been the actual seducer rather than the one innocently seduced" (Bender and Blau:514). A number of comic-industry defenders subsequently took up her insistence that the "normal" child was unharmed by social forces as diverse as incest and comic books, seeking to suggest that if a correlation existed between comic books and juvenile delin-quency, the fault lay not with the media but with the children who consumed the media because those children were "abnormal" or "maladjusted."

The remaining essays generally lacked the type of insights that could be found in Bender's work. Witty (1944) contributed an essay that failed to live up to the standard set by his previous writings on the subject and that essentially served as nothing more than a survey of U.S. Army training tech-niques reliant on visual aids such as filmstrips and comics. Sones's essay focused on comics and their utility for education, relying heavily on Witty's prior research as well as Thorndike's work. Sones suggested that comic books were useful tools for teaching poor readers the fundamentals of lan-guage acquisition because comics "employ a language that apparently is almost universally understood" (1944:233).

The claim that comic books were useful in the teaching of reading skills and vocabulary building generally relied on just one 1941 article, Thorndike's "Words and the Comics," which proponents of comic books cited endlessly in the following decades (Williams and Wilson 1942a; Gleason 1952; Emans 1960) despite the fact it became less and less applicable to ongoing controversies as the years passed. Thorndike's research into comic book vocabulary was, in fact, extremely limited. He studied the vocabulary in only four individual comics, all of which were published in 1940 by a single company, National, on whose advisory board he served. Thorndike found that each of the four comics he studied contained about ten thousand words plus another thousand beyond the most common. He concluded that the comic books offered a "substantial reading experience" that required the ability to read at about the fifth- or sixth-grade level for full comprehension (1941:113). While this study had obvious limitations regarding the size and representativeness of the sample, it still was one of the few efforts to approach comic books from a strictly scientific perspective in the wartime years. Most participants in the debate about comics—both pro and con—were content to rely on largely unsubstantiated claims based on personal interpretations, biases, and appeals to authority. Indeed, these sorts of claims would take center stage not only in social science journals but also more importantly in general-interest magazines.

Most historians of the comic book trace the birth of anti-comic-book concern to a single influential 8 May 1940 editorial in the *Chicago Daily News,* "A National Disgrace," written by Sterling North and widely reprinted. According to Margaret Frakes, in the two years that followed, the *Daily News* received more than 25 million requests for copies (1942:1351). This figure clearly indicates that something had changed in the discursive landscape. North's article was short and direct, a call to arms for concerned parents. He began by referring to comic books as "a poisonous mushroom growth" that took more than a million dollars out of the pockets of youngsters every month for "graphic insanity" (1940:56).

Examining 108 comic books for sale around Chicago, North made a strong distinction between the positive influence of newspaper comic strips and the negative impact of comic books when he concluded that 70 percent of the latter were "of a nature no respectable newspaper would think of accepting." The bulk of the comic books, North continued, made dime novels appear to be classic literature because the newer comic books were "badly drawn, badly written and badly printed—a strain on young eyes and young nervous systems—the effect of these pulp-paper nightmares is that of a violent stimulant. Their crude blacks and reds spoil the child's natural sense of color, their hypodermic injection of sex and murder make the child impatient with better, though quieter, stories." North concluded that "unless we want a coming generation even more ferocious than the present one, parents and teachers throughout America must band together to break the 'comic' magazine" (56).

The proposed solution was the same one suggested by most librarians and educators: a renewed emphasis on quality literature for children. North suggested plainly that the "antidote to the 'comic' magazine poison can be found in any library or good bookstore. The parent (and the teacher—ed.) who does not acquire that antidote for his child is guilty of criminal negligence" (56). These charges were repeated in March 1941 when North reprinted his original editorial with new commentary that stressed the importance of reviving oral storytelling traditions within the family (North 1941a) and again when he suggested in an article that the key to a child's healthy future lay not only with good books but with an active life of arts and crafts (North 1941b). North's articles, with their opposition of folk culture against the mass-produced elements of comic books and their status as an increasingly large cultural industry, paved the way for subsequent investigations of the comic book that placed the medium within traditions of anti-mass-culture commentary.

One of the most bizarre wartime defenses of comic books addressed head on the growing concerns about comic books and their relation to an increasingly mass society. William Moulton Marston, often credited as the inventor of the lie detector and the creator and writer of the *Wonder Woman* comic books for National, argued in *The American Scholar* that comic books could not be understood by intellectuals because they addressed the primal rather than the reflective parts of the brain (1944:36). Marston went on to make the unusual argument that Superman-style stories were good for children because they cultivated a wish for power: "Do you want him (or her) to cultivate weakling's aims, sissified attitudes? . . . The wish to be super-strong is a healthy wish, a vital, compelling, power-producing desire. The more the *Superman–Wonder Woman* picture stories build up this inner compulsion by stimulating the child's natural longing to battle and overcome obstacles, particularly evil ones, the better chance your child has for self-advancement in the world" (40). This perspective, which was ridiculed in a subsequent letter to the editor from noted literary critic Cleanth Brooks (Brooks and Heilman 1944:247–52), was not widely shared. Indeed, comic books were more likely to be chastised than celebrated for contributing to a climate of violence and fascism.

In 1945, for instance, *Time* reported that Walter Ong had condemned Superman as a Nazi and suggested that Wonder Woman reflected "Hitlerite paganism" ("Are Comics Fascist?" 1945:68). Similar complaints originated from a wide variety of sources. James Vlamos wrote in the *American Mercury* that comic books fester "the most dismaying mass of undiluted horror and prodigious impossibility ever visited on the sanity of a nation's youth" and suggested that comic books demonstrated to children "the nihilistic man of the totalitarian ideology" (1941:412, 416). Writing in the *Christian Century,* Frakes suggested that comic books were inculcating racism with their wartime caricatures of the Japanese and that the concept of the superhero was inherently fascist (1942:1349–50). Thomas Doyle reiterated these claims when he suggested that Superman reflected a Nietzschean ideology and that comic books generally represented a moral decadence that had defined the United States since the end of the First World War (1943:549–54). Finally, Lovell Thompson argued in the *Atlantic Monthly* that comic books were "feebly vicious material" whose readers had opted for a "goalless existence of decadence" in a "sub-hell where the devil himself is disciplined" (1942:128). The quick rise of widespread concern about the increasing moral decadence and potentially fascist spirit of the comic book points to the way that the medium was rapidly caught up in ongoing discourses about mass culture that predated the form itself and shaped the way that it was received by critics and ultimately the public. As the war concluded, these concerns did not abate but rather grew prodigiously to the point that the industry had no choice but to respond with a facade of restraint. The factors that contributed to postwar efforts at self-regulation can be seen in the intersection of comic books and the general critique of mass culture.

The rapid expansion of the comic book industry following the end of the Second World War was a cause for great concern for many commentators concerned with questions of mass culture. A 1948 article in the *Library Journal* was one of the first to point out the new scale of the so-called comic book problem. Citing figures gathered by the Ayers Newspaper Directory, the magazine reported that sales of comic books in the United States in 1946 had totaled more than 540 million copies, an average of 45 million each month. In comparison, a total of only 429 million books of all kinds had been sold in 1947 (Smith 1948:1651). Libraries and educators deemed it a major problem that comic books had surpassed books as the number 1 literary form in the United States, at least in units sold. Despite ongoing research that tended to conclude that no serious differences existed between children who read comic books excessively and those who read them not at all (Heisler 1947, 1948), the tone of articles about comic books increasingly tended toward moral panic. The *National Education Association Journal,* for instance, cited a case in which a six-year-old Pennsylvania boy was charged with shooting and killing his twelve-year-old brother for a comic book. The *Journal* argued that "what goes into the mind comes out in life," advocating the restriction of comic books and suggesting that freedom of the press "was never intended to protect indecency or the perversion of the child mind" ("Ubiquitous Comics" 1948:570).

Two solutions immediately suggested themselves. The first was the most extreme and was condoned by few. In 1948, comic burnings took place in a number of communities, including Chicago and Binghamton, New York ("Fighting Gunfire" 1948:54), but this practice was generally decried for its negative effects on children as well as for the fact that it promoted authoritarianism and had a negative impact on democracy (Tieleman 1949:299–300).

A toned-down version of this approach constituted the second option, as critics suggested forming organizations to fight for new legislation to control comic books. Jean Gray Harker, for example, suggested in the *Library Journal* that it was impossible to control what media children might come into contact with when they were separated from parental authority. Thus, librarians and concerned parents were duty-bound to clean up all comics. Harker's vow to battle the comic book industry was among the earliest explicit calls to action on the subject found in professional library journals: "*I'm* going to fight them! I will buy all the good books we can afford. I will encourage my children to go to the library, and I will discuss their reading with them. I'm going to talk to groups of parents in our local P.T.A.s. I shall ask conscientious parents and other citizens to urge swift passage of a state crime comic censorship law" (1948:1707). Less than two months later, however, the same publication editorialized against legislative action to clean up comic books. Suggesting that the problem of comic books was not only serious but also required realistic solutions, the *Library Journal* advocated taking a wait-and-see attitude with regard to new efforts within the comics industry to establish self-regulation ("What Is the Solution" 1949:180).

Three key exchanges drove the comic book industry toward self-regulation in 1947 and 1948. Each of these was a well-publicized critique of comic books, the combined impact of which led publishers to take actions intended to thwart further criticisms. In March 1948 a radio debate held in New York and aired nationwide pitted the *Saturday Review*'s John Mason Brown and novelist Marya Mannes against *L'il Abner* cartoonist Al Capp and *True Comics* publisher George Hecht ("Bane" 1948:70–72). Capp's defense of the comic strip, in which he argued that children are usually right about what is good for them, probably did little to defuse the attacks launched against the comics by Brown and Mannes. In his opening statement, Brown marshaled a number of typically highbrow condemnations of mass culture, terming comic books "the lowest, most despicable, and most harmful sort of trash" and enumerating a series of aesthetic objections to the form:

> As a writer, I resent the way in which they get along with the poorest kind of writing. I hate their lack of both style and ethics. I hate their appeal to illiteracy and their bad grammar. I loathe their tiresome toughness, their cheap thrills, their imbecilic laughter.
>
> I despise them for making only the story count and not the HOW of its telling. I detest them, in spite of their alleged thrills and gags, because they have no subtlety, and certainly no beauty. Their power of seduction, I believe, lies in the fact that they make everything too easy. They substitute bad drawing for good description. They reduce the wonders of the language to crude monosyllables, and narratives to no more than printed motion pictures. (Brown 1948:31)

Mannes argued from a similar position. In a 1947 *New Republic* article, "Junior Has a Craving," Mannes had condemned comics because they required no effort or concentration to read, suggesting that "comic books in their present form are the absence of thought. They are, in fact, the greatest intellectual narcotic on the market" (1947:20). Mannes's argument surpassed that of Brown insofar as she suggested that the negative impact of the comic book went beyond the merely aesthetic to include the political. Equating American enthusiasm for comic books with prewar German enthusiasm for Nazism, she warned that one consequence of comic books "might be a people incapable of reading a page of ordinary text. Another would be a society based on the impact of fist on a jaw. A third would be a nation that left it to the man in the costume. None of these prospects is exactly attractive" (23). Mannes further stated that whereas Charles Dickens had been a popular artist, Capp was nothing more than "a conveyor belt" ("Bane" 1948:70). The leveling of common anti-mass-culture arguments at comics in the postwar period formed the basis for the anti-comic-book drive. The factor that pushed comic book publishers toward self-regulation was the extension of the anti-mass-culture argument through reference to actual harm promoted in popular forums. Fredric Wertham provided evidence for these claims.

Two articles that appeared in the spring of 1948 had a tremendous impact on the postwar debate about comic books. The first of these was Judith Crist's *Collier's* profile of Wertham, "Horror in the Nursery" (1948), which emphasized a number of points about comics that Wertham would reiterate over the course of the following decade. First, Wertham stressed the mass nature of the comic book, contending that as many as 60 million copies were printed each month. Second, he criticized publishers' advisory board members as "psycho-prima donnas" who failed to do clinical work with children: "The fact that some child psychiatrists endorse comic books does not prove the healthy state of the comic books. It only proves the unhealthy state of child psychiatry" (23). Finally, Wertham announced that "the time has come to legislate these books off the newsstands and out of candy stores" and decried the fact that law enforcement officials were more likely to blame individual children for delinquency than to act against the social causes of criminality: "It is obviously easier to sentence a child to life imprisonment than to curb a hundred-million-dollar business" (23).

Shortly after Crist's article appeared, Wertham published an article in the *Saturday Review of Literature,* "The Comics . . . Very Funny! " (1948c), that gained widespread attention when it was condensed and published in the *Reader's Digest*, at that time America's most popular magazine. Wertham made his case that the common denominator in juvenile delinquency was comic books. He found this situation deplorable because existing social attitudes meant that children who were being seduced into delinquency were being punished, while the publishers, whom Wertham deemed truly culpable, remained free to reap extravagant profits. Wertham invoked traditional anti-mass-culture arguments when he noted that "comic books are the greatest book publishing success in history and the greatest mass influence on children." Furthermore, the illustrations that accompanied the article were labeled "Marijuana of the Nursery" (7), a clear reference to a phrase John Mason Brown had used in his debate with Al Capp. Wertham rejected seventeen specific arguments made by the comic book proponents ranging from the idea that only children with preexisting mental disorders were influenced negatively by comics and that comic books aided in the release of dangerous pent-up aggression to the assertions that law and order ultimately triumph in all comics and that they constitute a healthy outlet for children's fantasies. All of these suggestions, Wertham argued, were serious misreadings of Freud. Although he termed comic books a "systematic poisoning of the well of childhood spontaneity" (29), he stopped short in this instance of calling for legislative action against the comics. Nonetheless, others were already making that argument, and some states had begun to investigate the possibility of outlawing comic books. By the summer of 1948, a few months after the publication of Wertham's article, a number of publishers had banded together to bring some sort of self-regulation to the comic book industry.

The Association of Comics Magazine Publishers (ACMP) was officially created on 1 July 1948 when fourteen publishers with a combined circulation of more than 14 million comic books per month (approximately one-third of the industry) elected Phil Keenan president and agreed to abide by a self-imposed regulatory code ("Code for Comics" 1948:62). The new association appointed an advisory committee to "take positive steps toward improving comics magazines and making maximum use of them as a medium for education" ("Librarian Named" 1949:37). The executive director of the advisory committee was Henry E. Schultz, who was charged with insuring that members adhered to the code's directives. These strictures included rules relating to sex, crime, sadistic torture, vulgar language, divorce, and racism

("Purified" 1948:56). The credibility of the ACMP was severely undermined by a number of factors, not the least of which was the fact that the majority of comics publishers refused to join the organization. Both Dell and National, for instance, maintained that their in-house codes were more stringent than that of the ACMP and that the organization was therefore redundant. Other publishers simply resented having to pay screening fees to support the association ("New York Officials" 1949:978). Regardless of the reasons, the ACMP was largely seen as ineffective by both parents' organizations and legislators, who already had their own agencies in place. By the end of 1948, for instance, the National Congress of Parents and Teachers had "mapped a drive against lewd comics," and efforts to regulate comic books had been undertaken in Los Angeles, San Francisco, Detroit, and Dubuque ("Fighting Gunfire" 1948:55).

Efforts in certain cities and states ultimately failed to ban the publication and circulation of comic books at the end of the 1940s. Moreover, different drives sought differing aims where comic books were concerned. Some, as in St. Paul, Minnesota, and Cincinnati, Ohio, sought to influence publishers to produce acceptable comics and reduce offensive titles through the circulation of approved reading lists (Motter 1949; "What Comic Books Pass" 1949). Wertham explicitly rejected this approach to the problem, suggesting to Jesse Murrell of the Cincinnati Committee on Evaluation of Comic Books that the committee's ratings were overlenient and had actually "done a great deal of harm" (1953b). Regardless, the promotion of so-called good comic books remained a marginal concern as efforts to control the medium gained momentum.

An article in the *Horn Book,* for instance, suggested that Bible-based comics were an admission of failure in the war for children's reading habits ("At Long Last" 1948:233). That war stepped up a notch in the fall of 1948 when Los Angeles passed a county ordinance that banned the sale of all comic books that represented the commission of a crime to children under the age of eighteen ("Unfunny" 1948; "Not So Funny" 1948). Shortly thereafter, the state of New York, led by State Senator Benjamin Feinberg, sought to curb the circulation of comic books. Feinberg's bill, which would have required publishers to obtain permits before selling comic books, passed both the state House and Senate with strong majorities ("State Senate" 1949). This law brought the anti-mass-culture politics of New York news sources into conflict with their promotion of individualism. The *New York Times* agreed that comic books were "injurious to children" but nonetheless editorialized against the law as invasion of the free press ("Comic Book Censorship" 1949). Similarly, *The Nation* decried the "appalling" sales levels of comic books and suggested that they were driving an entire generation toward illiteracy but concluded that comic books were being scapegoated and that any real problems with them could be dealt with using existing postal regulations ("We Would" 1949).

Governor Thomas E. Dewey ultimately vetoed the New York bill as "overly vague" ("Comic Book Curb" 1949), and the Los Angeles County ordinance was ruled unconstitutional by the California Superior Court (Nyberg 1998:41). Anti-comic-book crusaders found some reason for optimism when Canada adopted a law restricting the circulation of crime comic books ("Canada's Comics" 1949; "Outlawed" 1949) and when the sale of crime comic books at U.S. Army post exchanges was halted because such publications went "beyond the line of decency" (Barclay 1949:26). Anti-comic-book crusaders were strengthened in their resolve by the decision to limit the sale of crime comic books to grown men in the armed forces while, as the *New York Times* noted in its lead paragraph on the story, "youngsters with ten cents will be able to go on buying them indefinitely" (Barclay 1949:26). The move also helped to cast doubt on social science researchers' pronouncement that comics had no ill effects on readers.

Two symposiums in the late 1940s articulated the divergent opinions about comic books at the close of that decade. The first, sponsored and hosted by Wertham, presented work by psychiatrists that suggested that comic books had a negative impact on child readers. The second, again appearing in the *Journal of Educational Sociology* and again edited by Zorbaugh, sought to defuse these suggestions. Wertham's symposium, "The Psychopathology of Comic Books," was held on 19 March 1948. Wertham's statement at the conference was edited and reprinted in the *Saturday Review* as "The Comics . . . Very Funny!" (Wertham 1948c), while the other presentations were published in the *American Journal of Psychotherapy,* on whose editorial board Wertham served. Aside from Wertham, the seminar presented the findings of four researchers, each of whom had serious reservations about comic books, particularly with regard to the way that they treated aggression.

Gerson Legman (1948) argued that comics focused on "impossible aggressions" such as torture and killing and that the violence found within comics was the primary reason for their tremendous success and rapid growth. Hilde Mosse (1948) continued this line of argument, disputing other psychiatrists' claims that comic books helped children release pent-up aggression in a cathartic manner. Rejecting Freud's assertions pertaining to the death instinct, Mosse suggested that early Freudian writings were more useful in this debate and that psychiatrists should not promote the venting of the death instinct in children but rather should work to affirm the life instinct. Mosse concluded by suggesting that aggression was not innate, as orthodox Freudians maintained, but was a social phenomenon that could be controlled. The problem with comic books, therefore, was that they interfered with emotional development by heightening frustration and aggression.

Paula Elkisch (1948) had done clinical studies of eighty children and their relation to comics and argued that comics not only heightened frustration in children but also created a conflict in readers that was the result of guilt about reading material that they realized was not suitable. Finally, Marvin Blumberg condemned comic books for the way in which they "smother violence with more violence, so when they attempt to battle social prejudices their emphasis and appealing sadism is so strong that the triumph of right at the end is a weak anticlimax" (1948:488). Collectively, these essays made the case that comics offered children unhealthy escapes from reality, taught violence as a solution to social problems, and stirred impulses that challenged the growth of socially useful behavior. While the commentators stopped short of equating comic books with the rise in juvenile delinquency, they did, nonetheless, lay the groundwork for such a conclusion by others.

At the opposite end of the spectrum on the comic book question, the *Journal of Educational Sociology* presented only the views of experts in the employ of comic book publishers or those with a very firm pro-comic-book message. Returning from the 1944 issue were Frank and Zorbaugh. Frank's essay, "Some Questions and Answers for Teachers and Parents" (1949b) privileged questions while offering few answers and took almost no positions at all. Instead she raised a number of concerns about comics and then answered each by noting that expert opinion was divided and that no conclusions could be drawn from the available data. Ultimately, she suggested, it was the duty of parents to guide the reading of their children.

Zorbaugh's essay sought to address the question of whether adults were truly concerned about children's reading or whether the press had whipped up the crisis. Zorbaugh concluded that a difference existed in the way that parents regarded comic books and comic strips and further suggested that only 36 percent of adults held unqualified positive views on comic books (1949:234).

Another essay, by Henry Schultz, suggested that the frenzy about comics was the result of scaremongering by Wertham, who was described as writing "vigorously and emotionally, if not scientifically and logically" (1949:215). Schultz went on to suggest that self-regulation by the ACMP, despite the fact that the organization oversaw only one-third of the industry, was the only "intelligent solution" (222). Interestingly, the issue failed to point out that Schultz was the ACMP's executive director and not, as the contributor's notes implied, a disinterested attorney.

The most forceful essay in the special issue was written by Frederic Thrasher, a member of the Attorney General's Conference on Juvenile Delinquency. In "The Comics and Delinquency: Cause or Scapegoat," Thrasher went on the offensive against Wertham's research as it was presented in the *Saturday Review* and *Collier's*. Citing Wertham as an example of a monistic or single-cause theorist, Thrasher suggested that Wertham's work presented "no valid research" and disregarded established research protocols (1949:195). To this end, Thrasher dismissed out of hand Wertham's contributions to the study of juvenile delinquency: "Wertham's dark picture of the influence of comics is more forensic than scientific and illustrates a dangerous habit of projecting our social frustrations upon some specific trait of our culture, which becomes a sort of 'whipping boy' for our failure to control the whole gamut of social breakdown" (195). Thrasher argued that the causes of antisocial behavior were complex and that many factors would have to be studied objectively to determine which were most important (200). That Wertham made exactly the same argument did not impress Thrasher. Thrasher simply ignored Wertham's ongoing claims that comics were only one of many factors contributing to juvenile delinquency by suggesting that he argued for monocausation even when he explicitly stated that he was not doing so (201). Furthermore, Thrasher condemned Wertham for failing to provide research data, specifically citing the *Collier's* article. That Wertham was not the author of that article and that *Collier's* could in no way be confused with a scientific journal in which research data might be appropriate for inclusion was of no concern. Thrasher went on to suggest that the inadequacies of Wertham's presentation in the *Saturday Review* included the lack of a complete overview of all comics published and the absence of a statistical summary of his cases (203).

Thrasher's rejection of Wertham's work ultimately hinged on two important points. First, Wertham's work had been publicized in nonscientific public-interest magazines rather than scientific or medical journals. Second, his psychiatric methodology was "open to question" because it was not identical to the case-study methodologies established by anthropology, psychology, or sociology (204). Thus, from Thrasher's standpoint, Wertham's conclusions could not be valid even if his data were presented in *Collier's* because Thrasher fundamentally disagreed with the proposition that psychiatric inquiry constituted a scientific methodology. Wertham would, in 1954, meet these objections in his most comprehensive study of comic books, *Seduction of the Innocent*. With its publication, the controversy over comic books headed toward its denouement.

Following the creation of the ACMP and the failure of anticomics ordinances in the late 1940s, the controversy about comic books began to settle down over the next few years. While many organizations adopted a wait-and-see approach to the ACMP and its attempted cleanup of crime comic books, efforts to control the lurid content of the form continued, albeit in a reduced form. The New York State Senate, for instance, followed up on Dewey's 1949 veto of anticomics legislation by holding closed-door hearings on the topic in June and August 1950. According to the *New York Times,* these meetings featured the testimony of judges, lawyers, and representatives of mothers' clubs in support of a renewed effort to draft legislation, while Schultz opposed any form of state regulation ("Witnesses Favor" 1950; "Oppose State" 1950).

At a subsequent closed-door hearing in December 1950, Wertham testified on the need to clean up the comic book industry and made specific recommendations regarding legislation. He argued that comic books constituted a "public health problem"—exactly the same argument that he would later make with regard to the problem of racial segregation in the

Delaware case—and further linked the two interests with his specific charge that comics taught race hatred to children:

> In the 40,000,000 to 80,000,000 crime comic books sold each month, Dr. Wertham told the committee, the hero is nearly always "regular featured and 'an athletic, pure American white man.' "
>
> "The villains, on the other hand, are foreign-born, Jews, Orientals, Slavs, Italians and dark-skinned races." ("Psychiatrist Asks" 1950:50)

A year later, at a public meeting to discuss a renewed effort at controlling comic books in New York, Wertham again called for a public health law that would restrict the sale of crime comic books to children aged sixteen or older ("Health Law Urged" 1950). The legislation that was ultimately adopted in February 1952 called for a ban on publications "principally made up of pictures, whether or not accompanied by any written or printed matter, of fictional deeds of crime, bloodshed, lust or heinous acts, which tend to incite minors to violent or depraved or immoral acts" (Nyberg 1998:48). Governor Dewey vetoed this law, like its 1949 predecessor, because he maintained that it would not stand up to a challenge on constitutional grounds ("Dewey Vetoes" 1952). At the same time that the comic book industry was winning battles in the legislative arena, it seemed that a shift in public opinion was also beginning.

As late as the fall of 1953, *Newsweek* magazine ran such articles as "More Friends for Comics," although that positive outlook soon shifted. The positive view of comics stemmed from a National Association for Mental Health affirmation that comic books had "a constructive influence on the young" and were not responsible for juvenile delinquency ("More Friends" 1953:50). This finding followed the conclusion of the Senate Crime Investigating Committee, which surveyed experts on juvenile delinquency in 1950 and reported that a majority of those surveyed doubted that comic books caused juvenile delinquency ("Many Doubt" 1950).

At the same time, the comic book industry mounted a successful public relations campaign aimed at convincing educators and librarians that comics had potential uses in education. Thus, the ACMP supported the objectives of the National Citizens Commission for the Public Schools to encourage grassroots participation in public schools throughout the country ("Comics to the Rescue" 1950). Ruth Bakwin expressed her concern about the "potentially educational" nature of comic books in a 1953 article on the psychological aspects of the form. Bakwin, who conducted no original research but cited industry-approved comics experts Bender, Frank, Sones, and Zorbaugh, argued that it was doubtful that comics were responsible for mental disturbances or that they affected language development or interest in reading. She concluded that comics offered a "high potential for education" that had theretofore been neglected (1953:635). Crime comic book publisher and former ACMP president Lev Gleason made a very similar argument in *Today's Health*. Citing a similar collection of experts (Gruenberg, Frank, Sones, Witty, Thorndike, and Bender), Gleason suggested that "now that the comics magazines have been popular for nearly 15 years, psychologists and educators have been able to make extensive studies of their effects. . . . Comics magazines, they declare, offer an amazing potential" (1952:40). Gleason articulated a number of assumed advantages and strengths of the comic book format before suggesting that most publishers strongly desired to improve the content of the comics but were waiting for parents to take a financial interest in the matter by supporting so-called good comics with their pocketbooks (54).

These pro-comic-book assumptions, and others, were re-reinforced by Frank in *Your Child's Reading Today* (1954), which devoted a chapter to comic books. Frank argued that the wholesale condemnation of comic books was unwarranted and could not be substantiated. Citing Thorndike's then fifteen-year-old research on vocabulary in the comics, she concluded, "comics have many plus values" (251). The most serious of the comic book critics' charges was the suggestion that irresponsible publishers were profiting from the inclusion of horror and sex in comic books, but she downplayed that conclusion by arguing that "experience and observation show that these are not the comics read and enjoyed by the vast number of children" (252).

Frank rejected the claims made by "wrathful critics" such as Wertham that comics led to juvenile delinquency, and she insisted that most psychologists and psychiatrists saw the need for more study of the question. At the same time, however, she suggested some definite psychological conclusions, including the idea that comic books did not create fears in children but simply brought existing fears to the surface. In this way, comics performed a service by alerting parents and psychologists to potential problems (253).

Finally, Frank reiterated her previous claims that comic books ultimately led children to "better reading" (255).Frank's position in regard to comics reading had not changed over the preceding ten years. She still maintained that comics were essentially harmless diversions and argued that it was the responsibility of parents rather than the industry or the state to oversee children's reading habits. Her arguments still relied on the twin assumptions that the majority of comics on the market were "good" and that comic book reading was simply a childhood stage through which children passed on the road to more ennobling literary values. However, these notions were not universal during the midcentury period.

A 1950 survey of juvenile delinquency experts conducted by the Senate Crime Investigating Committee raised a number of serious concerns regarding the medium. The notable opponents to comic books at this time included the American Medical Association, the American Legion, the General Federation of Women's Clubs, the National Council of Juvenile Court Judges, and the National Organization for Decent Literature. The ambivalence of a number of crime experts on the topic was perhaps best summed up by Federal Bureau of Investigation director J. Edgar Hoover when he argued that comics that were restrained in presentation and that conformed to prescribed standards of taste while teaching a true anticrime lesson were educational. At the same time, however, Hoover had some reservations, adding that

> crime books, comics and other stories packed with criminal activity and presented in such a way as to glorify crime and the criminal may be dangerous, particularly in the hands of an unstable child. A comic book which is replete with the lurid and macabre; which places the criminal in a unique position by making him a hero; which makes lawlessness attractive; which ridicules decency and honesty; which leaves the impression that graft and corruption are necessary evils of American life; which depicts the life of the criminal as exciting and glamorous may influence the susceptible boy or girl who already possesses anti-social tendencies. (U.S. Congress 1954:6)

Hoover's individualistic approach to juvenile delinquency suggested that comic books negatively affected only "susceptible" or "unstable" children. Thus, although this view was at odds with Wertham's conception of the influence of the form, it nonetheless helped spur ongoing interest in and research on the topic.

Thomas Hoult's "Comic Books and Juvenile Delinquency," published in 1949, and with its conclusions more widely circulated by a 1950 *Today's Health* article, challenged Florence Heisler's earlier findings that comics had little or no impact on their readers in the small town of Farmingdale, New York. Hoult dismissed Heisler's sample group as overly small and consequently unscientific (1949:280). His study compared the reading habits of 235 children arrested for juvenile delinquency in Los Angeles with 235 nondelinquent children matched to the first group by age, social and economic status, race, and education. Hoult found that the children charged with delinquency read 2,853 "harmful" comic books, while the nondelinquents had read only 1,786. He concluded that delinquent children read a greater number of comic books and significantly more "harmful" comic books than did nondelinquents. Hoult argued that this finding did not indicate a causative relationship between comic books and juvenile delinquency but was, nonetheless, significant finding and that "there is undoubtedly some connection that merits further careful investigation" (284). The popularization of these findings was even more forceful, concluding that comic books were as much a contributing factor to juvenile delinquency, as were slums, and suggesting that "we now have enough information to suspect that comic books dealing exclusively with criminal behavior tend to help keep the spirit of crime alive in delinquency areas" (Hoult and Hoult 1950:54).

Other research in the 1950s sought to draw conclusions about the relationship between comic books and juvenile delinquency through reference to content analyses. Morton Malter (1952), for instance, studied the content of 185 comic books published in the first two months of 1951 and concluded that Wertham was wrong to suggest that crime comics were the dominant genre unless one included Westerns depicting crime as crime comics (which Wertham did), in which case he was correct. A similar 1954 study conducted by Marilyn Graalfs concluded that scenes of violence accounted for 14 percent of all panels in comic books of all types and that as much as 26 percent of all panels in Western comics and 22 percent of panels in crime comics illustrated some form of violence. Graalfs further concluded that one-quarter of those panels depicted a person who was dead or injured (1968:92). All of this research, however, would be displaced in the spring of 1954 by the publication of the single volume that would dominate discussion of the relationship between comic books and juvenile delinquency from that point forward, Fredric Wertham's *Seduction of the Innocent.*

Writing about his participation as lead counsel for the National Association for the Advancement of Colored People in the Delaware desegregation case, Jack Greenberg recalled his expert witness:

> Wertham was of an imperious nature and quite temperamental, and everything had to be precisely as he wanted it. He insisted on testifying first, ahead of the other experts, offering the reason that by the time the trial began he would have examined the children and his testimony would be the most detailed, and he didn't want to face the burden of defending the testimony of preceding witnesses. He had an injured knee and until almost the last minute I couldn't be sure that he would show up. One point of tension was Wertham's view that comic books, particularly those that depicted sadism, violence, and racism, had a very harmful influence on children. As we discussed his testimony Wertham kept veering off into denouncing the malignant influence of comic books, and I kept trying to steer him back to the case at hand, thinking the comic book issue irrelevant and distracting. (1994:137)

That Wertham wished to equate the fight to end segregation with the fight to clean up the comic book industry cannot come as a surprise. Indeed, Wertham saw both of these social crises as problems for social psychiatry that could be dealt with through principles imported from mental hygiene intended to secure the public health by preventing future harm. Both segregation and comic books, Wertham believed, were part of a larger mosaic that contributed to social inequalities. He further insisted that each was a factor that could be isolated and dealt with in a scientific manner through legislation.

In fact, as Greenberg recounted, while being cross-examined on the witness stand, Wertham used the racist imagery in a copy of *Jumbo Comics* to draw explicitly the connection between the negative effects of state-sanctioned school segregation and comic books: "The children read that, and they are there indoctrinated with the fact that you can do all kinds of things to colored races. Now, the school problem partly, as you say, reinforces that, but it is very much more, because after all these commercial people who sell these things to children do so to make money. The State does it as acting morally . . . [s]o that the State really stabs very much deeper than these things do" (1994:138). For Wertham, therefore, these problems were roughly comparable and required similar solutions. The specificities of Wertham's commentary about comic books in the 1950s left little doubt as to the problems that he diagnosed and the corrective measures that he prescribed. His charges depended not only on his particular view of psychiatry but on the dominant thinking about mass culture and the mass society prevalent in the postwar era.

Although they were most explicitly enunciated in *Seduction of the Innocent*, Wertham's arguments about comic books were refined in a series of articles and speeches that began with "The Comics . . . Very Funny! " One week after that article appeared, Wertham spoke on a nationally aired CBS radio broadcast, *In My Opinion,* and his speech was subsequently reprinted in a Quaker journal, *Friends Intelligencer* (Wertham 1948a). This article clearly illustrates Wertham's intellectual debt to anti-mass-culture crusaders of the period. First he suggested that a "serious battle" was under way between American parents and "a small group of willful men making about ten million dollars a year profit—the owners of the comic-book publishing houses" (395).

Similarly, in a 1949 article published in *National Parent-Teacher,* Wertham relied on a traditional dismissal of comic books as lowbrow literature when he suggested that they were "smutty" and "unwholesome" and when he announced that "librarians have noted all over the country that since the enormous rise of comic books, children have been reading fewer good children's books" (1949j:7–8). Wertham's concern with the profit-minded nature of mass culture supported his argument relating to the substantial differences he perceived between violence in the comic books and violence in so-called great literature:

> Some fathers have told me that it "hasn't done any harm to my child; after all, when he reads Hamlet he doesn't see ghosts and want to put poison in my ear." The answer is easy: first of all, comic books are not as artistic as *Hamlet.* Second, there's only one *Hamlet* (and most children don't read it), whereas comic books come by the millions. Third, there has been no other literature for adults or for children in the history of the world, at any period

or in any nation, that showed in pictures and in words, over and over again, half-nude girls in all positions being branded, burned, bound, tied to wheels, blinded, pressed between spikes, thrown to snakes and wild animals, crushed with rocks, slowly drowned or smothered, or having their veins punctured and their blood drawn off. (396)

Here Wertham linked aesthetic preferences suggesting that Shakespeare was art while comic books self-evidently were not with the question of mass production and the representation of violence to conflate the three into a single argument against the comic book format.

This anti-mass-culture argument that set commerce in opposition to education reappeared in a 1954 article in which Wertham complained that "reading is the greatest educational force that mankind has ever devised. Comics, on the other hand, are the greatest anti-educational influence that man's greed has ever concocted. From this point of view comic books are part of a larger problem. We have reduced children to a market" (1954h:611). Wertham regarded the general notion of a commercialized culture for children as far more pressing than the specific question of comic books. Moreover, Wertham seemed to indicate that the problem was even greater insofar as mass culture was becoming increasingly acceptable to the guardians of children's culture.

Writing in *Religious Education,* Wertham suggested that "in former times smut and trash were frowned upon in children's reading. Either it was actively combated or it was minimized, curbed and barely tolerated. Nowadays it is not only defended, but is actually praised as being good for children!" (1954b:395). Wertham's commentaries of comic books during this time clearly need to be understood as existing generally in accord with the dominant definitions of culture that circulated in the period, particularly insofar as his arguments relied on a rejection of mass culture and a celebration of legitimated high culture. Wertham's near-exclusive focus in this era on comic books as degrading agents of mass culture stemmed from their particular form: "We selected comic books as a paradigm, because they lend themselves most easily to study of their contents and are most suitable for long-range investigation. One may easily miss significant aspects that are injurious in other media if one has not learned about them in pure culture in their crudest aspects, in such lower forms of mass media as comic books" (Wertham 1955e: 29). Further, Wertham clearly aligned himself with earlier traditions of literary-based dismissals of mass culture against what he depicted as a naively procomics position held by certain educators and child guidance experts in the employ of the industry.

At the same time, however, Wertham's critique of comic books also drew on a series of scientific principles that stemmed from his particular brand of psychiatry. Wertham's constant rejections of the work of experts employed by the comic book industry relied not simply on his constant tendency to point out that they lacked financial independence but also on a rejection of orthodox Freudianism and theories of innate aggression: "The apologists of comic books, who function under the auspices of the comic-book business (although the public is not let in on that secret), are sociologists, educators, psychiatrists, lawyers, and psychologists. They all agree that this enormous over-stimulation of fantasy with scenes of sex and violence is completely harmless. They all rely on arguments derived from misunderstood Freud and bandy around such words as 'aggression,' 'release,' 'vicarious' and 'fantasy world.' They use free associations to bolster up free enterprise" (Wertham 1948c:29).

Wertham's rejection of orthodox Freudianism and the theory of innate aggression that Bender and other defenders of the comic book promoted rested on the presumption that there was no such thing as neutral scientific inquiry. He further argued that child psychology had failed to take proper account of the mass media's enormous influence on children's lives. Specifically citing the failings of Frank and Gruenberg, Wertham wrote, "Much of what passes today as official child psychology is faulty for two reasons. In the first place it disregards ethical values, which can and should be taught, and which can be and are vitiated by outside influences. Instead of appreciating the role of ethics, it puts all the emphasis on the 'necessity' for unbridled self-expression for the child. Secondly, it is obsolete because it disregards the enormous influence of mass media, especially comic books" (1954b:398). To correct these sorts of lapses, Wertham proposed a fivefold analysis of the influence of comic books on children. Speaking in 1948 before the American Prison Association, Wertham (1948b) defined his approach as an analysis of typical cases: an analysis of comic books, an analysis of the scientific problems involved, an analysis of the methods of the comic book publishers, and an analysis of the practical steps that could be taken to address the findings of these analyses. This method would be replicated six years later in *Seduction of the Innocent* as Wertham worked to synthesize an approach to comic books that drew equally on the mass culture critique popular in the postwar period and on his idiosyncratic conception of a socially grounded psychiatric practice.

Writing to Ida McAlpine in September 1954, Wertham revealed that he wrote *Seduction of the Innocent* as "a non-technical book because I knew I could not budge the psychiatrists anyhow," since "after all, the really real character is 'laid down before [age] three,' so what harm can comic books do?" (Wertham 1954e:1–2). That *Seduction of the Innocent* was written for a lay rather than a scientific readership is evidenced by its loose structure: it touches on topics in one section and returns to them later. The book's first chapter, for instance, introduced the theme of comic books and juvenile delinquency but the topic was not dealt with concretely until the sixth chapter. Nonetheless, Wertham's foregrounding of that material in his introductory remarks highlighted the book's central concern.

Wertham opened his book by advancing an argument derived from his notion of social psychiatry, namely that understanding juvenile delinquency required understanding the social settings from which delinquency sprang. Furthermore, it was necessary to understand the delinquent's life history generally as well as the ways in which his or her life experience was specifically reflected in wish and fantasy. These facts, in Wertham's view, could be derived only through clinical social psychiatry of the type practiced at the Lafargue Clinic (1954i:3). The public viewed juvenile delinquency as a problem of individual behavior, but Wertham, grounded as he was in a more socialized view of behavior, rejected this view. To this end, Wertham explicitly rejected the philosophy of innate aggression that he insisted was the necessary underpinning of the individualistic view of delinquency. As he stated regarding a boy charged with the random shooting of a man at New York's Polo Grounds, "I do not believe in the philosophy that children have instinctive urges to commit such acts. In going over his life, I had asked him about his reading. He was enthusiastic about comic books. I looked over some of those he liked best. They were filled with alluring tales of shooting, knifing, hitting and strangling. He was so intelligent, frank and open that I considered him not an inferior child, but a superior one. I know that many people glibly call such a child maladjusted; but in reality he was a child well adjusted to what we had offered him to adjust to. In other words, I felt this was a seduced child" (11–12). He went on to suggest that society was cruel to children insofar as they were left "entirely unprotected" when they were shown crime, delinquency, and sexual abnormality in comic books, but the punishment that they received if they succumbed to such media's suggestions was more severe than if an adult similarly strayed from the path of virtue. This notion that children were preyed on and victimized by an adult culture that corrupted and then blamed them was a central motif throughout the book.

In the sixth chapter of *Seduction of the Innocent,* Wertham argued that juvenile delinquency did not simply happen naturally but was created by adults as a reflection of America's postwar social values: "Even more than crime, juvenile delinquency reflects the social values current in a society. Both adults and children absorb these social values in their daily lives, at home, in school, at work, and also in all the communications imparted as entertainment, instruction or propaganda through the mass media, from the printed word to television. Juvenile delinquency holds a mirror up to society and society does not like the picture there" (149).

Following the reasoning that delinquency was a social phenomenon, Wertham suggested that the rise of juvenile crime during the Great Depression pointed to the fact that adults were accessories insofar as they had created the economic climate that fostered childhood criminality. Wertham insisted that "the delinquency of a child is not a disease; it is a symptom, individually and socially. You cannot understand or remedy a social phenomenon like delinquency by redefining it simply as an individual emotional disorder" (156–57). To this end, Wertham suggested, juvenile delinquency needed to be studied in relation to other forms of social behavior. Moreover, Wertham's conception of delinquency as a social phenomenon allowed him to acknowledge the fact that delinquency was caused by a "constellation of many factors" (10), of which comic books represented only one. Although Thrasher accused Wertham of presenting a monocausationist theory of delinquency, he clearly regarded comics as only a "contributing factor" and not the actual cause of juvenile crime (10). Wertham stated this explicitly in a variety of ways and a number of times: "*Of course* there are other evil influences to which we expose children" (1954h:400); "Crime comics are certainly not the only factor, nor in many cases are they even the most important one, but there can be no doubt that they are the most unnecessary and least excusable one" (1954i:166). Indeed, Wertham bluntly answered the question of the single cause of juvenile delinquency in a response to the *Cincinnati*

Enquirer: "Juvenile delinquency has only one cause: adults. We adults sow the seeds of delinquent behavior" (Wertham 1954k:14).

Wertham opened his chapter on juvenile delinquency by quoting Adolf Meyer on the ridiculousness of refusing to act against a single factor simply because it was not the only factor (147), an argument that Wertham (1952) had also made in regard to school segregation. Wertham invoked the same metaphor to explain the need for a preventative public health approach to both problems. Wertham agreed with his critics when they suggested that not all children exposed to segregation or comic books would suffer psychological damage, but he dismissed the notion that no action should be taken to correct the situation: "I do not say that every child who reads comic books becomes a delinquent or becomes abnormal. Nor does the inhaling of tubercle bacilli (which we all do in a large city) mean that every one of us comes down with tuberculosis. And yet we forbid spitting in the subway. Not every piece of cheap, poisonous candy causes illness to the children who eat it, and yet we passed a pure food law to abolish bad candy. Don't you agree with me that the mind is as sensitive as the lungs and as the stomach—especially the mind of a child? " (1948a:396).

These comments were nearly identical to his remarks on school segregation: "Thousands of people in large cities inhale tubercle bacilli into their lungs. And yet only a relatively small number of these infected multitudes come down with the disease tuberculosis. We do not say that we do not have to pay any attention to the tubercle bacillus because enormous numbers of people do not become overly ill from it. The tubercle bacillus in cases not developing the disease is potentially injurious. This is scientific reasoning in the sphere of public health. In child psychiatry and child guidance, unfortunately, this type of reasoning is often lacking" (1952:97). Indeed, it is not surprising that Wertham would make the connection in these particular instances. During his testimony in the Delaware desegregation case, Wertham had used a copy of *Jumbo Comics* #153 to make a point about the creation of a racist culture in America. Drawing the magistrate's attention to the presence of explicitly racist imagery in the comic book, Wertham noted that segregated schools and offensive comic books were two of many harmful factors in the creation of race hatred in America and that the fact of multiple causation did not warrant inaction on one specific front but required a globalizing approach to the problem that would tackle individual problems as they arose, just as the Delaware court had tackled segregation as a negative influence (NAACP 1951:11).

Essentially, Wertham argued that juvenile delinquency was not an individual but rather a social phenomenon. Nonetheless, he concluded that action to control that factor was justified on the basis that it did not make any sense to refuse to treat a contributing factor even if it was not the only important factor. This reasoning derived equally from his political orientation evidenced in his work to end school segregation and from his notion of social psychiatry, which sought to combine preventative public health measures inspired by the mental hygiene movement with a liberal political perspective that considered individual behavior in relation to existing social structures. To make the argument that action against the comic books was necessary, however, Wertham necessarily had to demonstrate that they were, like the tubercle bacilli, a harmful factor and not simply a scapegoat.

One crucial line of argument in this regard stemmed from Wertham's condemnation of comics not simply as a contributing factor in juvenile delinquency but as a corrupting agent of mass culture. The second chapter of *Seduction of the Innocent* traced the history of the American comic book industry and suggested that he saw comic books as a problem because of their enormous pervasiveness. Estimating that between 75 and 80 million comic books were sold in the United States each month (1954i:29), Wertham argued that crime comics were the largest growth segment of the industry. He suggested that between 1937 and 1947 only nineteen comics could be classified as crime comics, which he defined as "comic books that depict crime, whether the setting is urban, Western, science-fiction, jungle, adventure or the realm of supermen, "horror" of super-natural beings" (20). By 1948, however, Wertham estimated that half of all new comics were pure crime books, while the other half were Westerns featuring criminal themes.

Moreover, like other critics of mass culture at the time, Wertham suggested that the themes of these crime comics tended to endorse an increasingly authoritarian society. He deplored examples of racism in jungle comics: "I have repeatedly found in my studies that this characterization of colored peoples as subhuman, in conjunction with depiction of forceful heroes as blond Nordic superman, has made a deep—and I believe lasting—impression on young children" (32). Moreover, ostensible heroes, such as Superman, tended to solve problems through the use of force and thereby taught children to be submissive to authoritarianism: "Superman (with the big S on his uniform—we should, I suppose, be thankful that it is not an S.S.) needs an endless stream of ever new submen, criminals and 'foreign-looking' people not only to justify his existence but even to make it possible" (34). All of this material could be found, he noted, in comics that sold hundreds of thousands of copies each month but went almost totally unread by people concerned with raising children. Wertham proposed to correct that oversight through a scientific methodology that would demonstrate definitively the negative impact of this form of mass culture. The bulk of *Seduction of the Innocent* was dedicated to that task.

Wertham set out to answer three questions in *Seduction of the Innocent:* Do comic books influence children's behavior? If so, how? And in what way and how long does the effect last (1954i:48)? In conducting the research to answer those questions, Wertham and his associates at the Lafargue Clinic rejected traditional social science methodologies in favor of a psychiatric approach. Wertham rejected the questionnaire methodology because it was inadequate: "To ask children a series of simple questions and expect real enlightenment from their answers is even more misleading than to carry out the same procedure with adults. The younger the child, the more erroneous are the conclusions likely to be drawn." Instead, Wertham opted to utilize "all the methods of modern psychiatry which were suitable and possible in the individual case" to determine the effects of comic books (1954i:49). Wertham incorporated the study of comic books into the general routine work of mental hygiene and child psychiatry at the Lafargue Clinic. This allowed "the largest cross-section of children" to be studied because they were referred to the clinic by the juvenile police bureau, by pediatric wards, and by private practices. Therefore a "large proportion" of the children studied were "normal children" who came to the clinic's attention for some social reason rather than because of a psychological concern (50).

In a January 1949 affidavit prepared for Los Angeles County counsel Harold Kennedy regarding the county's legislation to ban the sale of crime comic books, Wertham outlined the extent of his practice:

> I see about a thousand children a year, in clinics or in private practice. In the Mental Hygiene Clinic of the Queens General Hospital alone, there are about 400 new children every year under 13 years of age and about a

hundred from 13 to 19 years. A very large proportion of these children are normal children, referred for foster-home placement by such agencies as the N.Y. Founding Hospital, the Catholic Home Bureau, the Hebrew Orphan Asylum, the Big Brother Movement. I see also many normal children when I examine the children of adults who are referred to the clinic(s), or brothers and sisters. I also see children of superior endowment who are applicants for scholarships for special educational facilities. (Wertham 1949a:3)

Once inside the clinic, these children were examined in a variety of ways. They were the subjects of clinical interviews that were used to determine their life histories. Children received a number of standardized tests, including the Rorschach test, the Thematic Apperception Test, intelligence tests, and the mosaic test, which Wertham himself pioneered, among others (55–57). The results of these standardized tests, Wertham reported, pointed out that "children who suffer from any really serious intrinsic psychopathological condition, including those with psychoses, are *less* influenced by comic book reading" (57–58). Additionally, children were observed in playroom situations that demonstrated how comics were a social phenomenon whereby even nonreaders could be influenced through contact with comic book consumers (64).

These multiple approaches to the research, all of which were discounted by critics such as Thrasher as nonscientific and consequently invalid, ultimately directed Wertham to conclude that "not the experience itself, as an observer records and evaluates it, but the way it is reflected and experienced by the person himself, is what counts and what explains the psychological results" (78). To this end, Wertham suggested, only the clinical methodology used by psychiatry could get to the answers about the ways in which audiences actually used comics. In this way, Wertham argued that the study of media effects was best left to psychiatry and that it could not be properly assessed using methodologies that were ostensibly more scientific, disinterested, and objective. The renunciation of social-scientific methodologies that dominated the study of media and children in the midcentury era is the greatest single distinction between Wertham's work in *Seduction of the Innocent* and that of the social scientists who would minimize his contribution to the field.

In the fourth chapter of *Seduction of the Innocent*, Wertham again affirmed his belief that no direct causal relationship existed between comic books and juvenile delinquency (1954i:86). Nonetheless, he stressed several important effects that he felt generally characterized comic books. First, comics were "anti-educational" and interfered with normal mental growth (89). Adopting the arguments of the day, Wertham suggested that comics were not a legitimate form of art or communication and, therefore, that children had nothing to show for time spent reading comics: "since almost all good children's reading has some educational value, crime comics by their very nature are not only non-educational; they are anti-educational. They fail to teach anything that might be useful to a child; they do suggest many things that are harmful" (90).

A more pressing concern, however, stemmed from the fact that Wertham viewed comics as contributing to what he termed "moral disarmament," a process whereby the superego and the higher functions of social responsibility were blunted (91). As an "unparalleled distillation of viciousness," comics affected the child's "ethical image" by romanticizing force (92). Wertham, for instance, argued that there existed an "exact parallel to the blunting of sensibilities in the direction of cruelty that has characterized a whole generation of central European youth fed on the Nietzsche-Nazi myth of the exceptional man who is beyond good and evil" and the Superman conceit in comic books (97). This ethical confusion was reinforced, he argued, by the role of imitation. Wertham suggested that identification, the emotional aspect of reading, was corrupted by an ongoing confusion in most crime comics between the hero and the villain. He noted that comic books were conditioning children to identify with the strongest character in a given story, "however evil he may be" (116). This type of identification could, Wertham contended, intersect with a variety of preexisting tendencies and tip the balance of a child's predilections toward delinquency.

Wertham summarized the potential effects of comic books by arguing that they were a form of "mass conditioning" that exerted negative effects along the following lines:

1) The comic-book format is an invitation to illiteracy.
2) Crime comic books create an atmosphere of cruelty and deceit.
3) They create a readiness for temptation.
4) They stimulate unwholesome fantasies.
5) They suggest criminal or sexually abnormal ideas.

6) They furnish the rationalization for them, which may be ethically even more harmful than the impulse.

7) They suggest the forms a delinquent impulse may take and supply details of technique.

8) They may tip the scales toward maladjustment or delinquency. (118)

These general effects, however, were augmented by other influences specifically relating to areas such as sexuality and self-esteem that were the subjects of more narrowly focused chapters. Essentially, however, these side arguments only provided further evidence for Wertham's primary charges instead of outlining new sets of presumed effects of comic books on child readers. For example, Wertham condemned the representation of sexual violence in comic books for the way in which it created an ethical confusion in readers and contributed to potentially unnatural childhood development (175). Similarly, he charged that advertising in comic books that promised to reshape children's bodies through weight loss or muscle gain viciously played on childhood insecurities (198). Still, these remained subsidiary concerns of the larger charges against comic books, including the suggestion that comics interfered with the development of reading skills.

Seduction of the Innocent's fifth chapter specifically dealt with the effect of comics on literacy. "Retooling for Illiteracy" argued that "comic books are death on reading" (1954i:121). For Wertham, the problem of comics rested with the medium itself, regardless of the content: "The comic-book format, with its handled balloons scattered over the page, with its emphasis on pictures and their continuity, with its arrows directing the eyes from right to left or even up and down, with its many inarticulate words-that-are-not-words, interferes with learning proper reading habits" (127). The entire basis of Wertham's critique of comics as a detriment to the acquisition of proper reading skills lay on the idea that despite the problems associated with the lurid content of crime comic books, the medium itself was inherently problematic and was consequently irretrievable for a literate culture. Wertham adopted the traditional high-culture argument when he suggested that "the dawn of civilization was marked by the invention of writing. Reading, therefore, is not only one of the cornerstones of civilized life, it is also one of the main foundations of a child's adjustment to it" (121).

This argument began from the premise that reading was not an isolated function of the brain but was in actuality a highly complex performative act. This performance could be disrupted by several factors related to the synthesis of words and images in the comic book form. First, comics handicapped vocabulary by emphasizing the visual element rather than the proper word. Furthermore, irregular bits of printing in comics panels disrupted the acquisition of a normal left-to-right reading pattern. The pictures discouraged reading because people who had reading disabilities could grasp the narrative of a comic book exclusively through the visual elements—what Wertham termed a form of "picture-reading" (139). Wertham further argued that the poor-quality paper used to print comics at midcentury caused eyestrain for many readers. Consequently, Wertham concluded that despite the fact that reading disorders had existed before comics, they were a major contributing factor to contemporary reading disorders. This argument was often made against comics during this period and had been researched and confirmed as early as 1942 (Luckiesh 1942).

Wertham further tied the problem of the comic book format into his central argument when he announced the "relatively high correlation between delinquency and reading disorders; that is to say, a disproportionate number of poor or non-readers become delinquent, and a disproportionate number of delinquents have pronounced reading disorders" (136). Wertham further condemned comics' effect on literacy by reproducing the arguments of many early critics in the education and library field about the form—namely, that the mass production of comic books gave the genre an unfair advantage in competing with "good inexpensive children's books" (31). In reifying the traditional distinction between high and low cultures in the opposition of books and comics, Wertham clearly showed how much the anti-mass-culture debate had influenced him.

Having established his charges against crime comic books, Wertham then turned his attention to a refutation of the argument in favor of the form provided by other experts, specifically those he named as forming "the defense team" of paid experts in the employ of comic book publishers: Jean Thompson, Sidonie Gruenberg, Harvey Zorbaugh, Lauretta Bender, and Josette Frank (223). Wertham charged that these experts never addressed the comic books' content, preferring instead to deal only with vague generalities. By refusing to deal with specifics, Wertham suggested, these experts

were better able to marshal their many arguments that comic books were
harmless.

Wertham addressed each of these arguments in turn. He maintained, for
instance, that the suggestion that comic books constituted a form of contemporary folklore allowing children to experiment with reality failed to take
into account the fact that comic books, unlike fairy tales, were not symbolic:
"Children who play fairy tales would have a hard time having someone actually eat Red Riding Hood. But they can and do try to bind, gag, and stick each
other with sharp instruments as they see it so realistically depicted in comic
books" (241). Wertham noted that many orthodox Freudians and other psychiatrists had suggested that comics constituted a harmless release of aggression, but he responded by observing that this position represented a
misreading of Freud that lacked clinical proof of any kind (247). Wertham
insisted, "Freud himself never saw a comic book. And I am certain that he
would have been horrified—and even more horrified to learn that his name
is being used to defend them by some uncritical would-be followers" (270).
Wertham further suggested that several arguments forwarded by the experts
for the defense seemed to seek license for publishers to do anything that they
wished without responsibilities of any kind. The experts claimed, for instance,
that comics have no impact on shaping values except when they provide a
healthy moral message such as "crime does not pay." Comic book defenders
suggested that only children who were in some way predisposed to criminality were impacted by comic books, thereby placing the blame firmly on the
individual child rather than on the media. These experts claimed, following
Freud, that an individual's character was formed in the earliest years of life
and that any subsequent influence was negligible: "A child is not a stereotype
of his own past. To blame everything on very early infantile experiences is not
scientific but exorcistic thinking: Nothing could harm a child unless the devil
was already in him. Comic books do their harm early enough. Children of
three or four have been seen poring over the worst. Freud would not have
considered that too late for harm to be done" (245). These attitudes, Wertham
responded, condoned any and all behavior on the part of publishers and ultimately failed to take into account the fact that the roots of delinquency lay in
a balance of factors (246).

Ironically, critics often leveled this charge at Wertham, and he responded to
it at length in *Seduction of the Innocent*. He again acknowledged the concept

of multiple and complex causation: "Of course there are other factors beside comic books. There are always other factors." (242). He went on to suggest, however, that "the study of one factor does not obliterate the importance of other factors. On the contrary, it may highlight them. What people really mean when they use the let's-not-blame-any-one-factor argument is that they do not like this particular factor. It is new to them and for years they have been overlooking it. If they were psychoanalysts, they were caught with their couches up. They do not object to specific factors if they are intrinsic and noncommittal and can be dated far enough back in a child's life. They do not object to social factors provided they are vaguely lumped together as 'environment,' 'our entire social fabric,' 'culture' or 'socio-economic conditions' " (243). In a nutshell, Wertham concluded that the experts who claimed that comics had little or no influence over behavior were apolitical and unwilling to take a firm stand on any substantive issue, preferring instead to hide behind generalities or a psychiatric belief that stressed continuity over change. Wertham's conclusions about the effects of comic books, conversely, need to be understood as relating to his politically motivated and progressive ideas about the social uses of psychiatry and the possibilities for postwar liberalism in the face of an overwhelming insistence on individualistic explanations of human behavior.

Following a chapter that examined the success of anti-comic-book crusades in countries such as England, France, and Canada, Wertham opened his penultimate chapter by wondering about the collective responsibility of himself and his readers. He suggested that despite the pronouncements of the child guidance experts, comics were simply too large a problem for parents to deal with themselves; consequently, legislative action was required (301). Citing his participation for the defense in several censorship trials, Wertham insisted that he opposed censorship of any kind, which he defined as "control of one agency by another" (326). He maintained that efforts at self-regulation, such as the ACMP code, had "completely failed" (328) and called instead for a public-health-based law that would prohibit the display and sale of comic books to children under the age of fifteen. The justification for this law, Wertham argued, would be his clinical studies into the effect of comic books that gave "expression to the vague gropings of the more enlightened part of public opinion which seeks a curb on the rising tide of education for violence" (332). Wertham further noted that he had made this same sort of suggestion in reference to school desegregation and that the Delaware courts had adopted his logic in deciding to end racially based education practices. Wertham continued, "the analogy with the comic-book question is obvious. But whereas in the case of school segregation something new was accomplished, with crime comic books the same reasoning did not work" because many experts in delinquency "regard juvenile delinquents as if they were totally different from other children. Even liberal writers write of 'the mark of Cain which an evil destiny brands on some of our children.' They believe that emotionally strong children are unaffected, while only emotionally insecure children are exposed. This is pure speculation. It means the distinction between an invulnerable élite and a vulnerable common group. Reflect what snobbishness is involved" (337).

For Wertham, the distinction between censorship of material for adults and the restriction of material targeted at children was justified by the same logic that led to the desegregation of America's schools. Both were clearly public health problems that affected all children in important ways. He believed, however, that the cleanup of the comic book industry was retarded by the biases of American liberals who instinctively rejected the same arguments about culture that they had endorsed with respect to public policy in the schools. To this end, Wertham noted wryly that "crime comics are a severe test of the liberalism of liberals" (339). Moreover, in his conclusion, Wertham argued that the central problem of the mass media was not the comic books themselves but the society from which they sprang: "I had started from comic books, had gone on to study the needs and desires of children and had come to adults. I had learned that it is not a question of the comic books but of the mentality from which comic books spring, and that it was not the mentality of children but the mentality of adults. What I found was not an individual condition of children, but a social condition of adults" (394). Thus, Wertham affirmed the most basic tenets of his social psychiatry by subsuming his concerns about comic books within a larger concern about the general direction of postwar social life. That subsequent commentators responding to his work on comic books generally overlooked this progressivist intention can be seen by turning to an examination of the various ways that the scholarly and critical communities took up *Seduction of the Innocent.*

Detailed scientific refutations of Wertham's research were notably absent following the publication of *Seduction of the Innocent.* Indeed, the best

Congressional Digest could do was to reprint Frederic Thrasher's 1949 essay (Wertham 1954c; Thrasher 1954). The most obvious reason for this lack of scientific response was that Wertham's book effectively stifled much of the mid-1950s debate about comic books. Few of the defense team members whom he directly cited in his text, for instance, published significant responses to the book. Wertham had long criticized the so-called "experts for the defense," and while they also criticized him in the *Journal of Educational Sociology* and elsewhere, they rarely rose to the challenge of engaging directly with him.

Wertham's papers indicate that he had some contact with Zorbaugh and Frank following the publication of Judith Crist's article about his research in *Collier's*. In 1949 Zorbaugh invited Wertham, through a mutual acquaintance, to publish an article in a proposed third *Journal of Educational Sociology* special issue on comics, but Wertham declined the invitation, calling the issue "phony" and beneath reply (1950a). Following the release of *Seduction of the Innocent,* however, Wertham was very much back on the radar screen of the comics experts, particularly the Child Study Association (CSA). The CSA had two primary responses to Wertham's charges. First, the association issued a press release on 10 May 1954 clarifying its position on comic books and outlining the history of its efforts in the field. The CSA's press release pointed out that although the organization had maintained that "there is no competent evidence that reading about crime makes criminals," it had nonetheless condemned "vicious crime and horror comics as an offense against childhood. It has stated that they should be off the stands." This represented a departure from the CSA's 1949 suggestion that comics featuring real crime and sexually suggestive and sadistic pictures were "presumably not addressed to children—[were], perhaps, not even attractive to many of them" (CSA 1954:1–2). The press release went on to defend the CSA's paid advisory involvement with various comic book publishers.

Second, the CSA sent a lawyer's letter to Rinehart demanding two corrections to the book. The CSA objected to a footnote to page 223 in which Wertham mentioned experts "employed by the comic book industry." The CSA suggested that Gruenberg and Frank were not "employed" but "engaged" by various publishers. Second, the CSA denied the accuracy of a quotation attributed to the director on pages 374–75. In his written response, Wertham contended that his comments about the organization were "an understatement of the true facts," and he declined to make any changes (1954j). Wertham's papers contain no indication that the situation moved beyond this exchange, although he felt compelled to write to the CSA in December 1955 decrying the use of pressure methods to keep mentions of his research out of various magazines. In that letter, Wertham suggested, "If the Child Study Association has scientific material or scientific arguments against the research in my book, they should publish them in print and sign their name to it" (1955b). No such publications were forthcoming. Nonetheless, Wertham's interaction with the CSA was symptomatic of his engagement with many participants in the comic book industry at the time: threatening legal letters, responses from Wertham, no further action taken on the part of the industry, and no further research forthcoming from the experts.

Not surprisingly, the comic book industry's response to Wertham's writings was tremendously hostile and included hiring private detectives to investigate Wertham's past and harass his colleagues at the Lafargue Clinic in an effort to intimidate him into silence. A memo from Wertham to the clinic's staff that was copied to New York Police Commissioner Francis Adams quoted the publishing industry newsletter *Quest* in what Wertham took to be a threat: "The immediate enemy is Fredric Wertham, not some other publisher. He cannot be reasoned with. He must be discredited and rendered ineffective. This is a job for the bomb disposal squad, and comic book publishers should sit down and decide what to do about him. Will he go away? Probably not. He must be knocked out" (Wertham 1955c).

From the moment that he first began publishing commentaries on comic books, Wertham was inundated with letters from lawyers employed by irate publishers. In June 1948, Wertham received several letters from Albert Kanter, of *Classics Illustrated,* objecting to Wertham's characterization of that publication in his *Saturday Review* article "The Comics . . . Very Funny." After several letters and a threat of a libel suit from Kanter, the dispute boiled down to the question of whether blood was visible in an image of a man with his eyes gouged out in the *Classics Illustrated* version of Eugene Sue's *The Mysteries of Paris.* Wertham resolved the situation by retracting his statement that the image showed blood coming from beneath the bandage, noting that the blood is actually visible above the bandage (Wertham 1948g). In the spring of 1949, Ralph Daigh, the editorial director of Fawcett Publications, complained to *National-Parent Teacher Magazine* that Wertham had misrepresented

Fawcett's *Tom Mix* comic book as unduly violent in his article "What Are Comic Books? " Wertham responded to the charges after Fawcett threatened the magazine with a libel suit. His response, which analyzed the violence in the comic on a panel-by-panel basis, convinced *National Parent-Teacher Magazine* editor Eva Grant that the *Tom Mix* comic was barbarous and repulsive and that Wertham's assertions were temperate and evenhanded. Grant refused to retract any part of Wertham's article (Wertham 1949a).

Wertham took a different tack in dealing with complaints from Dell Publishing in 1953. When Dell complained about Wertham's comments on "good comic books" in his *Ladies' Home Journal* article "What Parents Don't Know about Comic Books," he responded by interrogating Dell about the specifics of the complaint. If Dell published one-third of all comic books in the United States, as the company frequently claimed, Wertham asked, how many comic books did the industry actually publish? How many did Dell publish, and how was this number broken down by different titles? He also inquired about whether Dell defined comic books representing mugging, pistol-whipping, or other forms of violence as "good comic books" (Wertham 1953b). Wertham's papers contain no record of any response to this letter from Dell.

Nonetheless, this was not Wertham's final interaction with Dell Publishing. In October 1953, Rinehart received several letters from comic book publishers, including National Comics, Dell, and Magazine Management, which published comics under a variety of different corporate names, protesting the announcement that Rinehart would publish *Seduction of the Innocent.* Writing to his literary agent, Wertham noted that "there have been great obstacles" leading to the publication of the book, including threatening letters written directly to Stanley Rinehart (1954f).

In March 1954, *Publisher's Weekly* printed a lengthy attack written in response to a three-page advertisement for *Seduction of the Innocent* that had run in an earlier issue. A response from Wertham (1954j) appeared in May, with Wertham specifically criticizing Dell (although the company's name was removed from the published version of the letter) and suggesting that what was sensational was "not Rinehart's advertisement, but the facts." In addition, Dell sent a number of letters and telegrams to Rinehart in March and April 1954 protesting the release of the book. These letters arrived as part of a wave over that two-month span as comic book publishers put

Rinehart on legal notice in preparation for potential lawsuits deriving from the allegations in the book. Among the publishers who sent legal letters to Rinehart were Whitman Publishing, Warner Brothers Cartoons, the Lone Ranger Inc., Edgar Rice Burroughs Inc., Dell Publishing, and a number of interested parties on behalf of Dell, such as Lee Duncan, the owner-trainer of dog star Rin Tin Tin. After the book's release, however, these publishers filed no libel suits. Whether this absence resulted from the strong text editing done by the Rinehart legal department in November 1953, the publishers' belief that the book contained no actionable or offensive elements, or a symptom of a new strategy devised by the comic book industry is impossible to determine. What is indisputable is that the comic book industry fought to suppress *Seduction of the Innocent* before its publication in April 1954 but ultimately took no legal action against the book after it was released to the public and greeted with overwhelmingly positive reviews.

Seduction of the Innocent received an incredible amount of press over the spring and summer of 1954. An enormous scrapbook in Wertham's papers contains hundreds—perhaps thousands—of reviews of the book from virtually every newspaper and magazine in the United States, Canada, and Britain. Wertham's agent suggested that the author had won a tremendous victory at the expense of his royalties, noting that the quantity of the reviews may have led interested parties to assume that they already had learned the book's argument without actually having to buy or read it. The book received glowing reviews from the educational and library journals that had long been split on the subject of comic book reading. The most enthusiastic review appeared in the *National Education Association Journal,* which celebrated Wertham's attempts to move beyond the study of individual cases and toward an understanding of the social causes of juvenile delinquency. Referring to the book as helping "to build the understanding essential to the growth and survival of our free democratic society," the editorial went on to pronounce *Seduction of the Innocent* the "most important book of 1954" and suggested that it should be in the library of every parent, teacher, preacher, and juvenile court judge (Morgan 1954:473).

Other professional journals were no less kind. The *Library Journal,* for instance, praised Wertham's work for its "substantial evidence" that could "not be laughed away" ("Non-Fiction" 1954:622), while the *American Journal of Psychotherapy* cited his "unusually praiseworthy effort to combat evil" (Wolf 1954:547). Mixed reviews could also be found, of course, but even these stressed the work's importance. Writing in the *Library Journal*, Thomas Zimmerman suggested that Wertham was an alarmist whose arguments would lead to an abridgment of freedom of the press. Arguing that "there is no easy answer," Zimmerman returned to librarians' earlier solutions to the comic book problem by suggesting that parents should address comics in their homes by presenting children with "good books" (1954:1607). Anita Mishler, writing in *Public Opinion Quarterly*, also raised concerns about the book, although she ultimately decided that it should be applauded "despite its shortcomings" (1955:117). She suggested, for instance, that despite the fact that Wertham's work was "more polemical than scientific," there was no doubting his central finding that comic books added nothing to the life of a child and his insistence that aggression should be productively channeled in a civilization rather than mindlessly released (116–17).

If *Seduction of the Innocent* consolidated the anti-comic-book sentiment in professional journals where it had been previously mixed, it also solidified opposition in religious magazines that had always been skeptical. In a two-part review of Wertham's book in June 1954, Harold Gardiner of the Jesuit journal *America* reiterated many of Wertham's arguments and declared that he had "never seen a more completely documented indictment" (1954a:321). He continued by stating, "this is a book that every Catholic parent ought to ponder" (1954b:342). A similarly toned review could be found in the pages of the *Catholic World* under the inflammatory title "Crime Comics Must Go!" The piece suggested that if crime comics publishers refused to clean up their product, they would have to be legislated out of existence as an "intolerable nuisance" (Sheerin 1954:19). These magazines raised strong moral objections to comic books, and both writers suggested that the Senate Subcommittee Investigating Juvenile Delinquency bore responsibility for recommending strong legislation that would accomplish the sort of control of comic books Wertham advocated.

While many nonreligious general-interest or public-affairs magazines concurred in this opposition to comics in the wake of the publication of *Seduction of the Innocent,* these publications nonetheless demurred on free speech grounds at the possibility of congressional action to regulate or clean up the industry. Few general-interest magazines, it seems, could afford to completely ignore Wertham's research. Sterling North, whose comments in

1940 had largely begun the midcentury anticomics crusade, called *Seduction of the Innocent* "the most important book of the year. Brilliantly written. Completely accurate. Thoroughly documented" (M.D.L. 1954:884). Winfred Overholser, a psychiatrist whom Wertham had condemned for participating in the Ezra Pound case, wrote in the *Saturday Review* that Wertham had presented "incontrovertible evidence" that the comic book was "a pernicious influence in the education of the young" (1954:16). The *New Yorker* dedicated seven pages to summarizing the findings presented in Wertham's work and concluded that it provided "potent ammunition" to use against Superman and his publishers (Gibbs 1954). The *Nation*, which had editorialized against the New York anti-comic-book legislation in 1949 while condemning comics, repeated its earlier stance. Arguing that comic books were fascist and racist, Ward Moore suggested that Wertham at the very least had circumstantial evidence about effects on his side. Moore, however, parted with Wertham where recommendations were concerned, arguing that censorship of any kind would be worse than the comic books that needed to be contained (1954:426–27).

Thus, the reactions to Wertham's research in professional, religious, and middlebrow magazines fell within a very narrow range. Few commentators dismissed the work outright, with the vast majority of reviewers noting that they agreed with the book's central findings if not its ultimate conclusions. Yet when the New York Intellectuals, scholars and critics who regarded themselves as the leading thinkers of the day, treated the book, they were more noticeably split on the work, and the vast majority of the opinion came down in opposition to Wertham despite the fact that he so clearly drew on critical presuppositions that they had collectively championed for decades.

Interestingly, three New York Intellectuals, Clifton Fadiman, C. Wright Mills, and Gilbert Seldes, who were most often at odds with the group as a whole were most supportive of Wertham's work. In choosing *Seduction of the Innocent* as an alternate selection of the Book-of-the-Month Club, Fadiman called it "the most shocking book to appear in this country since Upton Sinclair's *The Jungle*" (Gilbert 1986:104). The Book-of-the-Month Club subsequently declined to circulate Wertham's book, however, creating a scandal that he maintained had been engineered by his opponents. The club withdrew the book after distribution contracts had been signed because officials feared becoming involved in a lawsuit should the aggressive comic book industry opt to launch one (Wertham 1954f).

Seldes, long the most active advocate of the popular arts in the New York Intellectuals circle, found little to support in writing about comic books and their adult readers in the early 1950s. On a 14 May 1950 WNEW broadcast, Seldes (1950) sarcastically suggested that comic books should become the compulsory curriculum of American schools and that readers of Dickens should be severely punished. Seldes's argument stemmed from the finding that children could be cured of bad habits by forcing them to engage in that habit continuously until they tired of it, something that he hoped would cure American children of this particular interest. Seldes's 1951 book, *The Great Audience,* traced a history of anti-comic-book concern from Sterling North to Fredric Wertham. Seldes bemoaned the fact that "year after year Dr. Fredric Wertham brings forth panels showing new ugliness and sadistic atrocities; year after year his testimony is brushed aside as extravagant and out of date" (1957:91).

Mills subsequently matched Seldes's pre-*Seduction* support for Wertham's research project, praising the book in the *New York Times Book Review* for its "careful observations and sober reflections" and his "most commendable service to the public" (1954:20). Mills suggested that "any careful reader" would agree with Wertham's findings and that the questions that he raised should be the subject of further study. Mills's support of Wertham, who had been quoted approvingly on another topic in Mills's *White Collar* (1951:xi), may have resulted from their ongoing dedication to processes of social change in the 1950s, a dedication that many other critics had abandoned while adopting the politics of the postwar cultural consensus. Nonetheless, Mills was very supportive of Wertham and his work and wrote a brief note to him following the book's publication that read "Good luck: Hope you're read widely" (Gilbert 1986:103). These commentaries, however, would be the exceptions that proved the rule as far as the New York Intellectuals and Wertham were concerned, as other commentators cast a much more skeptical eye over his work.

Norbert Muhlen, writing in the influential journal *Commentary,* was probably the first of the New York Intellectuals specifically to address Wertham's work on comics. Muhlen's article, "Comic Books and Other Horrors: Prep School for Totalitarian Society?" (1949), combined many of the traditional postwar concerns about mass culture into a single article with specific reference to comics. Muhlen noted that the comic book was the least inhibited of all mass-cultural forms and that, as a consequence, it had become dedicated to "dehumanizing violence" (81). Characterizing the situation as "an American nightmare" (82), Muhlen noted that scientists had weighed in both for and against the comic book, leading to what he termed "a civil war among psychiatrists" (83). After assessing the charges made by both sides, Muhlen conceded that he remained unconvinced that, despite their obvious aesthetic defects, comics had demonstrably negative effects on their readers. Citing Wertham's earlier insistence on the complex causation of criminality in *Dark Legend,* Muhlen suggested that Wertham had become a monocausationist and betrayed his earlier writing (84).

Muhlen argued instead that comic books did not cause juvenile delinquency and offered the possibility that comics and juvenile delinquency might in fact stem from the same common root. This, of course, closely resembled the argument that Wertham asserted, but was at odds with the caricature of Wertham's argument often presented by his critics. Muhlen further approximated Wertham's arguments in suggesting that comic books were a child's education into violence and that the heroes of many comics were themselves totalitarian (85). Muhlen's closing comments were a distillation of general anti-mass-culture sentiment directed at comics. He suggested that the form was leading to the "robotization of the individual" similar to what had occurred in Germany and Russia (87). Thus, while Muhlen rejected Wertham's suggestion that comic books led to juvenile delinquency, Muhlen did believe that they were leading toward "an authoritarian rather than a democratic society" (87). Muhlen's very marginal distinctions between his beliefs and those of Wertham demonstrate both the degree to which the two writers drew on common assumptions about the place and effect of mass culture in the postwar period and the New York Intellectuals' need to stake out a unique position on cultural questions so they would not be accused of simply reiterating other people's arguments even in instances when distinctions among positions were almost negligible.

Muhlen again addressed Wertham's work following the release of *Seduction of the Innocent.* In a review for the *New Leader,* Muhlen characterized Wertham as a man who had long "crusaded for censorship and suppression of this type of juvenile literature." Muhlen's comments on the book were highly contradictory. On the one hand he called it "a repetitious, rambling, rhetorical staccato" (26) and condemned its reliance on alarmist generalities rather than facts and figures. On the other hand, Muhlen insisted that Wertham was generally right about what he had to say and that the dangers of comic books should not be underestimated. The key to this agreeing disagreement seemed to reside in Wertham's politics, which were completely at odds with the neoconservative tendencies of the postwar New York Intellectuals. Muhlen's review began on a point that no other review of the book even mentioned—Wertham's comments on Eastern European nations, including East Germany and the Soviet Union. Muhlen spent almost a quarter of his review on the question of Wertham's softness on these countries and the absence of crime comic books in that part of the world. For Muhlen, this provided evidence that Wertham was a completely unreliable commentator. Muhlen was skeptical of Wertham's attack on "Big Business interests" and contended that Wertham's critique on this front was misguided. Nonetheless, because of the New York Intellectuals' aesthetic disposition, Muhlen seemingly could not endorse comic books even as he disparaged Wertham. To this end, he wrote, "despite the lack of reliable data as to their circulation and influence on youthful minds, . . . it is plain that they depict a society in which the strong rule and right lies with the man who is most ruthless (if not sadistic) with his gun—in short, a totalitarian society. They also present a picture of man without faith or forgiveness—in short, an inhuman man" (27). To correct the problem, Muhlen recommended "educating the children against craving these books, and winning them over to other, better reading" (27)—exactly the same recommendation that librarians and other guardians of high culture had traditionally embraced as a cure-all for mass culture. Thus, from the point of view of the New York Intellectuals, Wertham was ultimately correct in his findings but entirely incorrect in the undergirding philosophy, and Wertham's left-leaning politics made his thinking on the comic book question entirely suspect in the eyes of Muhlen and others.

Reuel Denney, David Riesman's collaborator on *The Lonely Crowd*, wrote the *New Republic*'s review of *Seduction of the Innocent*, dismissing both the book and its author. Suggesting that Wertham was a "psychiatrist well known for his popularizing," Denney stated, "arguments from psychological experts are already suspect," thereby negating any claim to authority Wertham might have been able to maintain (1954b:18). Denney further argued that Wertham's theory of meaning creation was oversimplified insofar as it seemed to ascribe unambiguous meanings to images from comic books. Calling Wertham's writing "shop-worn," "high-pitched," "tedious," and "narrow," he criticized the book for failing to make its argument in a scientific fashion (18). In a subsequent response to a letter from Wertham (1954a:22) that corrected a factual matter and remarked on the "bilious" nature of the review, Denney pointed out that the "bile flow" in the review was "stimulated by the doctor's mixture" (1954a:22).

Denney's comments on Wertham were not restricted to the pages of the *New Republic:* Denney also wrote about Wertham at some length in *The Astonished Muse* (1957), arguing that the base idea for all condemnations of mass culture was the belief that it had usurped print, that print had usurped conversation, and that conversation had usurped contemplation (163). He further suggested that people who would replace mass culture with "good literature" were engaged in a form of moral panic. Chief among his examples of this type of thinking was Wertham, whom Denney charged with having "taken advantage of the sense of the 'media crisis' distributed among the older and parental groups to suggest shotgun definitions of the problem and its solution" (164). Denney argued that Wertham had associated comic books and juvenile delinquency "without evidence of any weight" (164). Further, Denney suggested that the audience for this type of panic were those parents who were cultural lowbrows, the least educated, and those who read the least. Finally, according to Denney, even if Wertham was genuinely sensitive to a real problem and even if his facts were true but poorly documented, he bore responsibility for introducing into discussions of the media a number of false assumptions because he had ignored cross-cultural complexities (165).

Other members of the New York Intellectual circle took similar swipes at Wertham throughout the 1950s. In addition to criticism from Leslie Fiedler and Robert Warshow, both of whom took great pains to reject Wertham's writings on culture and politics, Wertham was mentioned time and again in Bernard Rosenberg and David Manning White's volume, *Mass Culture.* Ernest Van Den Haag, for instance, snidely referred to *Seduction of the Innocent*'s tendency to utilize traditional "common sense" as psychological insight and nastily dismissed the book's political concerns: "Dr. Wertham in dressing Mom up as a psychiatrist also used some para-Marxist clichés from the attic" (1957:530). White similarly dismissed Wertham out of hand with the image of him "frightening the wits out of the Parent-Teachers Association of Scarsdale with his oversimplified message" (1957:13).

Wertham, it seems, was everywhere that the New York Intellectuals believed that they should be. As late as 1960, Daniel Bell still felt compelled to respond to Wertham's concerns about the relationship between comic books and juvenile delinquency. Arguing that juvenile delinquency was not on the rise in the 1950s but had been decreasing, Bell cited Wertham's findings on the "undeniably gory content of comic books" but dismissed them almost without comment, explaining, "comics may simply lead a child to escape from reality and to deaden his feelings about the brutality in the world" (1960:145). As with Muhlen, this was a narrow distinction because Wertham too argued that "undeniably gory content" of comics deadened a reader's feelings about brutality—indeed, that was one of his major claims. These responses clearly demonstrate, therefore, how the New York Intellectuals' commentaries failed to actively engage Wertham's arguments and instead rested on a rebuttal of a caricature that the New Yorkers themselves had constructed. The New York Intellectuals' most common attack on Wertham was to agree with his most basic premises regarding the inherently damaging qualities of mass culture but to dismiss his conclusions as unsupported by the data while generating no counterevidence for their assertions. The fact that the majority of the New York Intellectuals forcefully disagreed with Wertham and his findings caused little concern among the public. As the enthusiastic reception in the rest of the press demonstrated, *Seduction of the Innocent* had considerable impact in shaping the debate about comic books, even having its own demonstrable effects.

Seduction of the Innocent was released to the public on 19 April 1954, three days ahead of its planned publication date. At the same time, the Senate Subcommittee on Juvenile Delinquency, chaired by Senator Robert Hendrickson (Republican–New Jersey), which had been established 27 April 1953, was investigating the mass media's role as a contributing factor in youth crime. That the subcommittee's hearings on comic books virtually coincided with the publication of the book ensured a high visibility for both and made Wertham's work crucial to the study of the relationship between mass culture and juvenile delinquency. Wertham had criticized the subcommittee's earlier efforts in *Seduction of the Innocent*, dismissing Tennessee Senator Estes Kefauver, the ranking Democrat on the committee and author of its 1955 report, for his failure to become better informed on the comic book issue (1954i:346). This dismissal stemmed from Wertham's falling out with Kefauver after the 1950 Senate investigation of comic books with which Wertham had refused to cooperate once it became clear to him that no serious investigation of the medium was planned. In a letter to Arthur Freund, Wertham termed the 1950 Kefauver report "the greatest advertisement the crime comic book industry has had to date" (Wertham 1951), and Wertham's criticisms of the senator continued over the years. Nonetheless, when the subcommittee resumed its investigation into comic books on 21 and 22 April 1954 in New York, Wertham was one of the most notable experts called.

Wertham testified on the afternoon of 21 April 1954, the day before hearings opened to investigate Senator Joseph McCarthy's charges that communists had infiltrated the U.S. Army. His opening remarks and his responses to questions from the senators and the counsel for the subcommittee essentially reiterated his charges from *Seduction of the Innocent*, and Wertham stated that he would repeat any portion of that text under oath since every word was true (U.S. Senate 1954:877). After his statement of credentials and an explanation of his methodology, Wertham bluntly declared his belief that comic books were not the sole cause of youth crime: "nobody would claim comic books alone are the cause of juvenile delinquency" (871). Furthermore, according to Wertham's testimony, because children with morbid psychological problems were often wrapped up in their own psychic worlds, primarily "normal" children were negatively affected by comic books. This occurred, Wertham argued, by a process of seduction that he suggested dated back to ancient Roman tradition of bread and circuses:

> If you consult, as we have done, the first modern scientific psychologist who lived a long time ago, you will find the answer. That psychologist was St. Augustine. This was long before the comic book era, of course, but he describes in detail how when he was a very, very young man he was in Rome and he saw these very bloody, sadistic spectacles all around him, where the gladiators fought each other with swords and daggers, and he didn't like it. He didn't any part of it.

But there was so much going on and his friends went and finally he went and he noticed, as he expresses it, that he became unconsciously delighted with it and he kept on going.

In other words, he was tempted, he was seduced by this mass appeal, and he went.

I think it is exactly the same thing, if the children see these kinds of things over and over again, they can't go to a dentist, they can't go to a clinic, they can't go to a ward in a hospital, everywhere they see this where women are beaten up, where people are shot and killed, and finally they become, as St. Augustine said, unconsciously delighted. (872)

Wertham's argument about the seductive power of mass culture sat in opposition to the belief that only predisposed children were injured by comic books. He suggested that there was "no more erroneous theory about child behavior than to assume that children must be predisposed to do anything wrong" (875). Instead, he suggested that a number of factors, including comic books, conspired to seduce and betray America's youth and indoctrinate them with corrosive values. To this end, Wertham suggested that the propagandistic value of comic books was so strong that "Hitler was a beginner compared to the comic-book industry. They get the children much younger. They teach them race hatred at the age of 4 before they can read" (880). Faced with this crisis, Wertham repeated his call to isolate the single factor of comic books with national legislation based on the public health ideal that would prohibit the circulation and display of comic books to children under the age of fifteen. Wertham suggested that this type of law would bypass claims of censorship because publishers would remain free to produce material with violent or objectionable content for adult audiences, and children would even be able to see that material if their parents approved: "You see, if a father wants to go to a store and says, 'I have a little boy of seven. He doesn't know how to rape a girl; he doesn't know how to rob a store. Please sell me one of the comic books,' let the man sell him one, but I don't think the boy should be able to go see this rape on the cover and buy the comic book" (878). Wertham's testimony before the Senate subcommittee, therefore, placed his remarks in *Seduction of the Innocent* firmly in the public policy arena, where they stood as a notable benchmark in the history of governmental efforts to investigate the effects of the mass media and mass culture.

Immediately following Wertham came the comments of Bill Gaines, the publisher of EC Comics, noteworthy for their horror comics and for *Mad,* which would later parody Wertham as Frederick Werthless. For the press, Gaines's appearance represented the high point of the first day of the hearings, and his testimony was extensively quoted. Gaines opened by noting that because his father had started the modern comic book industry and because he personally had published the first horror comic book, he was the man to blame if blame were to be cast. However, he saw the comic book controversy entirely in terms of taste. Arguing that his company and others had provided millions of hours of entertainment for children, he suggested, "some may not like [comics]. That is a matter of personal taste. It would be just as difficult to explain the harmless thrill of a horror story to a Dr. Wertham as it would be to explain the sublimity of love to a frigid old maid" (U.S. Senate 1954:883).

Gaines defended a number of the comics stories that had been introduced into evidence earlier in the day by the subcommittee's executive director, Richard Clendenen, and by Wertham. After arguing that one of the EC stories that Wertham had condemned as racist actually sent an antiracist message to readers, Gaines was asked why he believed comics could send positive but not negative messages to readers. He responded by contending that there was no such thing as an unintentional message in comics: "when we write a story with a message, it is deliberately written in such a way that the message, as I say, is spelled out carefully in the captions. The preaching, if you want to call it, is spelled out carefully in the captions" (885). When pressed on the question of whether a foster child might experience fears or anxieties after reading a story in which foster parents were revealed to be werewolves, Gaines dismissed the possibility because "none of the captions said anything like 'If you are unhappy with your stepmother, shoot her'" (885). The most controversial aspect of Gaines's testimony came when he was asked what limits he, as a publisher of horror comics, put on what he would circulate to children. He responded that the only limits were those of his own sense of good taste. He was then presented with the cover of the most recent issue of one of his horror comics, which depicted a man with a bloody ax holding a severed woman's head and asked if that was in good taste. The subsequent exchange was quoted on the front page of the *New York Times* as well as in *Time, Newsweek,* and elsewhere (Kihss 1954a; "Horror Comics" 1954; "Are Comics Horrible? " 1954):

> **SENATOR KEFAUVER:** Do you think that is in good taste?
> **MR. GAINES:** Yes, sir; I do, for the cover of a horror comic. A cover in bad taste, for example, might be defined as holding the head a little higher so that the neck could be seen dripping blood from it and moving the body over a little further so that the neck of the body could be seen to be bloody.
> **SENATOR KEFAUVER:** You have blood coming out of her mouth.
> **MR. GAINES:** A little. (887)

The negative reaction to this particular exchange harmed the comic book defenders as much or more than anything that Wertham testified to, especially as it seemed to prove that comics publishers were out of touch with the concerns of the day. Gaines's testimony graphically reinforced Wertham's contentions that publishers were venally seeking to profit by peddling lurid material to children. Insofar as the first day's hearings would be reduced in the press coverage to an argument between Wertham and Gaines, it is difficult to imagine how the comic book industry could have profited in any way from the experience.

Other testimony presented by the twenty-two witnesses who came before the subcommittee did little to shore up the position of the comic book industry. Henry Schultz of the ACMP, for instance, was forced to admit that his organization's "seal has lost its imprint and its value in many ways" (U.S. Senate 1954:868). Testifying to rebut the arguments of Wertham and Harris Peck, both of whom suggested that comic books had a negative effect on readers, were Lauretta Bender and Gunnar Dybwad, executive director of the CSA. Asked if comics had negative effects, Dybwad refused to take a stand, arguing that widespread distribution of mass culture was symptomatic of larger problems in society and suggesting that he had not seen the clinical evidence to justify any claim either way (Nyberg 1998:75). Bender called horror comics "unspeakably silly" and suggested that children laughed at them and, moreover, that a child would not read any comic that caused him or her anxiety (Nyberg 1998:75). The testimony of Dybwad and

Bender was discredited, however, by Kefauver, who attacked the CSA for failing to disclose the fact that three of its members were, as Wertham had charged, paid consultants to the comic book industry: "You have deceived the public . . . by putting out advice to parents with the principal research and writing done by people in the pay of publishers, and you do not divulge these facts" ("Horror Comics" 1954:78). He went on to charge that the CSA had intentionally minimized the comic book problem by promoting industrial self-regulation and parental supervision as curatives in the place of legislation (Kihss 1954b:29).

Representatives of comic book publishers and the National Cartoonists Society put up little defense of the industry generally, and their comments tended to support Wertham's arguments, particularly as they pertained to mass culture. *Pogo* creator and society president Walt Kelly testified on behalf of newspaper comic strip artists, saying that while the organization opposed any legislative action with regard to comic books they did, nonetheless, recognize "the great danger of the magazines in question" (U.S. Senate 1954:893). Kelly insisted on a firm distinction between the highly censored and positive comic strip and the more dangerous and uncontrolled comic books. *Steve Canyon* creator Milton Caniff, appearing alongside Kelly, reinforced this opposition when he suggested that the two men were not attempting "to debate with Dr. Wertham, whose opinion we value very highly" but rather to make the point that newspaper strips served the public good through their tendency to entertain and to inform (U.S. Senate 1954:896). Kelly and Caniff resorted to a high/low split in comics formats by insisting on a clear distinction between the comic strip and comic book.

Helen Meyer of Dell Comics, then the largest publisher in the industry, furthered the high/low distinction within comic books when she drew a division between the work that her company published and that of companies like Gaines's EC. Meyer pointed out that Dell had never published crime or horror comics and was anxious to publicize that fact lest an overly broad anti-comic-book brush tar the company. She noted that Dell had refused to join the ACMP because she believed that that organization simply wished to use good publishers such as Dell as "an umbrella for the crime comic publishers," and she concluded, "we abhor horror and crime comics. We would like to see them out of the picture because it taints us" (Nyberg 1998:77). The hearings, therefore, firmly and very publicly reinforced the comic book's existing place within the general framework of postwar concerns about the effects of mass culture. David Park has correctly observed that in this regard, the hearings constituted a "symbolic display, a show trial" that addressed issues of taste more concretely than it did issues of harm (260). Wertham forcefully equated comic books and mass culture and then saw his argument buttressed from within the industry by Kelly, Caniff, and Meyer. Further, his opponents were either discredited as biased or were hoist on their own petards, as was the case with Gaines, thereby helping to prove to the public the merits of Wertham's long-standing charges. Faced with such a poor performance at the hearings, the comic book industry scrambled to make changes before the subcommittee could issue a negative report.

Editorial codes were not new in the field of comics. National, Dell, and Fawcett had had codes since the beginning of the 1940s, and the ACMP code had applied to about one-third of all comics publishers in the latter portion of that decade and into the 1950s before losing whatever force it had. The new code, however, would be stricter and more inclusive, covering almost all of the industry. On 17 September 1954, the *New York Times* ran a front-page photo of the new comic book "czar," Charles F. Murphy, whom the Times identified as a "vigorous campaigner against juvenile delinquency" who would "administer a code of ethics whereby publishers hope to purge the business of objectionable comics" (Harrison 1954:1). Murphy was to take office as director of the newly formed Comics Magazine Association of America (CMAA) on 1 October. He pledged that horror comics would be immediately eliminated from the industry through what he promised would be the strongest editorial code of any media form. The code would be written and presented to the public by 15 November (25). In the following week, Gaines announced that he was discontinuing the majority of his titles and replacing them with a "clean, clean line" ("Horror on the Newsstands" 1954:77). Gaines's subsequent refusal to join the CMAA was cited as "disturbing" by *America* ("Comic Book 'Czar' " 1954:3), which later termed the code "noble, if a little vague" ("Progress" 1954:114). That code was announced in the first week of November and applied to twenty-four of the twenty-seven existing publishers ("No More" 1954:55). Opting out were EC, Dell, and Gilberton, the publisher of the *Classics Illustrated* line of comic book adaptations of canonical literature. Responding to a comment in *America* that only code-approved comics should be sold to children, Dell's Walter Mitchell explained his company's refusal to participate:

> The reason Dell does not belong to the newly formed group is that, though it applauds the association's worthy objectives to eliminate "horror and terror" comics, it takes exception to the rest of its platform, i.e., merely to regulate (rather than eliminate entirely) love, crime and other comics of questionable nature.
>
> Dell can do much more good by staying out of the new group and by continuing to set a higher standard for the rest of the industry. (1954:308)

Gilberton's refusal stemmed from a similar objection rooted in the company's sense that the material that it published was of a superior quality and thus required no code approval because it relied so heavily on the educating and improving tendencies associated with literature (Sawyer 1987:8). For the majority of the industry, however, the code served to appease parents and magazine distributors. EC eventually joined the CMAA, and the organization deflected the charges made by Wertham and other critics. This was, of course, its single mission. As David Finn, the public relations adviser hired by the comic book industry in 1954, explained in his memoirs, "Public relations efforts to reduce the severity of criticism often disguise rather than reveal the essential conflicts involved. The purpose of such efforts is not to create an atmosphere in which the reforms demanded by critics will be made; it is to find a way to make the smallest possible concessions necessary to end the controversy. Only rarely is there a genuine willingness to face up to the real conflicts involved and to resolve them fairly" (1969:174). Finn acknowledged what many critics, Wertham included, had charged at the time, as concern with comic books abated in the wake of renewed self-regulation and the appearance of change.

While the Comics Code did not entirely end the U.S. debate over comics, it severely curtailed the discussion. Moreover, subsequent comments generally took on a different tone. Critics generally welcomed the advent of the code and appreciated the fact that the industry had taken these steps. Dorothy Barclay, writing in the *New York Times Magazine,* called the code seal of approval "a welcome sign" but warned parents to remain vigilant and to combat the effects of comics reading by providing children with good

books in the place of bad comics (1955:48). The *Christian Century* praised
the code for its challenge to mass culture and for its efforts to raise "the level
of popular taste" ("What About" 1955:389). Still other critics altered their
tone entirely. Humor, for instance, became one of the dominant discursive
modes around the crime comic book now that the question had been effectively settled. *Newsweek* columnist John Lardner argued that comic books
weren't bad but that the wrong people were reading them, and he suggested
that if criminals were learning crime techniques from the comics, as
Wertham argued, then the police needed to learn the same techniques from
the same comic books to thwart crime (1955:58). In England, which was wit-
nessing a tremendous public debate about the importation of American
horror comic books around this same time (Barker 1984), the *Spectator*
ran a contest honoring the best poem about horror comics ("The Boy"
1955:304). This lighthearted approach to the comic book question shows
that comics were no longer regarded as an entirely serious threat to the
nation's youth following the adoption of the Comics Code.

This is not to say, however, that criticism of the comics dissipated
entirely. Indeed, in the first year of the code, sporadic complaints about
comic books still continued to appear. Writing in the *American Mercury*,
Ruth Inglis noted that the *Classics Illustrated* line had gotten gorier in the
wake of its publisher's refusal to join the CMAA and subscribe to the code
(1955:120). Similarly, the *Wilson Library Bulletin* maintained its anti-comic-
books position, rooted as it was in the journal's anti-mass-culture stance.
Noting that the best thing that could be said for comics was that they could
not be proven to be definitively harmful, the *Bulletin* called comic books
"appalling," "odious," "abominable," and "virulent" before again concluding
that the surest way to control comics reading was to expose children to
good books (M.D.L. 1955:651). And, of course, Wertham remained a resolute
critic of the form.

In a postscript to his original anti-comic-book article, Wertham published "It's Still Murder" in the 9 April 1955 issue of the *Saturday Review*.
Subtitled "What Parents Still Don't Know about Comic Books," he renewed
his attack in light of the changes wrought by the Comics Code. He suggested that Kefauver had again betrayed American families by failing to
indict the comic book industry when he authored the subcommittee report
in early 1955 (1955a:11). Furthermore, the subcommittee had ultimately

endorsed the point of view that only predisposed children were affected by comic books, a decision that angered Wertham. He outlined his specific objections to the Comics Code and cited a number of transgressions that he had found in code-approved comics. Wertham concluded, "at present it is far safer for a mother to let her child have a comic book without a seal of approval than one with such a seal. If comic books, as the industry claims, are the folklore of today, then the codes are the fables" (48).

Wertham also advanced his attack in an article in *Religious Education* (1954b) in which he pointed out that the code administrator, Murphy, was a former crime comics publisher, having released titles such as *Tales of Horror* that emphasized "salaciously, suggestively drawn girls" (404). Furthermore, Wertham noted that Murphy was paid by the comics publishers and consequently that the independence of his office was seriously in doubt because exactly the same group of publishers who had previously run the failed ACMP would run the CMAA. Wertham disagreed with the code on straightforward, fundamental grounds:

> The comics publishers have had "codes" and "self-censorship" before, announced with great fanfare,—but never achieving anything except to delude some of the public into thinking something was being done, and that consequently *they* didn't have to bother about it any more. Whenever people begin to show signs of doing something themselves about controlling crime comics, the publishers come out with a "code" or something to divert attention, and avert action. You do not need a code to leave out harmful ingredients from comic books. All you need is to *do* it. All this talk about "codes" is just misleading. (405)

Despite his disapproval, however, the code endured and ultimately quelled the comic book controversy.

At the 1956 National Mass Media Awards sponsored by the Thomas Edison Foundation, comic books were honored for the first time alongside other media—radio, film, and television—for contributing to the nation's culture. Ironically, no code-approved comics were honored as Dell and Gilberton swept the awards, but the industry's ongoing self-regulation was nonetheless applauded as a productive step forward ("First Comic" 1956).

Wertham's concerns about crime comic books persisted, although he voiced those concerns far less frequently throughout the 1960s as he moved on to new projects. In a 1967 letter to the *New Statesman* regarding its review of Jules Feiffer's *The Great Comic Book Heroes,* Wertham argued that crime comic books remained important to the American comic book industry and that contemporary war comics were an "orgy of racism" (Wertham 1967). Nonetheless, by this time, general concerns about the effects of comic books on young readers had largely been displaced by a new medium that threatened an even more pernicious influence: television.

By 1960, discussions of comic books had all but disappeared from both the national media and professional journals. Writing in the *Elementary School Journal* in 1960, Robert Emans noted, "the controversy has apparently subsided. At least, it is not being aired in the nation's magazines. Little that now appears on the subject has the emotionality of the past" (1960:253). Although one of the reasons for this change was certainly the fact that the Comics Code continued to strongly influence the nation's comics publishers, another reason seems obvious as well. As early as 1950, critics had compared comic books and television as the mutually destructive twins of juvenile-targeted mass culture. Barclay (1950), for instance, noted that studies showed that children stopped reading comic books when their parents bought televisions. She suggested that both forms be replaced by good books.

In 1952 Paul Witty, who had conducted early effects research on comic books, warned parents about television's rapid growth and the probability that it constituted an "even greater problem" (1952:50). Three years later, he suggested that television had taken over as children's favorite leisure activity, and he warned that excessive television viewing correlated to low academic attainment (1955:18), although he had previously suggested that no such connection existed between comic books and scholasticism. These comments perpetuated traditional thinking about mass culture in the Cold War. Therefore, the rise of television in the late 1950s and 1960s clearly displaced comic books, not only as a form of entertainment for children but also as a source for concern among parents and cultural commentators. The Senate subcommittee that had investigated comic books in 1954 investigated television later that year, launching one of the first significant governmental forays into the study of the effects of television. In many ways, those studies helped lead to the development of the media-effects research paradigm as it has developed in the field of communication studies. By examining those studies in detail, the continuity between the anti-comic-book movement and the study of television effects becomes evident, as do the ways in that each grew out of a larger concern with mass culture generally.

CHAPTER FIVE
TELEVISION AND MEDIA EFFECTS

In his introduction to the 1949 edition of Joseph Klapper's influential study, *The Effects of Mass Communication,* Paul Lazarsfeld speculated about why the study of media effects was not yet a well-established academic specialization. For Lazarsfeld, the problem with the study of media effects was methodological. Where media effects had previously been debated by public intellectuals assured of the untested validity of their theses, the terrain now belonged to researchers trained in the social sciences who remained unconvinced. About media effects, therefore, Lazarsfeld suggested, "the main difficulty lies in formulating the problem correctly. For the trouble started exactly when empirical research stepped in where once the social philosopher had reigned supreme. To the latter there was never any doubt that first the orator and then the newspaper and now television are social forces of great power" (1949:1–2).

The shift that Lazarsfeld described was evident in early research by sociologists and communications scholars into comic books. Research undertaken by Katherine Wolf and Marjorie Fiske of Lazarsfeld's Bureau for Applied Social Research at Columbia University stressed, in contrast to Fredric Wertham's approach, children's individual and developmental needs. In "The Children Talk about Comics," Wolf and Fiske argued that "comics satisfy a real developmental need in normal children and are harmful only for children who are already maladjusted and susceptible to harm" (1949:50). Having conducted one-hour interviews with 104 children between the ages of seven and seventeen, Wolf and Fiske classified reader preferences along an age-based schema. They then determined the needs that they found to be satisfied by comic books in each age group. More importantly, however, the authors suggested that so-called normal children ultimately outgrew their interest in comic books while "maladjusted" children fixated on the medium. The source of maladjustment was not comics, however, but the family. Wolf and Fiske proposed that psychological or social maladjustment was present in children before they turned to comics: "The possible dangerous effects of comics on fans must not be overestimated. The child's problems existed before he became a fan, and the comics came along to relieve him" (35).

These findings, published in the Lazarsfeld and Stanton–edited volume *Communications Research, 1948–1949*, were far removed from those of Wertham, whose first comments on comic books appeared at almost exactly the same time. The distance between Wolf and Fiske's conception of a needs-satisfying media industry and Wertham's articulation of a debasing and corrupting culture delimited the postwar difference between empirically trained social scientists and what Lazarsfeld termed "social philosophers." That difference is the subject of this chapter and can best be illustrated by shifting the point of reference to the debate over television that emerged in the early 1950s and that has continued more or less to this day. Shifting the terrain from comic books to television highlights the transition from an aesthetic to an empirical model in the study of the mass media and popular culture. With the exception of Wolf and Fiske, comic books were rarely studied from research perspectives specifically rooted in the social sciences, and the dominant media-effects paradigm was little utilized in relation to discussions of the form. Social science researchers in the mid-1950s, conversely, quickly took up television as it emerged as the leading cause of concern in the domain of mass communication. In altering the object of study, therefore, research methods and approaches were also realigned. Just as comic books were rarely read through the specific lens of the media-effects paradigm, television was seldom regarded from any other perspective.

Concern about the influence of comic books on young readers dissipated as the critique of mass culture shifted with the coincidental rise of television and of empirically grounded social science mass media research in the postwar period. However, the media-effects paradigm that developed from the study of television was supported by an assumption rooted in preexisting critiques developed by Lazarsfeld's "social philosophers." They held that mass culture was atomizing and narcotizing and further that television represented its nadir. Television, as Patrick Brantlinger notes, is the mass medium that took the abolition of Walter Benjamin's notion of the "aura" of older cultural forms to its absolute limit (1983:249). It should come as no surprise, therefore, to discover television at the apotheosis of the anti-mass-culture critique.

Despite nostalgic depictions of the 1950s as television's golden age, the new medium clearly was regarded with the same sorts of apprehension and suspicion as previous mass cultural forms had been. In a widely quoted 1949 *Saturday Review* article, for instance, Norman Cousins wrote about television in much the same way that Wertham wrote about comic books. In fact, Cousins equated the two media when he argued that "the terror comic strips were bad enough, but they are rapidly on the way to playing squeaky second fiddles to television as prime movers in juvenile misconduct and delinquency" (1953:69). Cousins suggested that television was worse than comics because television was endorsed by parents, whereas comic books were not. Moreover, he invoked mass culture's threat to society when he bemoaned the perception that television had forsaken its democratic potential. What had displaced that potential, Cousins suggested, was "an invasion against good taste as no other communications medium has known," featuring a "mass-produced series of plodding stereotypes and low-quality programs" (70).

The *New York Times* television editor, Jack Gould, voiced similar sentiments. He argued that "television is getting pretty bad. The high hopes for video that were held by so many are vanishing before our eyes. The medium is heading hell-bent for the rut of innocuity, mediocrity and sameness that made a drab if blatant jukebox of radio" (1953:71). The common thread of these arguments against television are the themes that ran through all condemnations of twentieth-century mass culture: a belief that any new medium is crassly commercial, morally degrading, and targeted toward society's lowest common denominator. Social science researchers therefore conducted the initial studies of television and its role in American culture in the 1950s in the midst of a condemning and judgmental discursive field that had a great deal in common with the traditional critiques of mass culture advanced by literary critics and public intellectuals.

It should come as no surprise that Wertham was heavily involved in the debate about television as it came to eclipse concern over comic books in the late 1950s and into the 1960s. In 1959, Wertham and his publishing agent, James Street, began shopping a book manuscript that represented the culmination of the author's thinking on the intersection of youth, violence, and the mass media. "The War against Children" was structured almost identically to *Seduction of the Innocent,* and Wertham's conclusions strikingly resembled those drawn about comic books in the earlier volume. Wertham's optimism about television had waned significantly since he had first praised its "glorious future" in *Seduction of the Innocent.* In December of that year McGraw-Hill Books rejected the initial draft manuscript on the grounds that the book did not go far enough into the subject. The publisher requested a significant rewrite of the text, increasing the number of case studies cited, changing the organization and the writing style, and including more ideas for parents concerned about their children's mental health. Wertham spent three months restructuring the work and made a deal to excerpt it in the *Ladies' Home Journal,* drawing significant attention to the book in advance of publication. Ultimately, however, McGraw-Hill declined the book in March 1960, when the company's sales department indicated that the furor that had accompanied the November 1959 appearance of television quiz show cheater Charles Van Doren in front of the House Committee on Interstate and Foreign Commerce had exhausted the public's interest in the topic.

When McGraw-Hill rejected the manuscript, Wertham's agent turned to a number of other publishers, at least three more of whom declined the book during the summer of 1960. Rinehart, which had published *Seduction of the Innocent* and had more recently merged with Henry Holt, believed that the book would not be profitable. The publisher primarily feared that it would duplicate the success and nonsuccess of *Seduction of the Innocent.* That book had received more than a thousand positive reviews in the American press but sold few copies since it was so well discussed that people felt that they had no need to read it. Little, Brown declined the book because it would not be a "fence-buster" given that the subject had been so much discussed in recent years. Dutton suggested that the book dealt with an important area of public concern but that Wertham had not treated the subject with complete logic and effectiveness.

Whatever the reasons, Wertham's book never found a publisher. While he did publish much of his argument in popular magazines, newspapers, and scholarly journals over the course of the next half decade, the culmination of his thinking on media effects never received the public airing for which he might have wished. In that *Seduction of the Innocent* and "The War against Children" are almost identical in most important respects, the relative success of the former and total failure of the latter suggests that a sea change had occurred in the intervening six years. That change was the institutionalization of the media-effects paradigm by social-science-trained communications scholars working at U.S. universities. The field of mass communication research initially established itself as a unique tradition in the postwar period by narrowing its methodological scope and excluding competing and contradictory voices and approaches from the field. Wertham and the clinical method were one such exclusion.

Despite its lack of public exposure, Wertham's unpublished manuscript sheds a great deal of light on his thinking about media effects, and his published commentaries on television violence represent one road not taken in the development of American media-effects scholarship. In the 150-page text, Wertham outlined a thoroughgoing critique of the dominant communications paradigm that existed at that time, an alternative research paradigm, an analysis of the situation created by television, and a call to arms. He enumerated a series of charges against quantitative social science methodologies generally and specifically against the findings of the Hilde Himmelweit, A. N. Oppenheim, and Pamela Vince's *Television and the Child*.

Wertham deplored the fact that in the quantitative method, children were not examined but rather simply filled out questionnaires. Wertham suggested that this was "not the way to get true and intimate facts from a child" (1959b:46). He argued that the authors of *Television and the Child* had ignored significant mental health effects in favor of trifling effects such as the "disturbing" or "frightening" impact of television. He complained that the most important group of children, those under the age of eleven, had not been studied at all. Further, he alleged, the report was particularly misleading with regard to the effect on children of violence in Western programs: *Television and the Child*

> says that this violence is abstract and stylized and therefore innocuous and "readily acceptable." This pronouncement illustrates the difference between

the adult's offhand acceptance of what he *thinks* the child gets from television and the actual comprehension or lack of it by the child. It is a typical
adult response, and is not how the children see it. For example, the report
says that if the victim who has been shot clutches at his stomach, that
merely means that a shot has been fired from the front. Many children have
told me what it means to *them:* that the man is shot in the stomach because
that is one of the places where it hurts most." (47)

Wertham concluded that *Television and the Child* was an "industry-centered
rather than child-centered" report that had been designed and executed to
defend the television industry from criticism without addressing the actual
question of media effects. The book did so primarily through the adoption
of inadequate social-scientific models that inverted the social relations of
power.

   Throughout his manuscript, Wertham decried those media and communications experts who claimed that televisual violence caused no harm.
He noted that this was not a new argument and that similar claims had been
made to refute suggestions that poverty, disturbed families, poor teachers'
pay, crime comic books, unemployment, and war were factors in the development of juvenile delinquency. By rejecting the notion that these factors
influenced childhood development, Wertham argued that experts were
turning children into scapegoats: "Parents have been falsely assured that, in
Marya Mannes' words, crime and violence have nothing to do with crime and
violence. They are being told again and again that the only thing important
is what goes on in the child himself, and that everything depends on how he
was before he ever looked at television. In reality far more important is
what television was before the child ever looked and what ingredients of
sadism and brutality were put into it. What we are using as a scapegoat is
the child" (1959b:114).

   This tendency appeared most directly in the argument that only disturbed
or maladjusted children were susceptible. Wertham turned the tables on them
somewhat by challenging the methodological value of such conclusions
and demanding empirical proof. He countered that psychiatric evaluation
had proven that all children were impressionable and therefore susceptible
to media influence. By coupling media effects with a latent moralizing tendency on mass culture, Wertham highlighted a fundamental contradiction

in the claim that constructive or educational programs on television gave children constructive ideas but that destructive programs had no impact: "Children from good homes are supposed to be good, so that what they see on the screen does not disturb them. Children from bad homes are disturbed, so what they see on the screen makes no difference—if they were not influenced by that they would be influenced by something else" (117). This circular reasoning, Wertham argued, represented a fundamental stumbling block in the proper understanding of the individual child by bracketing social problems and perpetuating a divide between the "good society" and the bad that was a hallmark of the mass culture critics. Drawing yet again on his favorite metaphor from the health sciences, Wertham suggested that it was incumbent on society to try to protect all children from harm: "This disposes of the often heard claim that since so many children watch the screen without being demonstrably affected by it, there is no justification for believing that any children are affected. If physicians were to use that argument, medicine would be in a sad state. The vast majority of people who harbor the tubercle bacillus never get tuberculosis. Should we therefore disregard the existence of the tubercle bacillus?" (120). Thus, drawing on his experience as a medical practitioner, Wertham rejected the philosophical underpinnings of the dominant media-effects paradigm at the level of method and interpretation. In its place he proposed an entirely different analysis of media impact rooted in clinical psychiatry and populist social reform.

Wertham maintained that his clinical approach to the question of media effects had been producing results since 1949 and was best exemplified by his work on comic books in *Seduction of the Innocent*. In "The War against Children," Wertham addressed criticisms of his method—that it was unscientific because of the absence of control groups—by arguing that medical psychiatry foregrounds the sifting of stimuli in a dynamic psychological situation but that it does not do so with the "mathematical exactness and absolute precision" that is a requirement of some empiricists' narrow definition of science. With characteristic sarcasm, Wertham contended, "if we waited for that in action, in the study of human relations, we would still be living in caves. We could not even say with certainty that it is bad to covet your neighbor's wife. Nobody has ever undertaken a study on controlled cases" (1959b:51). Citing the work of C. Wright Mills, Wertham contended that really creative findings were not derived from quantitative statistical treatments of research questions. In Wertham's view, the media-effects debate needed careful methods of examination and rigorous clinical research. Statistical analyses of so-called objective tests were suspect on the one hand because they allowed nonstatistical factors to enter when the data were analyzed and on the other hand because they were only extensions of clinical examinations.

Wertham's arguments about the effect of television viewing on children were rooted generally in his work as a clinical psychiatrist and specifically in his work at the Harlem-based Lafargue Clinic. Nonetheless, he situated his findings within the context of work by scholars whom he admired. Thus, his unpublished television manuscript included approving references to Gilbert Seldes's suggestion that television was as powerful an influence on the development of children as schools were (1959b:57). He also drew on Dallas Smythe's research on the number of violent acts shown on television each broadcast day (14). Indeed, Wertham's arguments about television stemmed from the combination of the work of these scholars insofar as he was concerned with the power of television to shape young minds and the content of broadcasters' messages.

In the simplest terms, Wertham concluded that "screen violence conditions children to an attitude of violence" (62) through a subtle general process that gradually lowered the child's resistance so that other social factors, such as overprotection, could become pathogenic. Although to this day he has been routinely accused of exemplifying a monocausationist approach to the study of delinquency, Wertham was quite clear throughout "The War against Children" that delinquency was a complex social phenomenon, what he termed "a tapestry with many strands" (82). Television viewing did not cause delinquency or maladjustment but contributed to the situation in a number of significant ways, including the creation of an intellectual, moral, and/or sexual confusion about pleasure, reality, and fantasy (87) and the retardation of ethical development (96).

On this latter point, Wertham was clear that the root problem was not simply violence but the combination of violence and materialism represented by American commercial broadcasting. He argued that television advertising itself was designed to create an ethical problem in children by addressing them not as future producers but as current consumers: "In many homes there is a contest between family ethics and screen ethics. Parents must make up their minds whether they want to teach their children honesty or that one cereal is really much more nourishing than another brand, one filter cigarette so much safer than another, or one cosmetic a miracle above all others" (107). Thus, television placed children in an ethical bind between violence and manipulative consumption, a situation in which ethical confusion was twice confounded.

The net impact of television, therefore, was to heighten the most negative values that existed in contemporary society and to direct them at the audience least prepared to negotiate them. As Wertham summarized the situation, "At present adults blame the children if they are fascinated by bad programs. The industry blames the parents, telling them they can always turn off the set if they want to. The lawgivers do not accept the responsibility but ask the industry to regulate itself. It is a merry-go-round of irresponsibility" (145). Key to this conception were the communications scholars who argued a null inference theory of media effects. By providing the scientific foundation for the scapegoating of children, social scientific media-effects researchers helped drive a vicious circle that limited the long-term social utility of communications research generally.

Wertham's critique of violence on television began to emerge fully to the public only in the 1960s in the wake of his failure to find a book publisher. In a February 1960 *Ladies' Home Journal* article excerpted from the book manuscript, Wertham addressed what he cited as the ten most-frequently-asked questions about the effects of media violence. He continued his reasoning from *Seduction of the Innocent* and argued that the visual mass media were "not decisive or fundamental" causes of juvenile delinquency; however, they did play a "contributing part in the final tragedy" (1960:166). The real effect of mass media violence came in the form of a "subtle general conditioning" to violence, and researchers who insisted on blaming the family for delinquency while utterly failing to consider broader social influences made little progress in correcting the situation (166). On this point, Wertham firmly disagreed with the dominant hypothesis advanced by sociological media-effects research that only "maladjusted" or "predisposed" children were affected by television violence. He insisted that "*all* children are impressionable and therefore susceptible" (168). Wertham noted that medical science could not accurately predict which children exposed in an epidemic would develop the illness and which would remain well, but science had agreed therefore on the necessity to protect all children (170). A similar approach should be taken to address media violence.

In the years that followed, Wertham reiterated this argument on a number of occasions and in increasingly more mainstream venues. Writing again in the *Ladies' Home Journal* in August 1961, he argued that the mass media stimulated sex crimes, especially when sadism was present in pornography (1961:89). He repeated his belief that it was impossible to predict which children would be adversely affected by media violence in a 1962 letter to the *New York Times:* "in my psychiatric opinion, many children—whom we cannot identify beforehand—do not get over the education for brutality and violence with which we now so plentifully supply them" (1962a:28).

In another *New York Times* article published four years later, Wertham argued that television coverage of the war in Vietnam was hardening Americans to the war, not turning them against it. Suggesting that the deluge of media violence had made the war coverage look tame by comparison, he argued that fictional television violence and war reporting had begun to blend and strip the latter of its importance and impact. Television, Wertham argued, was no longer the best hope for human communication but rather had become a "vast machinery of hate" in which Americans viewed their enemies and potential enemies only in the worst possible light. Developing the argument he had made earlier in the year in *A Sign for Cain,* Wertham maintained that communication was the opposite of violence and that when people could not communicate with each other, they could not know one another. Such a situation inevitably led to hatred and violence (1966a:23).

Wertham's commentaries on media violence in the 1960s therefore clearly represented an extension of his book-length studies *A Sign for Cain* and *Seduction of the Innocent,* both of which grew out of his particular experiences as a psychiatrist and his strong belief in the clinical research methodology and the necessity of a public health approach to the treatment of violence at both the personal and international levels. This background ultimately would shape the way in which Wertham responded to the rise of a nonclinical social scientific media-effects tradition in the field of mass communication research.

The development of the media-effects paradigm in the study of mass communication and popular culture had at its roots the progressive and pragmatic dimensions of American empirical sociology. This intellectual project found its greatest expression in the Chicago School of Sociology in the first decades of the twentieth century, characterized by the work of researchers such as Robert Park, Charles Horton Cooley, John Dewey, and George Herbert Mead. Their studies of city-based microphenomena such as youth gangs came to define early American sociology as focused on research that held potentially ameliorative tendencies. Park, whose only book examined the role of the immigrant press in the adjustment of new populations, foregrounded the study of mass communication in sociology and has been called the first real theorist of the mass media (Rogers 1994:189). Park's involvement with the Payne Fund studies on the effects of motion pictures on youth, the first large-scale social science study of the mass media's impact on behavior and attitudes, certainly supports this claim.

The Payne Fund studies rested on the assumption that motion pictures were a moral problem that could be ameliorated by sociological and scientific intervention. The studies, therefore, were undertaken in an intellectual atmosphere influenced by oppositions between elite and mass culture that characterized the first half of the twentieth century. Indeed, the conclusions were presented in such a way as to reinforce the period's ongoing anti-mass-culture moralizing. W. W. Charters reported the Payne Fund studies' findings in a single volume, *Motion Pictures and Youth: A Summary*. Charters broke down the findings into two broad groupings: researchers who studied film content and attendance, and researchers broadly focused on media effects (1933:5). The effects researchers addressed their work to the influence of films on behavior and conduct, suggesting that a correspondence existed between movies and behavior. Children who were influenced by movies, he argued, were "maladjusted" before entering the theater (1933:16).

Nonetheless, the Payne Fund researchers were unwilling to place the blame entirely on the maladjusted child, reserving some genuine concern for the content of motion pictures. Charters stated bluntly, "crime pictures have a pronounced effect upon delinquents. Minor delinquencies are aggravated by these pictures in many cases; cues for criminal actions are presented and are sometimes copied by young delinquents" (54). Thus, while the Payne Fund studies rejected a theory of simple media-effects causation, they nonetheless provided a basis for the type of public policy advocacy that they had ostensibly rejected. The most important element that the Payne Fund studies brought to the debate, therefore, was the opening of the opportunity for sociologists and psychologists to claim both the mass media and children as viable objects of study. This tendency recurred in the debates around both comic books and television in the 1950s. Thus, the Payne Fund studies of motion pictures undertaken by sociologists at the University of Chicago laid the groundwork for what would become the media-effects paradigm in mass communication research in the 1950s and 1960s.

Three postwar books formed the model for the scientization of the mass culture critique in the form of the media-effects paradigm. These texts include the first two wide-scale English-language studies of television, Himmelweit, Oppenheim, and Vince's *Television and the Child* and *Television in the Lives of Our Children,* by Wilbur Schramm, Jack Lyle, and Edwin B. Parker (1961). The third is Joseph Klapper's general study of media effects, *The Effects of Mass Communication* (1960). Published over a four-year span, these three volumes marked the turn toward Parsonian sociology in the study of the mass media. The volumes' shared approach stressed objectivity through the use of statistical research methodologies and reference to scientific standards of validation. Moreover, they shared not only an approach to the questions under investigation but also a series of general conclusions. Each publication endorsed "the null inference" of media effects, or the suggestion that media have only a limited and minor impact on individual behavior (Comstock et al. 1978:388). Although later challenged by scholars of the mass media, this shared conclusion formed the initial assumptions of the media-effects paradigm and influenced subsequent developments in the field.

Perhaps the most important single finding of the study undertaken by British researchers Himmelweit, Oppenheim, Vince, and their associates was the fact that "television is used by different children in different ways" (1958:xiv). This blunt statement helped to shift discussion of television away from the broadly polemical and condemning statements of the past and toward a more nuanced and tentative understanding of the relationship between media and audiences. According to their findings, the most noticeable impact of television was its effect on leisure time. The authors suggested that television had displaced altogether some functionally similar activities while transforming others. Thus, the nature of childhood radio listening was altered as television programs displaced similarly themed radio programming, and comic book reading among children with television sets in their homes was "permanently reduced" (36).

The researchers concluded that television's appeal was significantly stronger than that of other aspects of mass culture but were loath to attribute significant effects to the new zenith of commercial culture. They noted, for instance, that while television did seem to impact the number of books and comics that children read, it did not affect their schoolwork (21). Traditional concerns about mass culture were not entirely obviated, however. For example, the authors expressed concern about the possibility that television was creating a generation of addicts, although again in this instance the blame fell squarely on the shoulders of the individual child whose "emotional insecurity and maladjustment seem to impel him towards excessive consumption of any available mass medium" (29). Obvious class biases clearly continued to inform this research despite its claims to scientific objectivity.

Schramm, Lyle, and Parker's conclusions in *Television in the Lives of Our Children* were very much in accord with the work of their British counterparts. In what has become a "classic statement" on media effects (Luke 1990:116), they suggested, "For *some* children, under *some* conditions, *some* television is harmful. For *other* children, under *other* conditions, it may be beneficial. For *most* children, under *most* conditions, *most* television is probably neither particularly harmful nor particularly beneficial" (1). Key to this understanding of selective influence was the idea that children are active selectors of media. Describing television as a "shiny cafeteria" from which choices were made, the authors contended that children "are most active in this relationship. It is they who use television, rather than television that uses them" (1–2). This conception of the child as an active participant in the viewing process directly challenged the mass culture critique's prior conceptions of the audience. These authors' minimized-effects thesis essentially argued that television had entered into a preexisting pattern of influences on children and presuming that any behavior of a child resulted solely from television would be incorrect (146).

The authors noted that critics had assumed but not proven a connection between television viewing and juvenile delinquency. Schramm, Lyle, and Parker responded that no single influence could be said to cause behavior and stated their belief "that the kind of child we send to television, rather than television itself, is the chief element in delinquency. According to our best current understanding of delinquency, the delinquent child (unless he is psychopathic) is typically not different from other children in standards or knowledge or intelligence, but rather in the speed with which he can rouse his aggressive feelings, and the intensity and violence of his hostility" (165–66). While the findings concluded that television was at best a contributory cause of youth violence, the authors ultimately condemned televised violence. They asked rhetorically, "Is this the best we can do? Is this the only way we can find to interest children and at the same time attract the large audiences that sponsors require? It seems to us that this might be a matter of pride as well as conscience for broadcasters. These are men of great skill and talent: is it really true that they find it necessary to appeal to large audiences of children with a stream of physical violence, abnormal excitement, and crime?" (177). Thus, ostensibly objective mass communication research still rested on the assumptions of quality and appropriateness that had defined the critique of mass culture for decades.

Klapper's *The Effects of Mass Communication* achieved the clearest distinction between social science research into the effects of mass communication and prior traditions of moralizing critique. As such, the book was the strongest statement of the null inference that ascribed little or no authority to the mass media in the postwar period. Sponsored by the television network CBS, Klapper's book argued that previous efforts to study mass communication had failed the public by providing either no answers at all or contradictory findings (3). He suggested that his phenomenistic approach would shift the terrain of the debate away from the "hypodermic theory" of direct effects toward a functionalist approach that regarded the media as an influence on rather than a cause of behavior.

This theory was derived from the work of Paul Lazarsfeld and Elihu Katz, who had developed the "two-step flow" theory of attitudinal change. This theory led Klapper to a series of generalizations about the media. First, he asserted that mass communication was not a cause of effects but a mediating factor in behavior. Second, mass communication reinforced existing predispositions rather than creating new ones. Third, the mass media's efficacy was determined by the context of the communicational situation (8).

Klapper also commented on theories of media effects that fell beyond the circle of attitudinal change. Noting that the effect of violent mass culture had been a prevalent social concern among "parents, educators and freelance writers" but not among "disciplined communications researchers" (135), he sought to dismiss the connection between the mass media and criminal behavior. In undertaking the reevaluation of the connection between media and delinquency, Klapper directly albeit cursorily and dismissively addressed Wertham's work on comic books. Klapper insisted, "it is undoubtedly true, as the critics claim, that some easily available comic books do or did deal with 'murder, mayhem, robbery, . . . carnage, . . . and sadism,' but the present author has yet to be convinced that they 'offer short courses' in these subjects, let alone in 'rape, cannibalism, . . . and necrophilia' " (137).

Significantly, Klapper rejected Wertham's argument in this instance based simply on Klapper's presumed authority as a researcher rather than on original research of any kind. In this regard it is difficult to distinguish ostensibly objective social science researchers from the uninformed freelance writers Klapper criticized elsewhere in his book. He simply dismissed all research into the relationship between the media and behavior that had preceded him, insisting that "nothing is known about the relationship, if any, between the incidence of violence in media programs and the likelihood that it will produce effects" (139). Instead, he suggested that the variety of claims about the effects of the mass media on behavior were conjectural and lacking in definitive findings of any kind (143). He claimed only that violence in the mass media served "some undefined function for particular personality types" (151). To this end, Klapper agreed with the findings of Himmelweit, Oppenheim, and Vince and Schramm, Lyle, and Parker in suggesting that the mass media were "by no means the sole nor the basic cause of the problems" (159). Together these three volumes established a dominant media-effects paradigm that held that the mass media had a negligible effect on behavior except in rare cases in which a child was predisposed toward violence.

The researchers who entered into the media-effects debate in the 1960s worked primarily in an experimental tradition as opposed to the sociological field-survey approach that characterized the work of both Himmelweit, Oppenheim, and Vince and Schramm, Lyle, and Parker. This approach was marshaled in support of two contradictory hypotheses throughout the 1960s. Albert Bandura was the first to demonstrate that violent media content had a negative effect on aggression in children by showing them ways to act, even if they did not subsequently act that way. At the same time, however, Seymour Feshbach showed that media had a positive impact on children by purging aggressive tendencies through catharsis (Comstock et al. 1978:129–40). This debate in behavioral psychology reopened the media violence question after sociologically oriented researchers had seemingly closed it but did little to resolve the subject.

Over the course of the decade, dozens of lab-based studies investigated the link between aggression and violent television content. The specialty of media-effects research in mass communication studies clearly bifurcated during the 1960s, opening the possibility for two competing yet equally recognized approaches to the question: a sociological perspective rooted in survey methodologies and a psychological perspective that utilized an experimental method. Neither of these traditions promoted critical thinking about the media, and both attempted to shut cultural critics out of the debate yet took research cues from those same critics.

Willard Rowland argues that this remodeling of communications research served the interests of the television industry by allowing it to fund bureaus that would train researchers in noncritical methodologies so that their findings would ultimately defend the television industry's interests (Rowland 1983:28). The flaw in the system, however, stemmed from the ongoing presence of cultural critics condemning media violence from a moral position and the American public's commonsense belief that some connection self-evidently existed between violence on the television screen and rising levels of juvenile delinquency.

The division between uncritical social science researchers and cultural critics widened throughout the 1960s and into the 1970s as a result of the institutionalization of media-effects research at a number of governmental hearings. The role of mass communication scholars at the Dodd subcommittee hearings in 1961, 1962, and 1964 helped to cement the role of researchers in governmental investigations on the mass media. Dodd's committee represented a later incarnation of the Hendrickson-Kefauver subcommittee under the direction of a new chair and featured some of the same witnesses, including Wertham. The subcommittee's June and July 1961 hearings centered on the question of violence on television—specifically, on the program *The Untouchables* and several other action-adventure shows. The following year Dodd challenged earlier network claims to responsible programming by citing evidence obtained from production companies that network heads had requested greater levels of sex and violence in programs. In 1964 a final day of hearings was held to discuss programs such as *The Outer Limits* and *Combat,* but the investigation had largely run out of steam by that time (Boddy 1997:171–72).

The Dodd subcommittee ultimately did not issue a final report and the investigation trailed off. Of note, however, was the subcommittee's three-pronged approach to the problem: public hearings, television monitoring by subcommittee staff members, and a review of the literature on media effects to date. Occupying one-third of the research agenda, the literature review provided an opportunity for scholars of mass communication to be publicly associated with research into television effects. Notably, the committee referenced Schramm, Lyle, and Parker's work. Schramm testified at the hearings and called for concerted funding to underwrite long-term effects research. While the Dodd subcommittee's interim report recommended funding such a research program, nearly a decade passed before significant government funds were allocated. The surgeon general's investigation into television violence ultimately became the force that positioned empirical mass communication research as the dominant paradigm once and for all.

In 1968, following Robert Kennedy's assassination, President Lyndon B. Johnson created the National Commission on the Causes and Prevention of Violence. The commission's mandate included the investigation of television's role in fostering a climate of violence in the United States. Although the committee paid close attention to contemporary research on media effects, its report made only minor policy suggestions, leaving the door open for a more meaningful future investigation that eventually came from the surgeon general. Inspired by the success of the surgeon general's report on cigarette smoking, Senator John Pastore (Democrat–Rhode Island) requested a similar investigation into television violence, a request that resulted in the Scientific Advisory Committee on Television and Social Behavior.

Endorsed by President Richard Nixon and announced on 16 April 1969, the advisory committee studied the problem of television violence for three years, spending $1.8 million, including the cost of twenty-three research projects underwritten by the National Institute for Mental Health's Television and Social Behavior Program. These research efforts fell into two broad categories: laboratory-based and field-based. These studies collectively demonstrated a strong connection between the viewing of television violence and subsequent aggressiveness among children (Cater and Strickland 1975:54). However, a May 1970 article in *Science* magazine disclosed the fact that the industry had held veto power over the committee members, raising suspicions about the eventual findings. The committee subsequently decided to produce a unanimous report to rebuild the credibility of the undertaking. The resulting compromise document forced the advisory committee to take a moderate stance on the question of television violence, ultimately resulting in no substantial changes to U.S. broadcasting policy. In Rowland's summary, "the 1974 hearings capped a quarter century of effort by politicians and regulators, broadcasting critics, academics, and a wide variety of public groups to secure legitimacy for the application of social science research methods and findings to the process of public policy making for broadcasting, while yet ignoring questions about whether such research would ever be likely to lead to substantive change in that policy" (1983:224). Thus, while the surgeon general's report produced no alterations in public policy, the undertaking clearly marked the arrival of mass communication research into media effects on the public stage. The funding of twenty-three projects to investigate television at governmental expense cemented media effects as the dominant paradigm. It was established as quantitative, short-term research that focused on the effects of viewing on individuals through experimental and field-based methodologies. Other approaches to the study of media effects seemingly were pushed completely out of the picture. The empirical approach's success in positioning itself as the sole viable approach to the topic essentially closed off the possibility of competing methodologies. One victim of this consolidation was Fredric Wertham.

Wertham certainly felt as if the surgeon general's report minimized the point of view that he had long stressed. In a 1972 article published in the *American Journal of Psychotherapy,* he condemned the report as "a betrayal of children and their parents, of responsible science, of public health, and of the people's trust in their governmental medical leadership" (1972:219). Wertham enumerated a number of significant objections to the report, including the absence of discussion of contrary findings and the absence of clinical methodologies. However, the preponderance of his objections stemmed from the report's insistence that only a "predisposed" portion of the audience was affected by television violence:

> the only-the-predisposed argument is an old cliché and timeworn alibi, long used by the media industries. It tries to put all the blame on the child and the audience. It is an excuse that evades the whole problem. One cannot scientifically lump all children into two groups, not predisposed and predisposed. Without at least some psychiatric underpinning (totally absent from the report) it just amounts to name-calling. We are supposed to take for granted some prior disability in the child. And is it not also simply prejudice against the poor, the underprivileged, the minorities? Who are these "predisposed"? Has any member of the Committee's research team examined them, and can he tell us by what criteria they were diagnosed? (217)

Wertham's condemnation of the surgeon general's report echoed a great deal of his post–*Seduction of the Innocent* writing on media violence, a topic with which he was centrally occupied during the 1960s and 1970s. While Wertham's criticisms of television shared much with his condemnations of comic books, his views are especially telling when compared to the dominant modes of conceptualizing the effects of television in the postwar period. In short, Wertham's arguments about television violence represent a road not taken in the history of American media-effects scholarship.

In a review of Robert Shayon's book *Open to Criticism,* Wertham noted that the study of environmental influences—including the mass media—on personal development had come to dominate research in psychiatry and sociology in the postwar era. This interest, however, had not led to greater control over mass media violence because "as they function at present regulatory agencies are agencies regulated by the industries which they are supposed to regulate" (Wertham 1971b:651). Wertham had criticized governmental inquiries into the effects of the mass media since the failure of the Hendrickson-Kefauver committee in 1954, and he had long maintained that industrial self-regulation was a sham.

Maintaining that position, he criticized the development of the film classification system in the late 1960s because he believed that it served to maintain the status quo and give license to libertarian viewpoints in which any content would be permissible in films (Wertham 1969b). Wertham's dismay at the failure of regulating agencies to take action on media violence and his contempt for the industry's self-imposed actions at the end of the decade went hand in hand with his rejection of the dominant media-effects paradigm. He argued that while laypeople regarded the effects of media violence as self-evident, communications researchers had worked hard to minimize or ignore the subject (1965:830). Specifically citing Schramm, Lyle, and Parker as researchers who had proposed that "mass media do not matter much in the life of a child," he gave three reasons why the null inference of media effects had become canonized. The first was the neglect of extrinsic environmental factors in psychopathology with the rise of psychoanalysis (830). Second, the questionnaire method employed by social scientists engaged in field research and developed as a tool for market research and public opinion polling was inadequate to the task of examining the mass media. Wertham suggested that the mass media were a quantitatively and qualitatively different form of influence that could not be measured statistically (831). Finally, he argued that social science researchers were simply influenced by the funding that research bureaus received from the media industry and consequently that these studies' findings were tainted (832). The only appropriate replacement for these defaults would be the adoption of a method that would entail "long-range clinical examinations and observations, preferably in conjunction with therapy, combined with projective tests and abbreviated psychoanalytical exploration" (833). This approach, he concluded, would highlight subtle long-range effects on attitude and personality that resulted from exposure to the mass media.

Wertham advanced this argument at greater length in an article published in the *American Journal of Psychiatry* (1962b). "The Scientific Study of Mass Media Effects" had originally been presented in October 1961 as a speech at a *Catholic World*–organized conference on "The Effects Controversy." Wertham clearly outlined the differences between his version of media effects and that of the null-inference social scientists. Wertham specifically set out to respond to the three most influential books on the topic: *Television and the Child, Television in the Lives of Our Children,* and *Effects of Mass Communication.* Wertham argued that *Television and the Child* represented "just another of the generalizations to the effect that the child's basic responses are determined entirely by the 'basic' personality of the child and not by the stimulation of the screen" (306).

Wertham noted that Himmelweit, Oppenheim, and Vince never examined the children discussed in the book and that the conclusions about their mental health were derived entirely from questionnaires, an approach that raised questions about the researchers' ability to place the blame for media-inspired violence on the immaturity of children whom the authors had never met (307). Wertham contended that *Television in the Lives of Our Children* was so full of generalizations that no research needed to have been undertaken at all, in this instance describing the use of questionnaires as inadequate and "unlife-like." Further, he maintained that these three volumes' use of statistical averages had downplayed the significance of negative effects and provided a "totally wrong impression. It is like claiming that there are no multi-millionaires or paupers by using the computation of the average American income" (307). Wertham singled out psychiatrist Lawrence Freedman's essay in Schramm, Lyle, and Parker's book because it was "all theory instead of clinical fact" and spent more time discussing children in the abstract than television in the specific (307).

Finally, Wertham completely dismissed Klapper's contention in *The Effects of Mass Communication* that "nothing is known about the relationship, if any, between the incidence of violence in media programs and the likelihood that it will produce effects" (Wertham 1962b:308). Because foundations and research agencies had underwritten all three volumes, argued Wertham, they provided evidence of a "currently approved trend" in mass communication research (308). The essential problem with these books, he maintained, was the empirical social science methodology that relied on primitive and subjective statistical measures (309). Clinical research that could incorporate the study of the whole child should be substituted for statistical field research. The thesis that maintained that children "are born that way" was fundamentally incorrect and had led to a series of erroneous conclusions (310). Concrete clinical analysis of all the causal connections in the creation of delinquency would, Wertham suggested, ultimately resolve the media-effects controversy.

These charges against empirical social science methodologies in media-effects research appeared time and again in subsequent articles by Wertham. In a 1964 *New York Times* piece, he maintained that only two incontrovertible facts existed about the media-effects controversy: the level of violence in American society had increased in the postwar period and a great deal of violence appeared on television (Wertham 1964b:11). The connection between these observations, Wertham argued, stemmed from the fact that television was a "school for violence" whose effects were long term and could not, therefore, be measured using questionnaire- or laboratory-based research methodologies.

In an article in *Twentieth Century* the same year, Wertham noted that governments the world over spent money to research ways to inflict violence through the use of the military but spent little money on research to prevent violence (1964a:32). To correct this oversight, he proposed the development of a field of "violentology" that would study all aspects of violence from comic books to riots and wars (34). This new science would require an appropriately new approach to the question because traditional mass communication research methodologies

> leave out what is truly human in the child or young adult. Formal replies to formal questions give only a partial and distorted picture. The best statistics cannot make up for that. Control groups, so valuable in physical sciences, are inappropriate for emotional and mental phenomena. Such studies as *Television and the Child* by Hilde Himmelweit, which uses the questionnaire–control group–statistical method without any examination of the children, minimize the effects and are misleading. The experimental method creates unlife-like artificial situations, remains entirely on the surface and does not reflect long-range effects. It is only the clinical method, the examination of children with modern methods, individually and in groups, with tests, a study of the social background and a follow-up, that reveals what really happens. (38)

At base, Wertham believed that the refusal to acknowledge a link between mass media violence and violent behavior in children lacked merit. He further argued that this refusal had become a shield behind which media producers and their apologists hid. He maintained that on the contrary, the assertion on which the dominant media-effects paradigm rested—that only "predisposed children" were at risk from media violence—had never been validated clinically (1968:199).

The essential difference between Wertham and the social science researchers who defined the media-effects paradigm in professional journals and at governmental hearings in the postwar period was the distinction between qualitative and quantitative research methodologies. As early as 1949, Frederick Thrasher had termed Wertham's psychiatric and clinical approach to the study of media effects unscientific, restricting that label exclusively for quantitative methodologies rooted in the Chicago School sociology at the beginning of the century. Wertham's disavowal of quantitative scholarship and adherence to a clinical method ultimately led to his complete absence from the research tradition. As the field of mass communication research established itself as a unique tradition in the postwar period, it did so by initially narrowing its methodological scope and excluding from the field competing and contradictory voices and approaches. Wertham and the clinical method were one such omission.

Wertham's final book, *The World of Fanzines* (1973), highlights the difference between Wertham and his opponents in the study of mass media and popular culture. Published when he was seventy-eight years old and long since retired, this book bore little resemblance to his other works except that it built on earlier statements that violence represented the antithesis of communication. Commissioned and financed by the Twentieth Century Fund, the book was, as its title suggests, a study of fanzines (fan magazines), primarily from a sociological or even anthropological point of view rather than from the perspective of a psychiatrist.

In his prospectus for the book, Wertham suggested that fanzines were "an important social phenomenon of our time worthy of being taken up . . . spontaneous efforts of young people to cope with their problems, to express their doubts and ideas, to experiment with their creative potentialities" (1969c:2). Wertham saw the study of fanzines as an extension of his lifelong work, which was concerned with listening carefully to what children had to say about the world in which they lived. Wertham stated that he had first learned of the existence of fanzines while working with Gino (of *Dark Legend*) in the 1930s but that he had not given them any thought until he began to receive them in the mail in the 1960s from fanzine editors aware of his position on comic books. Wertham had subsequently undertaken a systematic study of the medium, searching out more fanzines, subscribing to others, and even contributing occasional letters or articles and consenting to be interviewed. His interest in the form stemmed from his belief that fanzines represented a sincere and spontaneous form of communication.

Communications scholars and psychiatrists had neglected this medium out of a certain snobbishness that suggested that fanzines were unworthy of scholarly attention. He praised the fact that fanzines were not polluted by the greed and arrogance that dominated the mass media but instead were something "intensely personal" (35). As someone who had become increasingly concerned about the mechanization of daily life as his career wore on, Wertham regarded fanzines as a positive counterforce to the mass media.

The book traced the history of the fanzine's development as a medium of communication with particular emphasis on what he termed the three pillars of fanzines: science fiction, fantasy, and comic books. His discussion of comic books was particularly illuminating in relation to his work from the 1950s: he clearly distinguished between comic books—which he saw as the product of the economic crisis brought on by the American Depression of the 1930s—and comic strips, which he regarded as a legitimate art form whose roots lay in nineteenth-century Europe. This distinction between art and commerce led Wertham to praise fanzines concerned with comic books even as he was unwilling to recant his earlier position on comic books. Wertham valued the fact that the fanzines were free of censorship and commercial interests, two forces of which he was equally suspect. Moreover, Wertham regarded fanzines as distinct from the mass media because they were not "covered with the dust of dullness" but were written in ways that were fresh and unclichéd (87). Wertham concluded that fanzines occupied a space in the history of American culture that had been unfairly overlooked by historians, psychologists, and communications scholars. Assuming the psychiatrist's point of view, he answered the hypothetical question of whether participation in fanzine culture was psychologically healthy. He affirmed the value of the urge to create and to communicate with others. Fanzine work, Wertham suggested, was social rather than psychological, and fanzine writers and editors were not alienated from society but rather maintained a deep desire to communicate and socialize with others who shared similar interests. Given that the postwar era consisted of a consumer society, Wertham celebrated the fanzine for its outsider status. He conceptualized this refusal as a form not of opposition but of resistance and held that fanzine publishing was a form of implied social criticism. In the end, according to Wertham, "communication is the opposite of violence and every facet of communication has a legitimate place" (133).

Wertham's work on fanzines brought him into close contact with a large number of comic book fans who resented his previous work, particularly *Seduction of the Innocent*. His relationship to fandom in the late 1960s and early 1970s was, therefore, quite complex. Many fanzine writers assumed that he meant to pillory fandom and refused to sell him copies of their work. Wertham's papers, for example, contain a piece of notepaper to which was attached a quarter (which Wertham presumably had sent for a copy of a fanzine) with the note "Bug off quack" (Anonymous n.d.:1). These letters were reminiscent of the correspondence that Wertham had received in the early 1950s when he first began writing about comics, such as a handwritten missive from "The Dagger," complete with three skull-and-crossbones images, that spewed, "You big bums you are nuts. I hate you for saying that dick Tracy is bad for us. You rottin slobs you and your hole joint. Who ever let you out of the nut house must have been bats" (1952:1).

Other comic book fans responded respectfully but skeptically. Wertham continued to engage in protracted discussions with a large number of comic book fans in the late 1960s and early 1970s, including Russ Cochran, Alan Light, Gary Groth, Tony Isabella, and Mark Evanier, among many others. Wertham responded to questions about his research, corrected misunderstandings, and frequently sent offprints of his work to young comic book fans. In a few cases, Wertham sent copies of *A Sign for Cain* to fans who requested it (Wertham 1969a). Wertham's letters appeared in a large number of fanzines during this period, as did a number of interviews (Larson n.d.) and even some creative contributions, such as the poetry selections that he contributed to Donn Brazier's *Title* (Wertham 1974a).

When Wertham released *The World of Fanzines* in 1973, the book found generally positive reviewers in the arena that it studied. Dozens of surprised fanzine publishers responded favorably on two main grounds: first, that Wertham's work shed light on their activities; and, second, that it did so positively. In a particularly lengthy—and mixed—review of the book in *Rockets Blast Comicollector,* John Adkins Richardson noted that the book flattered fandom and consequently drew positive reviews from that group. Richardson raised a number of objections to Wertham's findings, noting that he downplayed the role of violence within fandom, but found the book "a superior job which should be of interest to serious students of popular culture and social psychology," although because it was published by a university press, "the average fan will think it is horribly overpriced" (1974:54).

Wertham's commentary on the world of fanzines provided a lens through which his criticism of mass culture and media violence could be properly refocused. Separated from the hyperbole and name-calling that accompanied the moral panic around comic books in the 1950s, Wertham's criticisms can be seen more accurately as a liberalist critique of the mass media's influence that sought not the end or even curtailment of a particular medium of communication but a reconceptualization of social relations. With *Seduction of the Innocent* and his other writings on the subject of the mass media, Wertham advocated a new series of social relations between adults and children, between individuals and society, and between art and commerce. With this in mind, it becomes clear that Wertham's contribution was excluded from more traditional approaches to media-effects scholarship on three counts.

First, Wertham was more critical of the capitalist media industries than the normative scholarship, much of which was funded by various media industries. Second, Wertham paid much greater attention to the ways in which audiences used the media over the long term than over the short term. Third, his conclusions suggested complex social arrangements rather than individualistic explanations. Wertham's approach to the study of media effects, therefore, can be seen to fall outside the dominant traditions of the social-scientific and behavioristic research paradigm as it developed in conjunction with government and industry research requirements in the decades following the end of the Second World War. His conclusions, which shared a number of significant biases with mass communication research findings, ultimately could not be reconciled with the dominant tradition because his dismissal of empirical methods and ongoing concern with the broadly cultural impact of the mass media found no correspondence in a field dominated by administratively informed scholarship.

Testifying before the Hendrickson-Kefauver subcommittee hearings in 1954, Paul Lazarsfeld informed the senators that mass communication research could not be seen as a panacea for the nation's problems:

> In the whole matter of the mass media there are questions of convictions and taste which can hardly be settled by research. At least for the time being

research cannot decide whether people should read good books rather than bad books, or whether they should listen to good music. One has to have convictions on the dignity of man, on the importance of matters of the mind, and one has to stand up and be counted on these convictions. If I see a cruel picture in a comic, or if I hear a stupid television program, I react negatively, even though I may not be able to back up my conviction with research findings. (1955:249)

Important here is Lazarsfeld's acknowledgment that the researcher's aesthetic convictions inform scholarly work even in instances where the scholar's biases are not supported evidentially. Equally crucial, however, was Lazarsfeld's telling qualification "at least for the time being," suggesting his belief that the questions that characterized critiques of mass culture might eventually be resolved empirically. In a similar vein, Leo Bogart argued the following year that while television "cannot really be blamed for turning children into criminals or neurotics," this finding of minimal effects was essentially beside the point. Bogart contended that "a much more serious charge is that television, in the worst aspects of its content, helps to perpetuate moral, cultural and social values which are not in accord with the highest ideals of an enlightened democracy. The cowboy film, the detective thriller and the soap opera, so often identified by critics as the epitome of American mass culture, probably do not represent the heritage which Americans at large want to transmit to posterity" (1956:273–74). Bogart's comments contrast what he perceived to be the illegitimate concern that television contributed to juvenile delinquency with the genuine worry that television was leading the United States away from its position as the seat of postwar enlightenment.

J. D. Peters suggests that the displacement that Bogart described was actually the driving force behind mass communication research in general: "If you could lay the classic texts of American mass communication research down on a psychoanalytic couch, you would find that they thought themselves talking narrowly about the mass media and their 'effects,' while they were in fact talking about the perils and possibilities of democracy" (1989:200).

It is no coincidence, following this logic, that the study of mass communication and popular culture in the United States should fully emerge between the wars and further that it should be consecrated as a legitimate field of study in an atmosphere riddled with concern about the corrupting influence of mass culture on democracy. While its roots may reside in the nineteenth-century distrust of mass culture, the formation of mass communication research was directed by the needs of the mass media industries and of government agencies that sought to regulate those industries according to values of individualism and laissez-faire capitalism. This development led toward a privileging of ostensibly objective research practices that would obviate the need for mass communication scholars to take a critical stance in relation to the industries that helped to legitimize and fund research in the field. Given such a situation, it seems unlikely that an unrepentantly committed social reformer such as Fredric Wertham could have ever found a place within the field's dominant traditions.

CONCLUSION

By the time of Wertham's death in 1982, his position within the burgeoning field of mass media studies was by no means secure. Indeed, his exit from the field can be traced through the codification of the research in some early textbooks. Shearon Lowery and Melvin De Fleur's 1983 *Milestones in Mass Communication Research: Media Effects* has played a key role in legitimizing the empirical paradigm in popular culture research. The book defined the importance of eleven key milestones in the history of this research, beginning with the Payne Fund studies and concluding with the surgeon general's report on television violence. Along the way, the authors highlighted contributions made by figures such as Paul Lazarsfeld, Wilbur Schramm, and, curiously, Fredric Wertham.

Lowery and De Fleur's text is one of the few instances in which Wertham and his work were incorporated into the history of mass communication research, albeit fleetingly. Consequently, the authors' comments signified a great deal about the way in which his work was received by generations of scholars writing after his death. Lowery and De Fleur argued that Wertham's work was "theoretically inconsistent" and that his position shifted at times from an argument rooted in selective influence based on individual differences to a view that stressed uniform effects. To this end, they suggested that Wertham's work in *Seduction of the Innocent* was "clearly a version of the old magic bullet theory" (262). They further argued that Wertham's insistence that comic books were not a causative but a contributing factor in juvenile delinquency represented a deliberate effort to mislead readers. They suggested that Wertham believed comics to be a causative factor but accused him of being unwilling to admit that belief (262).

A more serious charge in the eyes of Lowery and De Fleur, however, was the fact that Wertham's writings on comic books failed to live up to accepted standards of scientific validity: "the major weakness of Wertham's position is that it is not supported by scientifically gathered research data" (1983:262). They cited, for instance, Wertham's failure to include a comprehensive content analysis of all comic books published in the 1950s as evidence that his work was "biased, unreliable, and useless" (263). The perception that Wertham failed to provide "systematic evidence" can be seen as valid only if one assumes, as Lowery and De Fleur did, that the clinical methodology that he advocated and utilized was "by no means scientific" (263). These condemnations failed to acknowledge the fact that *Seduction of the Innocent* was in no way presented as a volume that adhered to generally accepted scientific reporting methods. Lowery and De Fleur further dismissed the clinical method as nonscientific as a matter of course. No argument for this dismissal was necessitated or made; it was simply accepted as a given. In this way, the received history of the media-effects paradigm unquestioningly dismissed nonempirical or critical work from the corpus of mass communication research. Indeed, the most recent edition of Lowery and De Fleur's *Milestones in Mass Communication Research: Media Effects* (1995) shed the chapter on *Seduction of the Innocent,* replacing those pages with new chapters addressing the uses and gratifications approach to the study of daytime serials and the Iowa study of hybrid seed corn. Wertham's name does not appear anywhere in this version of the textbook. With that, the elision of critical scholarship from the history of empirically grounded approaches to the study of media effects has been finalized.

For Lowery and De Fleur and other commentators, the legacy of Wertham's contribution to the postwar debates about the effects of mass culture resided not in the way in which his work impacted research into popular culture but in its effect on the U.S. comic book industry. It is important to see how his erasure as a scholar went hand in hand with a vilification of the man accused of undermining a whole cultural industry—some claim irrevocably. Lowery and De Fleur suggested that Wertham's ultimate contribution was not scholarly but social: he reinforced a "legacy of fear" about popular culture that ultimately led to the Hendrickson-Kefauver Senate hearings, the Comics Code, and the decline of comic books as a cultural form (265). Amy Kiste Nyberg challenges this simplified reading of the history of both anti-comic-book commentary and responses from industry and government. Her history of the development of the Comics Code points to a more complex interaction of forces. At the same time, however, even Nyberg does not refrain from scapegoating Wertham as an opportunist whose lasting contribution to American culture was the diminishment of the comic book form (1998:154).

This argument has become a common refrain among comic book readers, historians, and fans: Wertham killed comics. These observers persist in regarding Wertham as a malicious figure whose work destroyed the medium. In a *New Yorker* profile of cartoonist Jack Cole, for instance, Pulitzer Prize–winning cartoonist Art Spiegelman wrote that *Seduction of the Innocent* "triggered the Senate hearings and thereby toppled the industry" (1999:83). In what is possibly the most horrendously inappropriate overstatement ever made on this subject, comic book writer Mark Evanier has called Wertham "the Josef Mengele of funnybooks" (2003:189). This type of scapegoating and name-calling can only really be understood as a result of fannish anxieties over the comic book's historically degraded status in America's cultural hierarchy.

In the world of comic books, Fredric Wertham may never die. In 1977 an anti–Comics Code Authority underground comic book entitled *Dr. Wirtham's Comix and Stories* was launched. In 1985, Eclipse Comics launched a series of reprints of 1950s-published Standard Comics crime stories under the title *Seduction of the Innocent.* In *Dork* #10 (2003), Evan Dorkin presented the "true" story of Fredric Wertham, frustrated author of superhero comic books who vents his spleen at the industry that rejects his work by launching a personal vendetta. A 2004 episode of the superhero cartoon *Justice League* marked the fiftieth anniversary of Wertham's best-known work by featuring a villain quoting from an antisuperhero book, "The Innocent Seduced." Comic book fans, it seems, maintain the memory of Fredric Wertham as a kind of group wound that will never heal. They simultaneously celebrate and condemn his memory as a signifier of the travails that the industry has faced and overcome. This particular type of cultural memory seems peculiar to the field of comics. Television certainly has no evil icon on a par with Wertham. Nor is it easy to find examples of contemporary cinema that slyly refer to the Hays Code and especially to antifilm commentators such as W. W. Charters. Of course, this is easily explicable. Cinema overcame accusations regarding its degrading adolescence by proudly asserting its maturity. The American comics industry, conversely, has continually wallowed in its immaturity and has sought approval for doing so.

The continuing attacks on Wertham stem from a fundamental misunderstanding of his work. Out of print for fifty years, *Seduction of the Innocent* is better known than read. Further, the vast majority of Wertham's writings—in the form of articles and book reviews—remain uncollected and consequently are extremely difficult to read in any in-depth or systematic fashion. The parody of Wertham's argument—comic books cause juvenile delinquency—has been substituted for the actual argument in the minds of comic book fans and even in some textbooks dealing with popular culture. Bradford Wright, for example, wrongly asserts that Wertham cited a "causal link between comic books and juvenile delinquency" (2001:97). That Wertham never argued this conclusion is, for many contemporary commentators, entirely beside the point. Wright and others attack Wertham by confusing the notion of "some" with "all." Evanier argues that Wertham's work on fanzines in the 1970s represented "a complete, unacknowledged one-eighty from his earlier writings" (2003:190) because Wertham demonstrated that not all comic book readers became delinquents. Wertham, of course, never suggested that they would; indeed, his recurrent tuberculosis metaphor explicitly posited this. Simply because not all children would become delinquent was not a reason, according to Wertham, to attempt to reduce the numerous factors that contributed to delinquency, just as the fact that not all children would develop tuberculosis was not a reason to allow the virus to flourish unchecked. Evanier, Wright, and other contemporary critics expand Wertham's argument to realms that he quite consciously did not and then refute the false argument as self-evidently erroneous. Mass media and popular culture scholars simply continue to ignore him as inconsequential, offering his position in the field of comics as proof of his irrelevance.

Assessing *Seduction of the Innocent* in light of Wertham's other writings and of the intellectual climate of the period in which he was writing, the volume can be seen to have a number of clear strengths and serious shortcomings. The first serious advantage is the fact that it is the only book-length study of comic books published at the time of their greatest U.S. popularity. From a historical vantage point, it is the only sustained work from the postwar period that took comics seriously or treated them as if they were important in any way. Almost all the responses to *Seduction of the Innocent* were completely inadequate. While most negative reactions to the book shared the presumption that comic books were worthless trash—a position voiced even by commentators paid by comic book publishers—few brought their own analyses to the table. Wertham was regularly derided as "nonscientific," but no science was mobilized to counter his claims. Indeed, there was—and is—no scientifically based counterargument to *Seduction of the Innocent:* such an argument simply never materialized.

Wertham undeniably spent more time working on and thinking about the issues raised by comic books in the postwar era than any other single commentator, but his work has been dismissed by scholars on the rather spurious methodological grounds that mask lurking general aesthetic and moral presumptions about popular culture. Thrasher's rebuttal of Judith Crist's article on Wertham is the closest thing to a contemporary scientific rejection of Wertham's work, but it exists entirely at the level of the philosophical, as Thrasher had done no research and could point to no data to support his position. Ultimately, no findings refuted Wertham's contentions; authors mustered only assertions based on claims to authority. The rejection of *Seduction of the Innocent,* therefore, has taken place only on the assertive level of the public intellectual, not on the level of rigorous scientific rebuttal. Ironically, contemporary comics critics level persistent claims that Wertham was a bad scientist despite the fact that these critics are neither scientists nor professional researchers. Evanier simply calls Wertham's research "inane" (2003:179), for example, and Wright argues that there is "really no need to refute the arguments in *Seduction* point by point" (2001:162). This sort of nonrebuttal is an embarrassing example of the scholarly evasions that have for generations characterized responses to Wertham's work. Wertham's writings are more important than any of his critics because, unlike them, he systematically engaged with a clearly defined research problematic.

A second reason to admire *Seduction of the Innocent* is the fact that it so boldly flew in the face of the dominant political and social agendas of its age. Wertham was a liberal who was proud to put his career and reputation in jeopardy to speak out on important issues when others would not. From civil rights to the death penalty, from the Rosenbergs to international relations, Wertham took unpopular public stands on issues on which he was well ahead of the political curve. Wertham's findings on segregation in Delaware—which consisted of exactly the same proof as his research into comic books—were widely recognized as true at the time and still are today. Wertham demonstrated that addressing a single negative social factor, in this case segregation, could improve the lives of an entire population. Further, most contemporary readers of Wertham's work would likely concede that he was right in this case, even if his studies failed to meet the empirical standard demanded by Thrasher or Lowery and De Fleur.

At the same time, however, many of those readers are unlikely to concede that Wertham's conclusions about comic books are equivalent to his work on desegregation. For many, this is simply a case of a perfectly reasonable personal bias that deplores racism while wanting to celebrate a preferred form of entertainment. Yet the contradiction does highlight some interesting elements of Wertham's particular style of research. Wertham noted through extended discussions with his patients that certain social factors negatively affected psychological development. This work represented a fundamental break from the Cold War precepts of individualism that placed the blame for psychological illness squarely on the patient's shoulders.

A right-wing ideology that denies the reality of social causes for social problems lies at the core of rejections of Wertham's work even to this day. The celebration of individualism that was so central to the underground comics movement that produced artifacts such as *Dr. Wirtham's Comix and Stories* often acts as a mask for conservative political values. Wertham challenged the liberalism of Americans who had departed from the program of socially progressive reform, asking them to recognize the inherent biases of the postwar individualist consensus. It is interesting, therefore, to ask how the dominant criticism leveled against *Seduction of the Innocent* still clings to that particular ideology, as in Wright's claim that Wertham's endorsement of age-based ratings on comic books—such as those that have been widely adopted in the contemporary comic book industry—amounted to "a form of censorship" (2001:97). This criticism has explicit roots in a conservative idea that the profits of large publishing companies are more important than the mental health of children. Wertham's work challenged this type of thinking in the fields of psychiatry and social theory, and he continues to be demonized largely because his work rejects the individualist ideology.

The criticism of Wertham's work that holds the greatest weight certainly has to be the charge that the book is needlessly alarmist. Any thorough reading of Wertham's books and articles clearly demonstrates that *Seduction of the Innocent* was a departure from his other work, at least at the level of tone. Wertham was a charming and funny writer with a fondness for puns and sly jokes, but *Seduction* is largely free of humor. The overall tone is at times screeching. Many of his critics were absolutely correct to criticize this pervading sense of hysteria, and it does little to bolster his claims to scientific validity. It is unclear why Wertham felt that this overwrought style was necessary—his other publications for nonspecialist audiences evince little of this trait—but it is clear that it did him no long-term favors. At the same time, however, many of Wertham's critics use the alarmist tone simply to dismiss him altogether as a scholar and a critic. In essence, they refuse to engage with the arguments because they do not like the way these arguments are presented. This is an unscholarly dodge.

The most commonly seized upon claim in *Seduction* is the idea that Batman represents the "wish dream of two homosexuals living together" (Wertham 1954i:190). Cited endlessly, this claim is held up among comic book fans as self-evidently ludicrous, despite the fact that the argument is both relevant and convincing (see Medhurst 1991). Many Wertham critics treat this charge as if he wholly invented it despite the fact that he cites a number of clinical examples of patients whose reading of the Batman stories structure his interpretation. Wertham's disadvantage as a writer is patient confidentiality, which obviously restricted his ability to present data other than as anecdotal. Nonetheless, his papers are replete with examples of gay youths openly discussing the homoerotic subtext of the Batman and Robin relationship. Yet in a homosocial culture such as that of comic book collectors, these implications are taboo, and Wertham is denounced as an alarmist for even reporting the existence of these fantasies. In that way, Wertham's critical analysis is dismissed not because of its inherent homophobia—a common position in the an era when homosexuality was regarded as a mental illness—but because it is not homophobic enough. Thus, while much of *Seduction* plays to the prurient and alarmist aspects of American culture in an unhealthy manner, many of the critiques of Wertham's writing for this tendency are rooted in denial.

Where I personally depart from Wertham most directly is in his reliance on a critical distinction between high and low cultures. A generous reading might suggest that Wertham simply reiterated the ideologies that structured American thinking about culture in the twentieth century, but this downplays the degree to which Wertham's work helped to reinforce those particular modes of thought. Wertham's work on comics and television was rife with negative comparisons to the type of culture that he personally preferred as a reader and art collector. Moreover, his work does not particularly benefit from these biases. The high/low distinction as manifested in the United States has had a particularly negative impact on the culture of the majority of Americans. In privileging the culture of a self-imposed elite, the broader culture suffers. Further, it is high culture that has most aggressively championed the conservative culture of individualism—often through the figure of the artistic "genius"—against more inclusive and progressive social possibilities.

It is no coincidence that at the time of the comic book controversy the Central Intelligence Agency was funding international touring exhibitions of American modernist art that had been championed by conservative critics such as Clement Greenberg and Dwight MacDonald. Art, the product of an individual creative expression, existed in the postwar period in opposition to mass cultural kitsch, and the celebration of art acted as a hegemonic force in American culture. Wertham did not recognize this fact, and consequently his writings played into the burgeoning ideology of individualism that he otherwise rejected. Indeed, his influence as a public intellectual in many ways became central to this thrust because of his unproblematic use of this worldview. It is possible to suggest, of course, that key to Wertham's success as a commentator on popular culture was the fact that his work could easily be slotted into commonplace conservative rejections of mass culture, even if it did not fully endorse all of the implications of such a rejection.

That Wertham was unable to think his way out of this contradiction is not entirely surprising when one takes the time to consider the comic books of this period, a time when they were almost universally acknowledged as the quintessential example of a lowest-common-denominator culture, suitable only for the immature. While comic book publishers insisted that adults as well as children read comics, the publishers' actions clearly indicate that they were aggressively courting a children's market exclusively. Producing work by anonymous writers and artists, comic book publishers did everything in their power to maintain a children's audience. Fearing lost sales from price hikes because children's allowances were not growing at the rate of inflation, publishers frequently cut the page count of comic books rather than alter the price (a dime), which had been the industry standard since the mid-1930s. When industry sales leader Dell finally raised its prices to fifteen cents per issue in 1961, the company precipitated an internal financial crisis that ultimately resulted in Dell's demise, while competitors increased their cover prices only to twelve cents to maintain their young audiences.

Further evidence of the "low" nature of the comic books in this era, however, appeared between the covers. Featuring stories and images that "could not have appeared in even the most lurid of Hollywood B-movies" (Wright 2001:81), the majority of comics produced in this period were overtly racist and sexist as well as gory and violent. Jungle comics and war comics both traded extensively in racist and imperialist representations and ideologies. Romance comics and crime comics were ludicrously misogynist. Horror and crime comics contained images unlike any that could be found in any other medium. Indeed, it is telling that as early as 1949 the U.S. Army banned the sale of comic books on its bases, suggesting that the material was too gruesome for soldiers (Barclay 1949:26). Yet apologists for the comic book industry argued that this same material should be readily available to any five-year-old with a dime. This sort of incongruity gave life to Wertham's intervention into the debates about comic books, although contemporary critics of Wertham's work tend for the most part to play down this material by shifting the debate away from the worst of comics and toward what are regularly regarded as the best. In that way, once again, traditional high/low distinctions are cemented without scrutiny into their obvious social and political biases.

Discussion of Wertham's commentaries on popular culture—particularly comic books—is structured by historical amnesia. Comics retained from the postwar period are generally superhero comics, for which there remains a strong fan base; *Archie* comics, which remain strong sellers in the preteen market; and EC Comics, which have been comprehensively reprinted on more than one occasion. EC publisher Bill Gaines has recast the history of the Comics Code as an attempt to drive his "subversive" company out of business. A large number of commentators have come to accept as truth this myth, which gained force in early EC comics fan circles and subsequently spread.

Wright offers a particularly cogent example of this type of argument, beginning his discussion of EC by signaling its exceptionality ("There were comic book publishers, and then there was EC" [135]) and later calling the company "extraordinary" (136). Wright argues that Wertham, who used examples from EC comics several times in *Seduction*, consistently misread the EC books of which he was critical. Citing half a dozen short stories that Wright suggests demonstrated a strongly progressive social position, Wright claims that Wertham was deaf to the social criticism. Discussing a story called "The Whipping" with an ironic ending that finds a Ku Klux Klan–like group accidentally beating a bigot's daughter to death, Wright suggests that "EC addressed prejudice against . . . minorities" (140). Here his argument is simply an extension of Gaines's promotion of his company at the Senate hearings, where he accused Wertham of misrepresenting the politics of "The Whipping" by accusing the antiracist story of being racist. In this way, critics attempt to argue that Wertham was insensitive to art and to politics, suggesting that he has misread a simple story.

Wertham's reading of these texts, however, is—as an attentive reading of *Seduction* points out—rooted almost entirely in the readings of his patients. Wertham's work forcefully brings out the idea that reading is an active process and that texts are polysemic. Wertham pointed to examples of patients who found "hidden" erotic images in the shading of comic book figures, and he did it again when criticizing "The Whipping" and other such stories for racism. Wertham argued that many children read these books in unexpected ways, so that introducing a culture of racism, however satirically or ironically, in books marketed to children was fundamentally unhealthy.

Wertham's contention that not every child decoded the message that publishers such as Gaines saw as self-evident is a function of a take on reading that is much more complex and nuanced than the simple correspondence offered by Wright. Indeed, Nyberg tentatively supports a polysemic reading of "The Whipping" when she observes that "there are actually two stories being told," one by the images and one by the captions: that the story is antiracist only if one reads both sections. Reading selectively and ignoring the captions would result in a racist story, as Wertham maintains (1998:64). Similarly, Martin Barker rejects claims regarding the efficacy of the story as an instance of antiracist activism, arguing that the work's voice-over mitigates against the structure of the tale (1984:164). Gaines's suggestion, reiterated by Wright, that there is only one way to read a text is reductionist in the extreme, a fact recognized even at the time of the Senate hearings when Herbert Beaser challenged Gaines, pointing out that if it was possible that comic books could send "good" (i.e., antiracist) messages, could they not also send "bad" ones? Gaines responded that they could not, and subsequent commentators have structured their arguments to deny the possibility of the active reader to privilege the authorial intentionality of corporate comics production. For critics such as Wright, who praises EC comics as "liberating" (152), Wertham and, by extension, the Comics Code destroyed the only postwar-era company producing comics of value. The myth of quality that is attached to EC Comics, despite their repetitive "ironic" endings, has helped to structure the image of Wertham as a destroyer of the medium's potential. This represents a simpleminded reading of history that ignores the central fact that the Comics Code—which, in any case, Wertham did not advocate—did not destroy the medium's potential: comic book publishers did.

The mid-1950s were a period of tremendous contraction in the comic book industry. From 1954 to 1956 eighteen publishers left the comic book industry, and the number of titles published fell from more than 650 per month to just over 300 per month. Comic book defenders often see this reduction as a function of the Comics Code, but the case actually seems much more complex. Indeed, in the mid-1950s there seemed to be a "perfect storm" of events that damaged the comic book industry.

Specifically, three external forces converged to put pressure on comic book producers. First, the anticomics crusade in which Wertham was a central player shed unwanted light on the industry and alerted parents to the fact that comic books might not represent desirable reading for children. Second, in 1955 the American News Company, which distributed the vast majority of comic books in the United States, was broken up as a result of an antitrust action. Consequently, most publishers lacked a viable distributor, and many left the damaged industry as a result. Third, by 1955 the majority of American homes had television sets, and television became the primary visual-narrative entertainment form for both children and adults. All media in general and comic books in particular suffered in the wake of the wide-scale introduction of television in the 1950s.

Yet another, internal force also damaged the comic book industry: the refusal to grow up. Wright argues that "the code essentially dictated that comic books ought to be produced only for young children" (181), but this is almost entirely untrue. If anything dictated that comics were for young children, it was the twelve-cent price tag. Nonetheless, nothing in the Comics Code would have prevented comic book publishers from creating the type of mature, sensitive, and adult-themed texts that were so popular with, for instance, filmgoers or television viewers. In the mid-1950s, both film and television labored under production codes that were at least as restrictive as the Comics Code, but both attracted enormous adult audiences by developing material specifically for them. Comic book publishers— including EC—had never done so. Nothing in the Comics Code would have forbidden a comic book story of the moral complexity of midcentury Academy Award–winning films such as *On the Waterfront* or *Marty*. Wright's suggestion that the code ruled out adult stories reduces the category of adult entertainment to stories of vampires and werewolves—in short, to children's fare. Shortsighted publishers concerned with generating the easiest possible profits kept American comic books from developing an adult sensibility in the 1950s.

Ironically, the "adult age" of comic books arrived as comic book publishers adopted Wertham's suggestions. Wertham never advocated censorship but repeatedly called for age-appropriate labeling of comic books and a restriction on the ability of young children to buy certain inappropriate material. In the 1960s artists such as Robert Crumb took exactly this route. Crumb's publisher, Apex Novelties, labeled *Zap* #1, "Fair Warning: For Adult Intellectuals Only." Over the ensuing decades, publishers such as Fantagraphics and Drawn and Quarterly that specialize in comic books for adult audiences have taken pains to so label them. In 1991 DC Comics, the publisher of Superman and Batman, created a "Mature Readers" line of books, and in 2001 Marvel Comics, publisher of Spider-Man and the X-Men, followed suit. Fifty years after Wertham advocated age labels, publishers of all types commonly include such labels on their books. The result has been a dramatic increase in the number of comic books created for adult readers. Thus, the argument that Wertham condemned the comic book industry to childish irrelevance is entirely false. The possibility of creating mature works always remained present, but few artists and no publishers conceptualized this as a reasonable goal in the postwar era.

Of course, the lack of "serious" or "adult" comics has contributed mightily to the generally accepted idea that comic books are simply for children and do not constitute an important element of the cultural landscape. While the responsibility for this lack resides with comic book publishers and artists, Fredric Wertham has quite often taken the blame, however unfairly. Indeed, Wertham gets no respect as a researcher perhaps because comic books get no respect as a form; Wertham is consequently seen as having wasted much of his career worrying about a medium to which the majority of media scholars pay no heed. Comic fans, still caught up in the desire to earn respect for the medium, have cast Wertham as the villain who doomed comic books to a permanently lower status. If comics were not respected before Wertham, they were at least popular. After Wertham, they were neither. Ironically, however, Wertham is one of the only scholars—and certainly the only member of his generation—to have taken comic books seriously enough to consider their implications. This type of scholarly scrutiny was one of the prerequisites for the evolution of the form to legitimacy, although in seeking to manage the ensuing crisis while maintaining their profit margins the publishers sabotaged the possibility of growing the industry by attracting new audiences. Many fans and commentators mistakenly blame Wertham for this phenomenon.

Contrary to received opinion, Wertham was an important midcentury thinker who has been unjustly marginalized by three groups. Psychiatrists and social scientists have ignored his contribution to the study of media effects because the social basis of his thinking flew in the face of individualizing studies that tended to regard some media consumers as "abnormal." The New York Intellectuals and other cultural critics disdained his work despite its similarities to their own because Wertham's conclusions ultimately were rooted in a genuine sense of democracy, antiviolence, and progressive social thought that was increasingly anathema to the Cold War politics of individualism. Comic book fans despised him for his conclusions and because he did not like what they love: comic books. These critics regard comic books as more important than social relations. According to anti-Wertham comic book fans, any attempt to improve social relations among people that results in harm to the comic book industry is unjustified and unjustifiable because the individual as an artist or publisher is more important than society as a whole. This view takes the postwar ideology of individualism toward its ludicrous extreme.

Ultimately, Fredric Wertham aligned himself with the most defenseless portion of postwar American society, children. His critics have aligned themselves with an industry that targeted racist, sexist, and imperialist propaganda at minors. He was one man, operating out of a free clinic in Harlem, facing a multimillion dollar per year industry organization that hired private detectives to tail him and intimidate his staff. Yet comic book fans, cultural commentators, and social scientists have sought to portray Wertham as the reckless destroyer of a powerless cottage industry. This good-versus-evil narrative serves not to destroy the reputation and status of Wertham—social scientists and neoconservative cultural critics had already accomplished that—but to perpetuate comics' marginal status in the field of mass media and popular culture research. Knee-jerk reactions to critical commentary that posit comics as innocent victims of the establishment refuse socially and historically grounded analysis based on rigorous attention to evidence and complex theoretical understandings. In other words, comics' status as a medium forever stuck in adolescence is mirrored by an immature and overly defensive critical culture. By returning Wertham to the historiography of the media-effects paradigm and critically assessing the unique foundation of his arguments against comic books, the man and the medium gain much deserved recognition for their importance in the codification of new forms of mass culture in the postwar era.

WORKS CITED

Anonymous. N.d. Letter to Fredric Wertham. Box 155, folder 1. Papers of Fredric Wertham, 1818–1986. Library of Congress Rare Books and Special Collections Division, Washington, D.C.

Anttonen, Eva. 1941. "On Behalf of Dragons." *Wilson Library Bulletin,* March, 567, 595.

"Are Comics Fascist?" 1945. *Time,* 22 October, 67–68.

"Are Comics Horrible?" 1954. *Newsweek,* 3 May, 60.

Arendt, Hannah. 1951. *The Origins of Totalitarianism.* New York: Harcourt, Brace.

Aswell, Mary Louise White, ed. 1947. *The World Within: Fiction Illuminating the Neuroses of Our Time.* Intro. Fredrick Wertham. New York: Whittlesey House.

"At Long Last." 1948. *Horn Book,* August, 233.

Bakwin, Ruth. 1953. "The Comics." *Journal of Pediatrics* 42:633–35.

"Bane of the Bassinet." 1948. *Time,* 15 March, 70–72.

Barclay, Dorothy. 1949. "Army to Limit Sale of Comics." *New York Times,* 18 January, 26.

———. 1950. "Comic Books and Television." *New York Times Magazine,* 5 March, 43.

———. 1955. "That Comic Book Question." *New York Times Magazine,* 20 March, 48.

Barker, Martin. 1984. *A Haunt of Fears: The Strange History of the British Horror Comics Campaign.* Jackson: University Press of Mississippi.

"Baseball Is Ruining Our Children." 1954. *Mad Magazine,* August.

Bechtel, Louise Seaman. 1941. "The Comics and Children's Books." *Horn Book,* 1941, 296–303.

Bell, Daniel. 1960. *The End of Ideology.* New York: Free Press.

Bender, Lauretta. 1944. "The Psychology of Children's Reading and the Comics." *Journal of Educational Sociology* 18:223–31.

Bender, Lauretta, and Abram Blau. 1937. "The Reaction of Children to Sexual Relations with Adults." *American Journal of Orthopsychiatry* 7:500–18.

Bender, Lauretta, and Reginald S. Lourie. 1941. "The Effect of Comic Books on the Ideology of Children." *American Journal of Orthopsychiatry* 11:540–51.

Berelson, Bernard. 1961. "Who Reads Books and Why?" In *Culture for the Millions?* ed. Jacobs, 119–25.

Berger, Peter L. 1965. "Towards a Sociological Understanding of Psychoanalysis." *Social Research* 32:26–41.

Berliner, Arthur. 1983. *Psychoanalysis and Society: The Social Thought of Sigmund Freud.* Washington, D.C.: University Press of America.

Biel, Steven. 1992. *Independent Intellectuals in the United States, 1910–1945.* New York: New York University Press.

Blumberg, Marvin. 1948. "The Practical Aspects of the Bad Influence of Comic Books." *American Journal of Psychotherapy* 2:487–88.

Boddy, William. 1997. "Senator Dodd Goes to Hollywood: Investigating Video Violence." In *The Revolution Wasn't Televised: Sixties Television and Social Conflict,* ed. Lynn Spigel and Michael Curtin, 161–83. New York: Routledge.

Bogart, Leo. 1956. *The Age of Television: A Study of Viewing Habits and the Impact of Television on American Life.* New York: Ungar.

"The Boy Who Read Horror Comics." 1955. *The Spectator,* 11 March, 304.

Brantlinger, Patrick. 1983. *Bread and Circuses: Theories of Mass Culture as Social Decay.* Ithaca: Cornell University Press.

Brooks, Cleanth, and Robert Heilman. 1944. "On 'Why 100,000,000 Americans Read Comics.'" *American Scholar,* April, 247–52.

Brown, John Mason. 1948. "The Case against the Comics." *Saturday Review of Literature,* 20 March, 31–32.

Burnham, James. 1952. "Our Country and Our Culture." *Partisan Review,* May–June, 288–91.

"Canada's Comics Ban." 1949. *Newsweek,* 14 November, 62.

Cater, Douglass, and Stephen Strickland. 1975. *TV Violence and the Child: The Evolution and Fate of the Surgeon General's Report.* New York: Sage Foundation.

Charters, W. W. 1933. *Motion Pictures and Youth: A Summary.* New York: Macmillan.

Child Study Association of America. 1954. "A Supplementary Statement on the Relations of the Association to Comic Books." Box 3, folder 15. Papers of Fredric Wertham, 1818–1986. Library of Congress Rare Books and Special Collections Division.

"Code for Comics." 1948. *Time,* 12 July, 62.

"Comic Book 'Czar.'" 1954. *America,* 2 October, 2–3.

"Comic Book Censorship." 1949. *New York Times,* 25 February, 22.

"Comic Book Curb Vetoed by Dewey." 1949. *New York Times,* 20 April, 20.

"The Comics and Their Audience." 1942. *Publisher's Weekly,* 18 April, 1477–79.

"Comics to the Rescue of Education." 1950. *School and Society,* 20 May, 314–15.

Comstock, George, Steven Chaffee, Nathan Katzman, Maxwell McCombs, and Donald Roberts. 1978. *Television and Human Behavior.* New York: Columbia University Press.

Cornell, Julien. 1966. *The Trial of Ezra Pound: A Documented Account of the Treason Case by the Defendant's Lawyer.* New York: Day.

"The Couch Cult." 1950. *Time,* 11 September, 86–87.

Cousins, Norman. 1953. "Time-Trap for Children." In *Television and Radio,* ed. Marx, 68–71.

Crist, Judith. 1948. "Horror in the Nursery." *Collier's,* 29 March, 22–23.

"The Dagger." 1952. Letter to Fredric Wertham. Box 125, folder 3. Papers of Fredric Wertham, 1818–1986. Library of Congress Rare Books and Special Collections Division.

Dale, Douglas. 1951. "Pupil Segregation Held Health Drag." *New York Times,* 23 October, 23.

Daniels, Les. 1971. *Comix: A History of Comic Books in America.* New York: Outerbridge and Dienstfrey.

"Denies Favoring Soviet." 1951. *New York Times,* 30 May, 6.

Denney, Reuel. 1954a. "Correspondence." *New Republic,* 22 May, 22.

———. 1954b. "The Dark Fantastic." *New Republic,* 3 May, 18–19.

———. 1957. *The Astonished Muse.* Chicago: University of Chicago Press.

De Rossis, Louis. 1966. Review of *A Sign for Cain. Library Journal,* 10 October, 4678.

"Dewey Vetoes 'Objectionable' Comics Book Ban Measure." 1952. *Publisher's Weekly,* 26 April, 1766.

Doyle, Thomas F. 1943. "What's Wrong with the 'Comics'?" *Catholic World,* February, 548–57.

Dreyer, Barbara Ann. 1972. *The Influence of the Mental Hygiene Movement on the Education of Children during the Early Decades of the Twentieth Century in America.* Ann Arbor: University Microfilms.

Eliot, T. S. 1948. *Notes towards a Definition of Culture.* London: Faber and Faber.

Elkisch, Paula. 1948. "The Child's Conflict about Comic Books." *American Journal of Psychotherapy* 2:483–87.

Ellison, Ralph. 1953. "Harlem Is Nowhere." In *Shadow and Act,* 294–302. New York: Vintage.

Ellsworth, Whitney. 1949. "Comics Controversy." *Commentary,* March, 293–94.

Emans, Robert. 1960. "Treasure Island: The Classic and the Classic Comic." *Elementary School Journal,* February, 253–57.

"Escapist Paydirt." 1943. *Newsweek,* 27 December, 55, 58.

Evanier, Mark. 2003. *Wertham Was Right!* Raleigh, N.C.: TwoMorrows.

Ferman, Dorothy. 1950. "The Psychoanalytical Joy Ride." *The Nation,* 26 August, 183–85.

Fermi, Laura. 1971. *Illustrious Immigrants: The Intellectual Migration from Europe, 1930–1941.* Chicago: University of Chicago Press.

Fiedler, Leslie. 1952. "Afterthoughts on the Rosenbergs." In *An End to Innocence: Essays on Culture and Politics,* 25–45. Boston: Beacon.

———. 1957. "The Middle against Both Ends." In *Mass Culture,* ed. Rosenberg and White, 537–47.

"Fighting Gunfire with Gunfire." 1948. *Newsweek,* 20 December, 54–55.

Finn, David. 1969. *The Corporate Oligarch.* New York: Simon and Schuster.

"First Comic Book Awards." 1956. *America,* 14 April, 47–48.

Fox, Sanford J. 1966. "A Constructive Look at Destruction." *Saturday Review of Literature,* 19 November, 40–41.

Frakes, Margaret. 1942. "Comics Are No Longer Comic." *Christian Century,* 4 November, 1349–51.

Frank, Josette. 1944. "What's in the Comics?" *Journal of Educational Sociology* 18:214–22.

———. 1949a. *Comics, Radio, Movies—and Children.* New York: Public Affairs Committee.

———. 1949b. "Some Questions and Answers for Teachers and Parents." *Journal of Educational Sociology* 23:206–14.

———. 1954. *Your Child's Reading Today.* New York: Doubleday.

Fremont-Smith, Eliot. 1966. "We Are Not Alone." *New York Times,* 19 September, 41.

Freud, Sigmund. 1927. *The Future of an Illusion.* Trans. W. D. Robson-Scott. New York: Liveright.

Fuller, Edmund. 1966. "Reading for Pleasure." *Wall Street Journal,* 21 September, 18.

Gans, Herbert. 1974. *Popular Culture and High Culture: An Analysis and Evaluation of Taste.* New York: Basic Books.

Gardiner, Harold C. 1954a. "Comic Books: Cultural Threat?" *America,* 19 June, 319–21.

———. 1954b. "Comic Books: Moral Threat?" *America,* 26 June, 340–42.

Gay, Roger C. 1937. "A Teacher Reads the Comics." *Harvard Educational Review* 7:198–209.

Gibbs, Wolcott. 1954. "Keep Those Paws to Yourself, Space-Rat!" *New Yorker,* 8 May, 134–41.

Gilbert, James. 1986. *A Cycle of Outrage: America's Reaction to the Juvenile Delinquent in the 1950s.* New York: Oxford University Press.

Gleason, Leverett. 1952. "In Defense of Comic Books." *Today's Health,* September, 40–41, 52–54.

Gorman, Paul R. 1996. *Left Intellectuals and Popular Culture in Twentieth-Century America.* Chapel Hill: University of North Carolina Press.

Gould, Jack. 1953. "A Cut-Rate Nickelodeon." In *Television and Radio,* ed. Marx, 71–74.

Graalfs, Marilyn. 1968. "Violence in Comic Books." In *Violence and the Mass Media,* ed. Otto Larsen, 91–96. New York: Harper and Row.

Graebner, William. 1991. *The Age of Doubt: American Thought and Culture in the 1940s.* Boston: Twayne.

Greenberg, Clement. 1957. "Avant-Garde and Kitsch." In *Mass Culture,* ed. Rosenberg and White, 98–110.

Greenberg, Jack. 1994. *Crusaders in the Courts: How a Dedicated Band of Lawyers Fought for the Civil Rights Revolution.* New York: Basic Books.

Gruenberg, Sidonie Matsner. 1944. "The Comics as a Social Force." *Journal of Educational Sociology* 18:204–13.

Hale, Nathan. 1995. *The Rise and Crisis of Psychoanalysis in the United States: Freud and the Americans, 1917–1985.* New York: Oxford University Press.

Harker, Jean Gray. 1948. "Youth's Librarians Can Defeat Comics." *Library Journal,* 1 December, 1705–7, 1720.

Harrison, Emma. 1954. "Magistrate Is Made Comics 'Czar.'" *New York Times,* 17 September, 1, 25.

"Health Law Urged to Combat Comics." 1951. *New York Times,* 4 December, 35.

Heisler, Florence. 1947. "A Comparison of Comic Book and Non–Comic Book Readers of the Elementary School." *Journal of Educational Research* 40:458–64.

———. 1948. "A Comparison between Those Elementary School Children Who Attend Moving Pictures, Read Comic Books, and Listen to Serial Radio Programs to an Excess, with Those Who Indulge in These Activities Seldom or Not at All." *Journal of Educational Research* 42:182–90.

Hill, George E. 1941. "Taking the Comics Seriously." *Childhood Education*, May, 413–14.

Hill, George E., and M. Estelle Trent. 1940. "Children's Interests in Comic Strips." *Journal of Educational Research* 34:30–36.

Himmelweit, Hilde, A. N. Oppenheim, and Pamela Vince. 1958. *Television and the Child: An Empirical Study of the Effect of Television on the Young.* London: Oxford University Press.

Hoberek, Andrew. 1998. "Race Man, Organization Man, *Invisible Man.*" *Modern Language Quarterly* 59:99–119.

Hook, Sidney. 1952. "Our Country and Our Culture." *Partisan Review,* September–October, 569–74.

"Horror Comics." 1954. *Time,* 3 May, 78.

"Horror on the Newsstands." 1954. *Time,* 27 September, 77.

Hoult, Thomas. 1949. "Comic Books and Juvenile Delinquency." *Sociology and Social Research* 33:279–4.

Hoult, Thomas, and Lois Hoult. 1950. "Are Comic Books a Menace?" *Today's Health,* June, 20–21, 53–54.

"How Much of a Menace Are the Comics?" 1941. *School and Society,* 15 November, 436.

Hughes, H. Stuart. 1961. "Mass Culture and Social Criticism." In *Culture for the Millions?* ed. Jacobs, 142–47.

———. 1975. *The Sea Change: The Migration of Social Thought, 1930–1965.* New York: Harper and Row.

Inglis, Ruth A. 1955. "The Comic Book Problem." *American Mercury,* August, 117–21.

Jacobs, Norman, ed. 1961. *Culture for the Millions? Mass Media in Modern Society.* Princeton, N.J.: Van Nostrand.

Jacoby, Russell. 1987. *The Last Intellectuals: American Culture in the Age of Academe.* New York: Basic Books.

Jay, Martin. 1973. *The Dialectical Imagination: A History of the Frankfurt School and the Institute of Social Research, 1923–1950.* Boston: Little, Brown.

Jumonville, Neil. 1991. *Critical Crossings: The New York Intellectuals in Postwar America.* Berkeley: University of California Press.

Kihss, Peter. 1954a. "No Harm in Horror, Comics Issuer Says." *New York Times,* 22 April, 1, 34.

———. 1954b. "Senator Charges 'Deceit' on Comics." *New York Times,* 23 April, 29.

———. 1958. "N.A.A.C.P. Awaits U.S. School Move." *New York Times,* 15 September, 12.

Kinneman, Flida Cooper. 1943. "The Comics and Their Appeal to the Youth of Today." *English Journal* 32:331–35.

Klapper, Joseph. 1960. *The Effects of Mass Communication.* 2d ed. New York: Free Press.

Kornhauser, William. 1959. *The Politics of Mass Society.* New York: Free Press.

Lardner, John. 1955. "How to Lick Crime." *Newsweek,* 7 March, 58.

Larson, Randall D. N.d. "An Interview with Fredric Wertham, M. D." *Fandom Unlimited,* no. 1.

Lazarsfeld, Paul F. 1949. Introduction to *The Effects of Mass Media: A Report to the Director of the Public Library Inquiry,* by Joseph Klapper, i–xi. New York: Bureau of Applied Social Research, Columbia University.

———. 1955. "Why Is So Little Known about the Effects of Television on Children and What Can Be Done?" *Public Opinion Quarterly* 19:243–51.

———. 1961. "Mass Culture Today." In *Culture for the Millions?* ed. Jacobs, ix–xxv.

Lazarsfeld, Paul F., and Robert K. Merton. 1957. "Mass Communication, Popular Taste, and Organized Social Action." In *Mass Culture,* ed. Rosenberg and White, 457–73.

Lears, Jackson. 1989. "A Matter of Taste: Corporate Cultural Hegemony in a Mass-Consumption Society." In *Recasting America,* 38–57.

Legman, Gerson. 1948. "The Comic Books and the Public." *American Journal of Psychotherapy* 2:473–77.

Lerner, Max. 1952. "Our Country and Our Culture." *Partisan Review,* September–October, 581–85.

"Let Children Read Comics; Science Gives Its Approval." 1941. *Science News Letter,* 23 August, 124–25.

Lethbridge, Nemone. 1967. "Promoting Violence." *New Statesman,* 17 November, 688.

"Librarian Named on Comics Advisory Committee." 1949. *Library Journal,* 1 January, 37.

Lowenthal, Leo. 1961. "An Historical Preface to the Popular Culture Debate." In *Culture for the Millions?* ed. Jacobs, 28–42.

Lowery, Shearon, and Melvin De Fleur. 1983. *Milestones in Mass Communication Research: Media Effects.* New York: Longman.

———. 1988. *Milestones in Mass Communication Research: Media Effects.* 2d ed. New York: Longman.

———. 1995. *Milestones in Mass Communication Research: Media Effects.* 3d ed. New York: Longman.

Luckiesh, Matthew, and Frank K. Moss. 1942. "Legibility in Comic Books." *Sight-Saving Review* 12:19–24.

Luke, Carmen. *Constructing the Child Viewer: A History of the American Discourse on Television and Children, 1950–1980.* New York: Praeger, 1990.

M.D.L. 1954. "Talking Shop . . ." *Wilson Library Bulletin,* June, 884.

———. 1955. "Talking Shop . . ." *Wilson Library Bulletin,* April, 651.

MacDonald, Dwight. 1944. "A Theory of Popular Culture." *Politics,* 1 February, 20–23.

———. 1957. "A Theory of Mass Culture." In *Mass Culture,* ed. Rosenberg and White, 59–73.

Malter, Morton S. 1952. "The Content of Current Comic Magazines." *Elementary School Journal,* May, 505–10.

Mannes, Marya. 1947. "Junior Has a Craving." *New Republic,* 17 February, 20–23.

"Many Doubt Comics Spur Crime, Senate Survey of Experts Shows." 1950. *New York Times,* 12 November, 1, 61.

Marable, Manning. 1991. *Race, Reform, and Rebellion: The Second Reconstruction in Black America, 1945–1990.* 2d ed. Jackson: University Press of Mississippi.

Marston, William Moulton. 1944. "Why 100,000,000 Americans Read Comics." *American Scholar,* January, 35–44.

Martin, Ralph G. 1946. "Doctor's Dream in Harlem." *New Republic,* 3 June, 798–800.

Marx, Herbert L., ed. 1953. *Television and Radio in American Life.* New York: Wilson.

May, Larry, ed. 1989. *Recasting America: Culture and Politics in the Age of Cold War.* Chicago: University of Chicago Press.

McCarthy, Sister M. Katharine, and Marion W. Smith. 1943. "The Much Discussed Comics." *Elementary School Journal,* October, 97–101.

Medhurst, Andy. 1991. "Batman, Deviance, and Camp." In *The Many Lives of the Batman: Critical Approaches to a Superhero and His Media,* ed. Roberta E. Pearson and William Uricchio, 149–63. New York: Routledge.

Meerloo, Joost. 1968. Review of *A Sign for Cain. American Journal of Psychotherapy* 22:115.

Meeropol, Robert, and Michael Meeropol. 1975. *We Are Your Sons: The Legacy of Ethel and Julius Rosenberg.* Boston: Houghton Mifflin.

Mills, C. Wright. 1951. *White Collar: The American Middle Classes.* New York: Oxford University Press.

———. 1952. "Our Country and Our Culture." *Partisan Review,* July–August, 446–50.

———. 1954. "Nothing to Laugh At." *New York Times Book Review,* 25 April, 20.

Mishler, Anita L. 1955. Review of *Seduction of the Innocent. Public Opinion Quarterly* 19:115–17.

Mitchell, Walter B. J., Jr. 1954. "Dell Needs No Watchdog." *America,* 11 December, 308.

Moore, Murray. 1973. Review of *The World of Fanzines. Knip Knop* (self-published fanzine), no. 1.

Moore, Ward. 1954. "Nietzsche in the Nursery." *The Nation,* 15 May, 426–27.

"More Friends for Comics." *Newsweek,* 27 November 1953, 50.

Morgan, Joy Elmer. 1954. Review of *Seduction of the Innocent. NEA Journal,* November, 9:473.

Mosse, Hilde. 1948. "Aggression and Violence in Fantasy and Fact." *American Journal of Psychotherapy* 2:477–83.

Motter, Alton M. 1949. "How to Improve the Comics." *Christian Century,* 12 October, 1199–1200.

Muhlen, Norbert. 1949. "Comic Books and Other Horrors: Prep School for Totalitarian Society?" *Commentary,* January, 80–87.

———. 1954. "The Case against Comics." *New Leader,* 17 May, 26–27.

———. 1966. Review of *A Sign for Cain. America,* 24 September, 352–53.

National Association for the Advancement of Colored People. 1951. "Psychiatrist Tells Court School Segregation Harmful." *News from NAACP,* 25 October, 1–25.

"New York Officials Recommend Code for Comics Publishers." 1949. *Publisher's Weekly,* 19 February, 977–78.

"No More Werewolves." 1954. *Newsweek,* 8 November, 55.

"Non-Fiction." 1954. *Library Journal,* 1 April, 622.

North, Sterling. 1940. "A National Disgrace." *Childhood Education,* October, 56.

———. 1941a. "The Antidote for Comics." *National Parent-Teacher,* March, 16–17.

———. 1941b. "The Creative Way Out." *National Parent-Teacher,* November, 14–16.

"Not So Funny." 1948. *Time,* 4 October, 46.

Nyberg, Amy Kiste. 1998. *Seal of Approval: The History of the Comics Code.* Jackson: University Press of Mississippi.

"October 26." 1966. *Publisher's Weekly,* 12 September, 87–88.

"Oppose State Regulation." 1950. *New York Times,* 9 August, 24.

Ortega y Gasset, José. 1993 [1932]. *The Revolt of the Masses.* New York: Norton.

"Outlawed." 1949. *Time,* 19 December, 33–34.

Overholser, Winfred. 1954. "Want a Laugh?" *Saturday Review of Literature,* 24 April, 16.

Park, David. 2002. "The Kefauver Comic Book Hearings as Show Trial: Decency, Authority, and the Dominated Expert." *Cultural Studies* 16:259–88.

"Parnassus, Coast to Coast." 1956. *Time,* 11 June, 65–70.

Partisan Review. 1952. "Our Country and Our Culture." May–June, 282–86.

Pells, Richard. 1985. *The Liberal Mind in a Conservative Age: American Intellectuals in the 1940s and 1950s.* New York: Harper and Row.

Peters, J. D. 1989. "Democracy and American Mass Communication Theory: Dewey, Lippmann, Lazarsfeld." *Communication* 11:199–220.

Plummer, Brenda Gayle. 1996. *Rising Wind: Black Americans and U. S. Foreign Affairs, 1935–1960.* Chapel Hill: University of North Carolina Press.

Powdermaker, Hortense. 1957. "Hollywood and the U. S. A." In *Mass Culture,* ed. Rosenberg and White, 278–93.

"Progress in Comic Book Cleanup." 1954. *America,* 30 October, 114.

"Psychiatrist Asks Crime Comics Ban." 1950. *New York Times,* 14 December, 50.

"Psychiatry in Harlem." 1947. *Time,* 1 December, 50–52.

"Purified Comics." 1948. *Newsweek,* 12 July, 56.

R.G. 1949. "The Author." *Saturday Review of Literature,* 7 May, 10.

Rabassiere, Henry. 1957. "In Defense of Television." In *Mass Culture,* ed. Rosenberg and White, 368–74.

Rahv, Philip. 1952. "Our Country and Our Culture." *Partisan Review,* May–June, 304–10.

"Regarding Comic Magazines." 1942. *Recreation,* fall, 689.

Reibman, James. 1990. "The Life of Dr. Fredric Wertham." In *The Fredric Wertham Collection: Gift of His Wife Hesketh.* Cambridge, Mass.: Busch-Reisinger Museum, Harvard University.

Richardson, John Adkins. 1974. Review of *The World of Fanzines. Rockets Blast Comicollector,* no. 106, January, 52–54.

Richardson, Theresa R. 1989. *The Century of the Child: The Mental Hygiene Movement and Social Policy in the United States and Canada.* Albany: State University of New York Press.

Riesman, David, with Reuel Denney and Nathan Glazer. 1950. *The Lonely Crowd: A Study of the Changing American Character.* New Haven: Yale University Press.

Rogers, Everett. 1994. *A History of Communication Study: A Biographical Approach.* New York: Free Press.

Rosenberg, Bernard, and David Manning White, eds. 1957. *Mass Culture: The Popular Arts in America.* New York: Free Press.

Ross, Andrew. 1989. *No Respect: Intellectuals and Popular Culture.* New York: Routledge.

Rosten, Leo. 1961. "The Intellectual and the Mass Media: Some Rigorously Random Remarks." In *Culture for the Millions?* ed. Jacobs, 71–84.

Rowland, Willard. 1983. *The Politics of TV Violence: Policy Uses of Communication Research.* Beverly Hills, Calif.: Sage.

———. 1988. "Recreating the Past." *Communication* 10:121–40.

S. J. K. 1941a. "The Comic Menace." *Wilson Library Bulletin,* June, 846–47.

———. 1941b. "Libraries, to Arms!" *Wilson Library Bulletin,* April, 670–71.

Savage, William W. 1990. *Commies, Cowboys, and Jungle Queens: Comic Books and America, 1945–1954.* Hanover, N.H.: Wesleyan University Press.

Sawyer, Michael. 1987. "Albert Lewis Kanter and the Classics: The Man behind the Gilberton Company." *Journal of Popular Culture* 20:1–18.

Schramm, Wilbur, Jack Lyle, and Edwin B. Parker. 1961. *Television in the Lives of Our Children.* Stanford, Calif.: Stanford University Press.

Schultz, Henry E. 1949. "Censorship or Self-Regulation?" *Journal of Educational Sociology* 23:215–24.

Seldes, Gilbert. 1950. *The Lively Arts.* WNEW radio broadcast, 14 May. Box 112, folder 4. Papers of Fredric Wertham, 1818–1986. Library of Congress Rare Books and Special Collections Division, Washington, D.C.

———. 1957. "The People and the Arts." In *Mass Culture,* ed. Rosenberg and White, 74–97.

Sheerin, John B. 1954. "Crime Comics Must Go!" *Catholic World,* June, 161–65.

Smith, Ruth Emily. 1948. "Publishers Improve Comic Books." *Library Journal,* 15 November, 1649–53.

Sones, W. W. D. 1944. "The Comics and Instructional Method." *Journal of Educational Sociology* 18:232–40.

"Speaking of Operations." 1946. *Time,* 18 February, 66.

"State Senate Acts to Control Comics." 1949. *New York Times,* 24 February, 17.

Strang, Ruth. 1943. "Why Children Read the Comics." *Elementary School Journal,* February, 336–42.

Suchoff, David. 1995. "The Rosenberg Case and the New York Intellectuals." In *Secret Agents: The Rosenberg Case, McCarthyism, and Fifties America,* ed. Marjorie Garber and Rebecca L. Walkowitz, 144–70. New York: Routledge.

"Superman Scores." 1942. *Business Week,* 18 April, 54–56.

Sussmann, Warren. 1989. "Did Success Spoil the United States? Dual Representations in Postwar America." In *Recasting America,* ed. May 19–37.

"This Week." 1966. *Christian Century,* 14 September, 1116.

Thompson, Lovell. 1942. "How Serious Are the Comics?" *Atlantic Monthly,* September, 127–29.

Thorndike, Roger. 1941. "Words and the Comics." *Journal of Experimental Education* 10:110–13.

Thrasher, Frederic M. 1949. "The Comics and Delinquency: Cause or Scapegoat?" *Journal of Educational Sociology* 23:195–205.

———. 1954. "Do the Comic Books Promote Juvenile Delinquency? Con." *Congressional Digest,* May, 303, 305, 314.

Tieleman, Adrian. 1949. "Comic Books and Democracy." *Educational Administration and Supervision,* 35:299–301.

"'Tis True, 'Tis Comics and Comic 'Tis 'Tis True." 1941. *School and Society,* 10 May, 598.

Tocqueville, Alexis de. 1957. "In What Spirits the Americans Cultivate the Arts." In *Mass Culture,* ed. Rosenberg and White, 27–34.

"The Ubiquitous Comics." 1948. *National Education Association Journal,* December, 570.

"Unfunny Comic Books Barred in Los Angeles." 1948. *New York Times,* 23 September, 38.

U. S. Congress. Senate. 1954. *Juvenile Delinquency (Comic Books): Hearings before the Senate Subcommittee on Juvenile Delinquency.* 83d Cong., 2d sess., 21–22 April, 24 June 1954.

———. 1998. "Juvenile Delinquency (Comic Books)." In *World Encyclopedia of Comics,* ed. Maurice Horn, 861–902. New York: Chelsea House.

Van Den Haag, Ernest. 1957. "Of Happiness and Despair We Have No Measure." In *Mass Culture,* ed. Rosenberg and White, 504–36.

Vlamos, James Frank. 1941. "The Sad Case of the Funnies." *American Mercury,* April, 411–16.

Warshow, Robert. 1957. "Paul, the Horror Comics, and Dr. Wertham." In *Mass Culture,* ed. Rosenberg and White, 199–211.

———. 1962. "The 'Idealism' of Julius and Ethel Rosenberg." In *The Immediate Experience,* 33–43. New York: Anchor Books.

"We Would Be the First to Acknowledge." 1949. *The Nation,* 19 March, 319.

"Wertham Assails Ezra Pound Ruling." 1949. *New York Times,* 27 November, 33.

Wertham, Fredric [F. I. Wertheimer]. 1919a. "The Yoga-System and Psychoanalysis: Part One." *The Quest,* 10:182–96.

——— [F. I. Wertheimer]. 1919b. "The Yoga-System and Psychoanalysis: Part Two." *The Quest,* 10:316–35.

———. 1928. "1828–1928." Unpublished manuscript. Box 158, folder 6. Papers of Fredric Wertham, 1818–1986. Library of Congress Rare Books and Special Collections Division, Washington, D.C.

——— [Frederic Wertham]. 1937. "The Catathymic Crisis: A Clinical Entity." *Archives of Neurology and Psychiatry* 37:974–78.

———— [Frederic Wertham]. 1938. "Psychiatry and Prevention of Sex Crimes." *Journal of Criminal Law and Criminology* 28:847–53.

———— [Fredrick Wertham]. 1941. *Dark Legend.* New York: Book Find Club.

———— [Frederic Wertham]. 1943. "While Rome Burns." *New Republic,* 24 May, 707–8.

———— [Frederic Wertham]. 1944. "Unconscious Determinant in *Native Son.*" *Journal of Clinical Psychopathology and Psychotherapy* 6:111–15.

———— [Frederic Wertham]. 1945a. "Psychosomatic Study of Myself." *Journal of Clinical Psychopathology and Psychotherapy* 7:371–82.

———— [Frederic Wertham]. 1945b. "Quis Custodiet, Ipsos Custodes?" *New Republic,* 22 October, 538–40.

————. [Frederic Wertham]. 1945c. "Thrombophlebitis with Multiple Pulmonary Emboli: Psychiatric Self-Observations." *American Journal of Medical Sciences* 226:166–73.

———— [Frederic Wertham]. 1945d. "Who Will Guard the Guardians?" *New Republic,* 29 October, 578–80.

———— [Frederic Wertham]. 1946. "The First Great Psychological Novelist." *Book Find News,* November, 10–12.

———— [Frederic Wertham]. 1947a. "The Dreams That Heal." *New Republic,* 3 November, 25–27.

———— [Frederic Wertham]. 1947b. "Theatre Arts Bookshelf." *Theatre Arts,* July, 9–10.

———— [Frederic Wertham]. 1947c. "War OR Peace?" *New Republic,* 27 January, 37–39.

———— [Frederic Wertham]. 1948a. "Are Comic Books Harmful to Children?" *Friends Intelligencer,* 10 July, 395–96.

————. 1948b. "The Betrayal of Childhood: Comic Books." In *Proceedings of the Seventy-eighth Annual Congress of Correction, American Prison Association,* 57–59. New York: Central Office.

————. 1948c. "The Comics . . . Very Funny!" *Saturday Review of Literature,* 29 May, 6–7, 27–29.

————. 1948d. "The Cult of Contentment." *New Republic,* 29 March, 22–29.

————. 1948e. "Escape into Ethics." *New Republic,* 3 May, 26–27.

————. 1948f. Review of *Glass House of Prejudice. American Journal of Psychotherapy* 2:497–98.

————. 1948g. Letter to the editor. *Saturday Review of Literature,* 10 July. Box 125, folder 3. Papers of Fredric Wertham, 1818–1986. Library of Congress Rare Books and Special Collections Division, Washington, D.C.

————. 1948h. "Psychiatry for the Average Reader." *New York Times Book Review,* 4 January, 3, 16.

————. 1949a. Affidavit prepared for Los Angeles County Counsel Harold W. Kennedy. January. Box 113, folder 5. Papers of Fredric Wertham, 1818–1986. Library of Congress Rare Books and Special Collections Division, Washington, D.C.

————. 1949b. "The Air-Conditioned Conscience." *Saturday Review of Literature,* 1 October, 6–8, 26–27.

————. 1949c. "Freud Now." *Scientific American,* October, 50–54.

———— [Frederic Wertham]. 1949d. "It's Murder." *Saturday Review of Literature,* 5 February, 7–9, 33–34.

————. 1949e. "Let the Salesman Beware." *New York Times Book Review,* 15 May, 4, 12.

————. 1949f. Letter to Eva H. Grant, 4 July. Box 113, folder 6. Papers of Fredric Wertham, 1818–1986. Library of Congress Rare Books and Special Collections Division, Washington, D.C.

————. 1949g. "A Reply to Philip Wylie." *Saturday Review of Literature,* 30 July, 7–8, 35.

————. 1949h. "The Road to Rapallo: A Psychiatric Study." *American Journal of Psychotherapy* 3:585–600.

————. 1949i. *The Show of Violence.* Garden City, N.Y.: Doubleday.

————. 1949j. "What Are Comic Books?" *National-Parent Teacher,* March, 10–12.

————. 1950a. Letter to Arthur Freund, 14 June. Box 111, folder 6. Papers of Fredric Wertham, 1818–1986. Library of Congress Rare Books and Special Collections Division, Washington, D.C.

————. 1950b. "Short-Cut to Joy." *Saturday Review of Literature,* 22 April, 38.

————. 1950c. "What to Do Till the Doctor Goes." *The Nation,* 2 September, 205–7.

————. 1951. Letter to Arthur Freund, 2 January. Box 113, folder 3. Papers of Fredric Wertham, 1818–1986. Library of Congress Rare Books and Special Collections Division, Washington, D.C.

————. 1952. "Psychological Effects of School Segregation." *American Journal of Psychotherapy* 6:94–103.

———— [Frederic Wertham]. 1953a. "The Ivory Couch." *Saturday Review of Literature,* 31 January, 16–17.

————. 1953b. Letter to Jesse L. Murrell, 29 December. Box 159, folder 13. Papers of Fredric Wertham, 1818–1986. Library of Congress Rare Books and Special Collections Division, Washington, D.C.

————. 1953c. "A Psychiatrist Looks at Psychiatry and the Law." *Buffalo Law Review* 3:41–51.

————. 1953d. "Psychiatric Observations on Abolition of School Segregation." *Journal of Educational Sociology* 26:333–36.

———— [Frederic Wertham]. 1954a. "Correspondence." *New Republic,* 22 May, 22.

————. 1954b. "The Curse of the Comic Books: The Value Patterns and Effects of Comic Books." *Religious* Education 49:394–406.

————. 1954c. "Do the Comic Books Promote Juvenile Delinquency? Pro." *Congressional Digest,* May, 302, 304, 310.

————. 1954d. Letter to Frank E. Karelsen, 11 June. Box 3, folder 13. Papers of Fredric Wertham, 1818–1986. Library of Congress Rare Books and Special Collections Division, Washington, D.C.

————. 1954e. Letter to Ida McAlpine, 4 September. Box 59, folder 7. Papers of Fredric Wertham, 1818–1986. Library of Congress Rare Books and Special Collections Division, Washington, D.C.

————. 1954f. Letter to Richard Condon, 24 February. Box 120, folder 4. Papers of Fredric Wertham, 1818–1986. Library of Congress Rare Books and Special Collections Division, Washington, D.C.

————. 1954g. "Nine Men Speak to You: Jim Crow in the North." *The Nation*, 12 June, 97.

———— [Frederic Wertham]. 1954h. "Reading for the Innocent." *Wilson Library Bulletin*, 22 September, 610–13.

————. 1954i. *Seduction of the Innocent.* New York: Rinehart.

————. 1954j. "Wertham Replies to Criticism of Ad." *Publisher's Weekly*, 1 May, 1889.

————. 1954k. "Why Do Some Teen-Agers Become Delinquent?" *Cincinnati Enquirer*, 12 October, 18.

————. 1954l. "Why Do They Commit Murder?" *New York Times Magazine*, 8 August, 8, 49–50.

————. 1955a. "It's Still Murder: What Parents Still Don't Know about Comic Books." *Saturday Review*, 9 April, 11–12, 46–48.

————. 1955b. Letter to Frank E. Karelsen, 14 December. Box 3, folder 13. Papers of Fredric Wertham, 1818–1986. Library of Congress Rare Books and Special Collections Division, Washington, D.C.

————. 1955c. Memorandum to the members of the staff, 14 February. Box 125, folder 3. Papers of Fredric Wertham, 1818–1986. Library of Congress Rare Books and Special Collections Division, Washington, D.C.

————. 1955d. "The Psychology of the Criminal Act and Punishment." *University of Chicago Law Review* 22:569–81.

————. 1955e. " 'Superman' Bedreigt de Jeugd." *Elseviers Weekblad*, 31 December, 29.

————. 1956. *The Circle of Guilt.* New York: Rinehart.

————. 1959a. "10 Ways a Child May Tell You He Is Headed for a Troubled Teen Age." *Ladies' Home Journal*, March, 62–63, 194–200.

————. 1959b. "The War against Children." Unpublished manuscript. Box 149, folder 4. Papers of Fredric Wertham, 1818–1986. Library of Congress Rare Books and Special Collections Division, Washington, D.C.

————. 1960. "How Movie and TV Violence Affects Children." *Ladies' Home Journal*, February, 58–59, 165–70.

————. 1961. "Sex Crimes Can Be Prevented." *Ladies Home Journal*, August, 46–47, 88–90.

————. 1962a. "Children and TV Violence." *New York Times*, 12 July, 28.

————. 1962b. "The Scientific Study of Mass Media Effects." *American Journal of Psychiatry* 119:306–11.

————. 1963a. "Society and Problem Personalities: Praetorian Psychiatry." *American Journal of Psychotherapy* 17:404–16.

————. 1963b. "Three Hundred Years of Psychiatry, 1535–1860." *American Journal of Psychotherapy* 17:513–15.

————. 1964a. "Can We Study Violence Scientifically?" *Twentieth Century*, winter, 32–38.

————. 1964b. "School for Violence." *New York Times,* 5 July, 11.

————. 1965. "Mass Media and Sex Deviation." In *Sexual Behavior and the Law,* ed. Ralph Slovenko, 829–49. Springfield, Ill.: Thomas.

————. 1966a. "Is TV Hardening Us to the War in Vietnam?" *New York Times,* 4 December, 23.

————. 1966b. *A Sign for Cain: An Exploration of Human Violence.* New York: Macmillan.

————. 1967. "Horror for Sale." *New Statesman,* 14 July, 7.

————. 1968. "What Do We Know about Mass Media Effects?" *Corrective Psychiatry and Journal of Social Therapy* 14:196–99.

————. 1969a. Letter to Edward Romero, 2 November. Box 156, folder 11. Papers of Fredric Wertham, 1818–1986. Library of Congress Rare Books and Special Collections Division, Washington, D.C.

————. 1969b. "The Sound of the Trumpet." *Journal of the Producers Guild of America* 11:37–40.

————. 1969c. "Youth Speaks." Box 156, folder 12. Papers of Fredric Wertham, 1818–1986. Library of Congress Rare Books and Special Collections Division, Washington, D.C.

————. 1971a. "Human Violence Can Be Abolished." *Johns Hopkins Magazine,* summer, 34–39.

————. 1971b. "Open to Criticism." *American Journal of Psychotherapy* 25:650–52.

————. 1972. "Critique of the Report to the Surgeon General from the Committee on Television and Social Behavior." *American Journal of Psychotherapy* 26:216–19.

————. 1973. *The World of Fanzines: A Special Form of Communication.* Carbondale: Southern Illinois University Press.

————. 1974a. Letter to Donn Brazier, 28 December. Box 177, folder 12. Papers of Fredric Wertham, 1818–1986. Library of Congress Rare Books and Special Collections Division, Washington, D.C.

————. 1974b. "Potential Victims." *The Sciences,* May, 3.

————. 1976. Review of *Simple Justice: The History of Brown v. Board of Education and Black America's Struggle for Equality. American Journal of Psychotherapy* 30:507–9.

Wertham, Fredric [Frederic Wertham], and Lili Golden. 1941. "A Differential-Diagnostic Method of Interpreting Mosaics and Colored Block Designs." *American Journal of Psychiatry* 98:124–31.

Wertham, Fredric [F. I. Wertheimer], and Florence E. Hesketh. 1926. *The Significance of Physical Constitution in Mental Disease.* Baltimore: Williams and Wilkins.

Wertham, Fredric [F. I. Wertheimer], and Adolf Meyer. 1923. "Concerning Psychoanalysis." *Archives of Neurology and Pathology* 24:191–97.

Wertham, Fredric [Frederic Wertham], and Florence Wertham. 1934. *The Brain as an Organ: Its Postmortem Study and Interpretation.* New York: Macmillan.

"What about the Comic Books?" 1955. *Christian Century,* 30 March, 389.

"What Comic Books Pass Muster?" 1949. *Christian Century,* 28 December, 1540–41.

"What Is the Solution for Control of the Comics?" 1949. *Library Journal,* 1 February, 180.

White, David Manning. 1957. "Mass Culture in America: Another Point of View." In *Mass Culture,* ed. Rosenberg and White, 13–21.

Whyte, William H. 1956. *The Organization Man.* New York: Simon and Schuster.

Williams, Gweneira, and Jane Wilson. 1942a. "They Like It Rough: In Defense of Comics." *Library Journal,* 1 March, 204–6.

———. 1942b. "Why Not? Give Them What They Want!" *Publisher's Weekly,* 18 April, 1490–96.

"Witnesses Favor Comic Book Curbs." 1950. *New York Times,* 14 June, 29.

Witty, Paul. 1941a. "Children's Interest in Reading the Comics." *Journal of Experimental Education* 10:100–4.

———. 1941b. "Reading the Comics—A Comparative Study." *Journal of Experimental Education* 10:105–9.

———. 1942. "Those Troublesome Comics." *National Parent-Teacher,* January, 29–30.

———. 1944. "Some Uses of Visual Aids in the Army." *Journal of Educational Sociology* 18:241–49.

———. 1952. "Comics and Television: Opportunity or Threat?" *Today's Health,* October, 18–19, 49–53.

———. 1955. "Comics, Television, and Our Children." *Today's Health,* February, 18–21.

Witty, Paul, and Anne Coomer. 1942. "Reading the Comics in Grades IX–XII." *Educational Administration and Supervision* 28:344–53.

Witty, Paul, Ethel Smith, and Anne Coomer. 1942. "Reading the Comics in Grades VII and VIII." *Journal of Educational Psychology* 33:173–82.

Wolf, Katherine, and Marjorie Fiske. 1949. "The Children Talk about Comics." In *Communications Research, 1948–1949,* ed. Paul F. Lazarsfeld and Frank Stanton, 3–51. New York: Harper.

Wolf, William. 1954. Review of *Seduction of the Innocent. American Journal of Psychotherapy* 8:543–47.

Wright, Bradford W. 2001. *Comic Book Nation: The Transformation of Youth Culture in America.* Baltimore: Johns Hopkins University Press.

Zilboorg, Gregory. 1950. "Ignorance—Amateur and Professional." *The Nation,* 2 September, 207–9.

———. 1951. *Sigmund Freud: His Exploration of the Mind of Man.* New York: Scribner's.

———. 1955. *The Psychology of the Criminal Act and Punishment.* New York: Hogarth.

Zimmerman, Thomas L. 1954. "What to Do about Comics." *Library Journal,* 15 September, 1605–7.

Zorbaugh, Harvey. 1944a. "Editorial." *Journal of Educational Sociology* 18:193–94.

———. 1944b. "The Comics—There They Stand!" *Journal of Educational Sociology* 18:196–203.

———. 1945. "Comics—Food for Half-Wits?" *Science Digest,* April, 79–82.

———. 1949. "What Adults Think of Comics as Reading for Children." *Journal of Educational Sociology* 23:225–35.

INDEX

class, 44, 87. *See also* children, as
  maladjusted
classicism, 54
Classics Illustrated, 146, 161, 163
Clendenen, Richard, 158
clinical studies: advocated by Wertham,
  37, 173–74, 184–85, 189; critique of,
  196
Cochran, Russ, 191
Cold War: and the intellectual, 74–75;
  and mass communications
  research, 4, 12; and race relations,
  88–89
Cole, Jack, 197
colonialism, and violence, 100
Comfort, Alex, 71
comic books: burning of, 116; censorship of, 116–17, 144 (*see also* Association of Comics Magazine
  Publishers); and *Circle of Guilt,*
  92; commentators on, 4; crime,
  12, 134, 136–37, 139, 144, 145; cultural critics of, 130–32, 160–61;
  defenders of, 108, 114–15, 125–27
  (*see also* Bender, Lauretta; Frank,
  Josette; Gruenberg, Sidonie M.;
  Zorbaugh, Harvey); and fanzines,
  190; and illiteracy, 113, 117–18, 130,
  140–41; industry of, 110, 114, 120,
  146–47, 205–8; and juvenile
  criminality, 4, 118–19, 123–28; as
  literature, 110–11; as lowbrow
  literature, 130; in the postwar
  period, 105, 106, 115–18; and the
  1950s, 105, 124–29; and wartime
  critiques of, 105–8, 113–14;
  Wertham's impact on, 196–98
Comics Code Authority (CCA), 6,
  161–64

Comics Magazine Association of
  America (CMAA), and Comics
  Code, 161–62, 165, 197, 205
comic strips, 160, 190
"Comics . . . Very Funny!, The"
  (Wertham), 118–17, 121, 130, 146
Committee for Cultural Freedom, 81
communism, 12; anti, of Wertham, 77;
  threat of, 76, 78–79
Communist Party, 88
"Concerning Psychoanalysis"
  (Wertham), 20
consumption, and postwar society,
  79
Cooley, Charles Horton, 177
Court of General Sessions, 26
Cousins, Norman, 169
Crist, Judith, "Horror in the Nursery,"
  118, 145, 199
Crowd, The (Le Bon), 42
Crumb, Robert, 206
culture: and cultural pluralism, 75; and
  democratic values, 54–55, 75, 76;
  and individualism, 75, 79–81,
  102–3, 200, 201, 207; popular, 4,
  13–15, 57; utopian, 54; and
  violence, 71. *See also* elite culture;
  mass culture
Cycle of Outrage, A (Gilbert), 51

Daigh, Ralph, 146–47
Dark Legend (Wertham), 10, 17, 26,
  27–29, 63–65
Darrow, Clarence, 9, 16
Daumier, Honoré, 71
DC Comics, 206
De Fleur, Melvin, 195–96
Delaware, school segregation in, 93–97,
  135–36